HOW TO DO MORE IN LESS TIME

THE COMPLETE GUIDE TO INCREASING YOUR PRODUCTIVITY AND IMPROVING YOUR BOTTOM LINE

SECOND EDITION

ALLISON C. JOHS AND DANIEL J. SIEGEL

AMERICAN BAR ASSOCIATION
Law Practice Division

Cover design by Cory Ottenwess/ABA Design

Printed in the United States of America.

27 26 25 24 23 5 4 3 2 1

A catalog record for this book is available from the Library of Congress.

Discounts are available for books ordered in bulk. Special consideration is given to state bars, CLE programs, and other bar-related organizations. Inquire at Book Publishing, ABA Publishing, American Bar Association, 321 N. Clark Street, Chicago, Illinois 60654-7598.

www.shopABA.org

Contents

About the Authors

Allison C. Johs, Esq., is president of Legal Ease Consulting, Inc., where she provides coaching and consulting services for lawyers and law firms on practice management and marketing, including productivity, law firm operations, billing, client service, business development, and social media.

After leaving her position as administrative partner at one of Long Island's premier law firms in 2005, Ms. Johs started Legal Ease Consulting, Inc. to help lawyers build better law practices. A former practicing lawyer and law firm manager, she understands the law firm environment and the daily pressures faced by lawyers trying to manage and build their business while practicing law and successfully serving their clients.

Ms. Johs is a nationally recognized speaker, presenting workshops and programs in both public and private settings. She is the author of numerous published articles on practice management, business development, and marketing. She writes the *Legal Ease* blog (www.legaleaseconsulting.com) and the Simple Steps column for *Law Practice* magazine. Her website, Lawyer Meltdown (www.lawyermeltdown.com), provides resources and information for lawyers about managing and building their practices. She is the coauthor, with Dennis Kennedy, of *Make LinkedIn Work for You: A Practical Handbook for Lawyers and Other Legal Professionals* (2019), as well as a number of other books published by the ABA Law Practice Division.

Daniel J. Siegel, Esq., has been called the "Geek Lawyer" and is known for using technology in innovative ways to help get better results for clients. When, in 2005, Attorney Siegel had the opportunity to open his own law office, he opened the Law Offices of Daniel J. Siegel, LLC, as well as Integrated Technology Services, LLC, a practice management consulting firm that teaches lawyers and their staff how to use technology to make their practices more effective and efficient.

In everything he does, Mr. Siegel combines his knowledge of law and procedure with cutting-edge technology, while recognizing that technology can enhance, but not replace, the people skills needed for success. It is this passion that has led his firm to represent hundreds of lawyers as appellate counsel and as professional responsibility/ethical guidance counsel. The same passion drives his efforts to improve the workflows of lawyers everywhere.

A Philadelphia native, and diehard Philadelphia sports fan, Mr. Siegel is the author of 14 other books, including *The Ultimate Guide to Adobe Acrobat DC*, *Checklists for Lawyers*, and the first edition of this book, all published by the American Bar Association Law Practice Division. He is also the author of *Changing Law Firms: Ethical Guidance for Pennsylvania Law Firms & Attorneys*, published by the Pennsylvania Bar Institute, and *Pennsylvania Workers' Compensation Law—The Basics*. Mr. Siegel can be reached at dan@danieljsiegel.com or by phone at (610) 446-3457.

Acknowledgments

The first edition of this book, published in 2014, was an outgrowth of two programs—Dan's "How to Do 90 Minutes of Work in 60" and a program I did for many years under different titles, but always focusing on productivity strategies lawyers could use in their day-to-day work. Putting those two program concepts together has made them both stronger and, we hope, more useful for lawyers in their quest to get more done in less time and focus on their most important priorities. With the pandemic in 2020 creating a sea change in how everyone (not just lawyers) performs their work, we thought it was about time for a second edition of this book. My thanks again to Dan for being willing to put our two concepts together into one book and for the hours of work it took to bring this book back to life; it is amazing to see the change that has taken place in less than ten years.

Thanks to the staff at the ABA and especially to Sarah Craig for the many hours she spent working with us to make the second edition of this book a better version than the first. She is truly the consummate professional and has been a steady guiding force throughout the process. Thanks, too, to the Law Practice Division and especially to the Book Publishing board and our reviewers, Marcia Wasserman and Richard Ferguson, who made excellent suggestions to improve the final product.

Last, but certainly not least, thanks to my husband Fred Johs, who is my partner in more ways than one and whose belief in me seems to know no limits.

— Allison Johs

The most common question I get isn't about my legal skills, or my tech skills, it's always about how I manage to juggle my law firm, my consulting firm, and the many other activities with which I am involved. The reason is more than the fact that I type fast, it's that I use tools—some might call them tricks, but I see them as the Leatherman tools that keep me going. I love getting things done more efficiently, so I can do more—and still be home for dinner every day.

This book grew from my program "How to Do 90 Minutes of Work in 60" into much more, thanks to the exceptional insights from my friend and colleague Allison, without whom this book might be seen unfairly as merely another tech book for geeks. Working with Allison is a joy, and learning from her is an additional benefit.

But in the end, efficiency matters only if the quality is high and there is time to relax, even if that means watching another disappointing season of Phillies baseball. Because when I'm watching baseball, or doing something else to relax, I know that it is with my family, who support me in every way possible. My wife Eileen and my sons Bradley and Douglas never complain about my activities and always encourage me. Thank you also to the ABA staff for all you do and for offering Allison and me an outlet to share our perspectives, and to my staff, Pam Myers and Christa Frank High, who might prefer if I focused a bit more on the office.

And finally to you, the readers and the attendees of my 90 in 60 programs, who take the time to comment, to compliment, and to offer your thoughts.

—Dan Siegel

Introduction

If you're like many lawyers we work with, you work long hours and still feel that you don't have enough time to complete your work, let alone accomplish important tasks like marketing and business development, training, mentoring, or strategic planning. Those lawyers often tell us they feel trapped, unable to dig out from what seems like never-ending piles of paper or work to be completed. But then they look around and see other lawyers seemingly accomplishing the same work and still going home for dinner and having time on the weekend for other, nonwork activities. How do *those* lawyers find the time?

Everyone gets exactly the same 24 hours in every day. If you're struggling, the problem often isn't that you don't have enough time; the problem is that either you aren't managing your activities effectively enough to fit within the time you have available or you aren't using the tools you have as efficiently as possible.

This book will help you tackle both.

MANAGING ACTIVITIES

Managing your activities well means eliminating or minimizing obstacles to productivity, including:

- Allowing others' priorities to control your day.
- Failing to appropriately estimate how long tasks will take to complete.
- Allowing constant interruptions.

- Using to-do lists inappropriately
- Planning poorly
- Simply not knowing the most efficient way to accomplish what you need to accomplish

In an article in the *Harvard Business Review*,[1] the authors note that using alternative methods to accomplish goals can boost productivity:

> Some forward-thinking companies have taken a different approach entirely. They expect their leaders to treat time as a scarce resource and to invest it prudently. They bring as much discipline to their time budgets as to their capital budgets. These organizations have not only lowered their overhead expenses; they have liberated countless hours of previously unproductive time for executives and employees, fueling innovation and accelerating profitable growth.

But while most will agree that time is a valuable resource, a great deal of time is wasted every day in workplaces, including law offices. And these time-wasters don't disappear when workers are working from home, especially if they are working parents. According to a study conducted by Mopria Alliance in 2021, employees are distracted approximately every 30 minutes, and parents who work from home face about 10 percent more distractions than parents working in an office and almost 50 percent more distractions than individuals working from home who are not parents.[2]

WHAT ARE THE BIGGEST TIME-WASTING CULPRITS?

Multiple surveys[3] agree that significant workplace time-wasters include:

- **Time spent online**
- **Meetings or conference calls**, especially those that meander or in which more time is spent discussing work than actually executing it, or too

1. Michael Mankins, Chris Brahm & Greg Caimi, *Your Scarcest Resource*, HARV. BUS. REV., May 2014, http://hbr.org/2014/05/your-scarcest-resource/; Michael E. Porter & Nitin Nohria, *How CEOs Manage Time*, HARV. BUS. REV., July–Aug. 2018, https://hbr.org/2018/07/how-ceos-manage-time.
2. *Distracted Working*, MOPRIA ALLIANCE (2021), https://mopria.org/Documents/Mopria-Distracted-Working-Survey-2021.pdf.
3. *Id.*; *New CareerBuilder Survey Reveals the Most Common and Strangest Productivity Killers at Work*, CAREERBUILDER (June 11, 2015), https://press.careerbuilder.com/2015-06-11-New-CareerBuilder-Survey-Reveals-the-Most-Common-and-Strangest-Productivity-Killers-at-Work; *2014 Wasting Time at Work Survey*, SALARY.COM (Mar. 19, 2014), http://www.salary.com/2014-wasting-time-at-work/.

many meetings with short gaps in between that aren't long enough to accomplish anything significant

- **Coworker distractions**
- **Email and instant messaging**
- **Interruptions**
- **Ineffective multitasking**
- **Disorganized workspace**

As you can see, a common theme among time-wasters is that they involve distractions. But it isn't just the distractions themselves that negatively affect productivity. Udemy conducted a study of workplace distractions,[4] which revealed that "[n]oisy, interruption-prone offices make employees unmotivated, stressed, and frustrated. Employers could boost morale—and their bottom line—by giving people training for staying productive despite distractions."[5]

But do general workplace studies apply to lawyers and other knowledge workers? In 2020, a study conducted by the Economist Intelligence Unit commissioned by Dropbox[6] found that U.S. knowledge workers lost 28 percent of their working hours to distractions, averaging a loss of 581 hours per knowledge worker per year. Some of the biggest distractions were interruptions from colleagues; checking, reading, and responding to work-related email; and work-related meetings. The same study showed that almost half of workers said they can focus more when working from home, and 42 percent reported spending more time on deeply focused work while working from home.

Just imagine if you could turn even a portion of that unproductive time into productive time!

TOOLS: TECHNOLOGY AND PRODUCTIVITY

Although technology is supposed to make our lives easier, in some ways technology has only added to our "time management" problems. A Branded Research, Inc., study conducted in 2018 for reMarkable found that people waste eight hours—a full workday—every week checking notifications and that 75 percent

4. *Udemy in Depth: 2018 Workplace Distraction Report*, https://research.udemy.com/research_report/udemy-depth-2018-workplace-distraction-report/ (last visited Aug. 10, 2022).
5. *Id.* at 2.
6. Out of Office: Potential $1.2 Trillion Opportunity in Improving Focus in Knowledge Work, Shows Study Commissioned by Dropbox (Oct. 13, 2020), https://dropbox.gcs-web.com/news-releases/news-release-details/out-office-potential-12-trillion-opportunity-improving-focus.

of people said notifications resulted in procrastination and decreased focus.[7] There is little doubt that in the past four years, that problem has only gotten worse. Compounding the situation is the pandemic and the expectation by some employers and clients that remote work means being "always available" for work.

According to a 2011 article in *Entrepreneur* magazine,[8] in addition to email, the top technology time-wasters include:

1. To-do list apps
2. Social media
3. Instant messages
4. Talking on the phone

Remarkably, more than a decade later, these remain among the top time-wasters,[9] and it's possible that with the increase in remote work and reliance on software and applications at work, these items are even more time consuming than before.

HOW THIS BOOK CAN HELP

This book addresses many of the time-wasters discussed in these studies, from interruptions to emails, to-do lists, meetings, and more. At their core, all of these time-wasters are the result of a combination of two things:

- An inability to *identify the right activities* (inability to say no, lack of direction, interruptions—both human and electronic) and
- An inability to *perform those activities efficiently* (procrastination, ineffective delegation, lack of organization, inefficient use of technology).

7. Press Release, reMarkable, PR Newswire, Seventy-Five Percent of Americans Admit Digital Notifications Hurt Work Focus, New Survey Reveals (Nov. 8, 2018), https://www.prnewswire.com/news-releases/seventy-five-percent-of-americans-admit-digital-notifications-hurt-work-focus-new-survey-reveals-300746148.html.
8. Andrew Kardon, *5 Tech Time Wasters and How to Avoid Them*, ENTREPRENEUR (Oct. 1, 2012), http://www.entrepreneur.com/blog/224526.
9. Rose Leadem, *7 Time Wasters Taking Away from Your Productivity*, CALENDAR (Jan. 22, 2019), https://www.calendar.com/blog/7-time-wasters-taking-away-from-your-productivity/; Rachel Blakely-Gray, *8 Common Workplace Productivity Killers (and What You Can Do about Them)*, JEFFBULLAS.COM (Apr. 28, 2020), https://www.jeffbullas.com/workplace-productivity/; *10 Big Productivity Killers at Work & How to Avoid Them*, CAREERBUILDER (Jan. 14, 2021), https://www.careerbuilder.com/advice/infographic-the-10-biggest-productivity-killers-at-work; Brandi Calero-Holmes, *10 Distractions That Kill Workplace Productivity*, BUS. NEWS DAILY (Aug. 3, 2022), https://www.businessnewsdaily.com/8098-distractions-kiling-productivity.html.

Productivity is about first knowing what to do (ensuring you are focusing on the right things) and only then about getting those things done in the most efficient way possible.

You can be efficient at organizing the supply closet, but if that task isn't the highest use of your time and energy, your efficiency isn't going to improve your overall productivity. You're being efficient but not effective, because you're not focusing your energy on the right things. There's not much benefit to doing the *wrong things* efficiently.

In Part I of this book, you'll learn strategies for conquering your feelings of overwhelm and taking back control of your day. You'll find out how to determine what you should spend your time on and how to eliminate or delegate the remaining tasks. You'll discover why deadlines are important and how to use them effectively, as well as how to use your calendar as one of your most important defenses in the battle to be productive. In short, you'll learn to identify—and focus on—the *right things*.

Once you've determined which tasks you should undertake, then it's time to focus on working as efficiently as possible to get that work done. Toward the end of Part I, you'll learn how to conduct meetings effectively (whether virtual or in person) and create systems for increased efficiency.

In Part II, we'll show you some time-saving technology tips and solutions you may not have heard about. This section of the book will show you how to do things the *right way*. Think of it as your guide to efficiency.

The technology time-saving tips in this book focus on many of the software programs lawyers use on a daily basis. According to the 2021 ABA Legal Technology Survey Report, Windows is the primary operating system used in law firms, with 77% of all lawyers using Windows.[10] In our experience, most lawyers are continuing to use Word, Outlook, and the other programs in the Microsoft Office 365 suite, as well as Adobe Acrobat. As such, our technology tips focus on these programs, but they also include far more general tech time-savers.

Since the first edition of this book was released in 2014, the way lawyers practice law has undergone significant changes, many of which are the result of the COVID-19 pandemic that began in 2020 and only seems to be abating as we write this in 2022. Lawyers rely on technology more today than ever before. They have shifted their practices to more cloud-based platforms and

10. https://www.americanbar.org/groups/law_practice/publications/techreport/2021/ssf/

implemented more remote work options and hybrid work environments, and they conduct more client meetings and document signings virtually. Two years after the beginning of the pandemic, these changes are not likely to go away.

While these changes are positive (and, in many cases, long overdue), some of them add layers of complexity that can also negatively impact lawyers' productivity. In this edition of the book, we discuss how to set up your home office for maximum productivity and how to manage hybrid work.

If you can save six minutes per day with these time-saving tips (and that is a highly conservative estimate), you will save 30 minutes per week (more than 25 hours per year) doing routine, repetitive activities. At $150 per hour, this means that you can recoup more than $3,750 per year in billable time, time that can be devoted instead to client service—or, perhaps, to family and other personal priorities.

Let's get started.

Part I
DEVELOPING GOOD PRODUCTIVITY HABITS

Chapter 1

SET GOALS AND PRIORITIZE

Productivity and organizational expert David Allen, author of *Getting Things Done*, bases his productivity recommendations on the general principles that in order to be productive, you must capture all of the things you have to manage, determine how best to deal with them, and then learn how to focus on the most important items.

In other words, first it's about identifying the "right things." Too often, lawyers fall into the trap of expending time and energy on the "wrong things" because they seem urgent or simply because they happen to be in front of them; the telephone is ringing, the email arrives in our inbox, or a colleague or staff member knocks on the door. But, as we discuss later in this chapter, those urgent items aren't always the right things.

How do you identify what the right things are?

SET GOALS

It's hard to decide what the right things are without first defining your goals. The first step toward becoming more productive is to decide what you need to accomplish. Only then can you determine how you are going to get there. Even if you have no control over your firm's goals, you can (and should) set your own short- and long-term business goals.

The central theme of this book is personal productivity, which means we'll be concentrating mostly on individual shorter-term and micro-level goals and actions to improve your day-to-day efficiency and effectiveness. Long-term and firm-wide goal setting are also extremely important, but they are not the main focus of this book. It does, however, bear mentioning that all of your short-term goals should be in alignment with your long-term, big-picture goals and ideally in line with your firm's goals as well.[1]

Goal-Setting Guidelines

You're not likely to stay on track with goals you don't think are important, so set goals that mean something to you. Your goals should be tied to the core values and principles of your practice and the services you provide to your clients.

If you are new to setting goals, begin with something attainable but not too easy to reach. Taking on too many goals at once, or setting unrealistic goals, will overwhelm you and may slow—or even halt—your progress. Although you don't want to make your goals too easy, you can always add more if you do reach your goals early. Or you can go home for the day, recharge, and enjoy some time away from work.

Your goals need to be realistic and achievable within a specific time frame. They should be measurable so you can see if you are making progress and so you can identify what else needs to be done to meet the goal. Some experts call these kinds of goals "SMART" goals.

SMART is an acronym for

S—Specific—State the goal clearly and concisely. Vague statements about "improving" or "increasing" are not enough—make them concrete.

M—Measurable—It should be easy to tell whether you've reached your goal and, if not, how far off you were.

A—Actionable/Achievable—Goals only work if you can do something to achieve them; they cannot be dependent on the actions of others, on market forces, or on anything else you cannot control.

R—Relevant—The goal should be tied to something important for you personally or for your firm. A specific, measurable, actionable goal that isn't one you are invested in achieving is not likely to make a substantial impact. How will the goal improve your bottom line, advance your career, or improve your clients' lives? Make sure your goals, if achieved, will make a real difference. Focus on the benefits. The relevance component of your goal should answer the question, "Why am I doing this?"

1. All goals should also be related to the firm's values, vision, and mission. To learn more about solidifying your values and creating firm vision and mission statements, check out Allison's Vision and Mission Statement workbook: https://www.lawyermeltdown.com/products-services/product-vision-mission-workbook/ (last visited Aug. 11, 2022).

T—Timed—A measurable goal is no good if you don't know when to measure or how long you anticipate it will take to reach the goal. Set deadlines for yourself or benchmarks you must reach on the way to attaining the goal. Without deadlines or time expectations, it's too easy to put goals on the back burner, as we will see in Chapter 6.

Examples:

Vague Goal: Get more clients.
SMART Goal: Add three new estate planning clients within the next three months.

Vague Goal: Improve the firm's website.
SMART Goal: Update all attorney bios and practice area pages on the firm's website to reduce legalese and incorporate keywords by October 1.

Vague Goal: Improve client service.
SMART Goal: Obtain client feedback on every engagement.

In addition to performance-based goals, you may want to set goals that focus more on learning and mastery than on performance, particularly for newer lawyers or lawyers taking on new practice areas or initiatives.

There are some experts who claim that setting goals can actually be harmful,[2] asserting that goal setting can lead to "unethical behavior, over-focus on one area while neglecting other parts of the business, distorted risk preferences, corrosion of organizational culture, and reduced intrinsic motivation." When goals are set without reference to firm values, culture, ethics, and overall objectives, or if goals are set externally by someone else, it is easy to see how these problems could arise. When realistic goals are set internally, based on values, they should support the organization and the individual.

Done right, goal setting should consider the firm's and individual lawyer's culture and values. Review of those goals and the progress made toward them should always be done with the understanding that there may be competing values or activities that need to be considered. Setting goals is necessary to articulate the direction for a law firm or individual lawyer and to help to measure performance and progress. Even the naysayers concede that incentives and goals are useful.

2. HBS Working Knowledge, *Why Setting Goals Can Do More Harm Than Good*, Forbes (Jan. 2, 2013), http://www.forbes.com/sites/hbsworkingknowledge/2013/01/02/why-setting-goals-can-do-more-harm-than-good/.

Make Goals Concrete

The act of mentally setting a goal likely won't improve your productivity on its own. Reducing your goals to writing will not only help you to clarify them but also make them more concrete and reinforce them in your own mind. Sharing your goals with others can provide further reinforcement.

A study performed by Dr. Gail Matthews at the Dominican University of California[3] found that participants who wrote down their goals accomplished significantly more than those who did not. Those who sent commitments to a third person accomplished significantly more than those who did not. Results were further improved when participants not only wrote down and shared their goals, but also sent weekly reports about their progress.

The study showed that overall, people and businesses that simply write down goals are 50.4 percent more likely to achieve their goals than those who don't. The success rate increases even further with regular progress reports to measure how they are doing against their goals. People are 77.6 percent more likely to achieve their goals when they complete planned progress reports.

Goals mean nothing without execution; they need to be paired with *actions*. Once you have your SMART goals in place, documented, and shared, it's time to choose the *right activities* to pursue in order to reach those goals. This requires you to begin by setting priorities to determine what is most important.

IDENTIFY PRIORITIES

The Jar of Rocks

There are many different versions of the story of the jar of rocks (just Google "jar of rocks" and you'll come across numerous text versions, YouTube demonstrations, and more), but the elements are all essentially the same:

> A professor stands in front of his class and pulls out a large glass jar, which he proceeds to fill with large rocks. When he can no longer fit any more rocks in the jar, he asks the class if the jar is full. The class responds in the affirmative.
>
> The professor then brings out a container of pebbles, which he empties into the jar of rocks. The pebbles fill the spaces between the

3. Gail Matthews, Dep't of Psych., Dominican Univ. of Cal., The Impact of Commitment, Accountability, and Written Goals on Goal Achievement, Podium Presentation at the 87th Convention of the Western Psychological Association (2007), https://scholar.dominican.edu/psychology-faculty-conference-presentations/3/.

> rocks. Again, he asks the class if the jar is full. Again, they respond affirmatively.
>
> Next, the professor empties sand into the jar, which settles between the pebbles. Once more, he asks the class whether the jar is full. Now the class is not so sure.
>
> Finally, the professor brings out a pitcher of water, which he pours into the jar until some begins to overflow. This is when he tells the class that the jar is full.

The jar represents your available time, and each item placed in the jar represents tasks or projects that take up part of that time. The large rocks represent the most important items in your life or your practice; they are things you most need to accomplish—and often the items that are most often neglected. Now imagine that the professor had first filled the jar with water. It would have been impossible to fit any of the other items in the jar.

The small stuff (pebbles, sand, and water) will manage to find its way in between the larger rocks, but you have to put the large rocks in first, or you'll never get them in. In order to fit the most important tasks or projects into your day, you first need to identify what they are; you need to define the activities that are of highest value to you so that you can spend time on those tasks first. In short, you need to prioritize.

Prioritizing is a skill that is particularly critical for lawyers to learn, because lawyers are so often working under deadlines imposed by others, whether they are established by a court, by statute, or by the circumstances of the deal or matter the lawyer is working on. In addition, clients in legal matters are often anxious or highly emotional—the outcome of their legal matter will likely have a significant impact on their lives, families, or businesses. These circumstances place pressure on lawyers, which often results in a failure to prioritize effectively.

Purpose + Result = Priority

Prioritizing tasks helps you to get out of the "reactive mode" by determining in advance where the majority of your time and energy should be spent. Ensuring that each task has a legitimate **purpose** (*i.e.*, it helps to advance your goals—or your clients' goals) is one way to prioritize. Another way to think about this concept is focusing on the outcome or anticipated **result** of the task, rather than on the task itself.

You probably avoid some tasks that should be priorities because you don't like to do them. For example, you may not enjoy creating billing entries or sending out bills, but they should be priorities because you can't get paid without them. Focusing on the outcome (getting paid) instead of the task itself (reviewing your bills) may help you to stop avoiding those tasks. Sometimes the tasks you avoid can be delegated, but sometimes they can't because you're the only one who can do them. (We'll talk more about delegation in Chapter 4.) When unpalatable tasks cannot be delegated, focusing on the outcome can be all the motivation you need to get them done.

If the task has an important purpose and a high-value result, make it a priority.

Stephen Covey's "Importance vs. Urgency" Matrix

Readers of Stephen Covey's *The 7 Habits of Highly Effective People* know that "urgent" tasks tend to get done, regardless of whether they are important. Some tasks are both urgent and important. For example, when you have a scheduled meeting with a client or a hearing date for a motion, somehow the preparation work gets done on time. Those tasks are important, and the deadlines create urgency and provide a framework within which to structure your activities.

Figure 1.1, Covey's Importance vs. Urgency Matrix, illustrates this concept. Tasks that fall within the upper right quadrant, those that are both urgent and important, tend to get done first, but often tasks in the lower right quadrant, those that are urgent but not important, can take precedence over those in the upper left, important but not urgent tasks. That is why it is so important to take control of setting your own priorities and, if necessary, creating urgency around those tasks. (We'll talk about how to do that in Chapter 6.)

Figure 1.1 Importance vs. Urgency Matrix

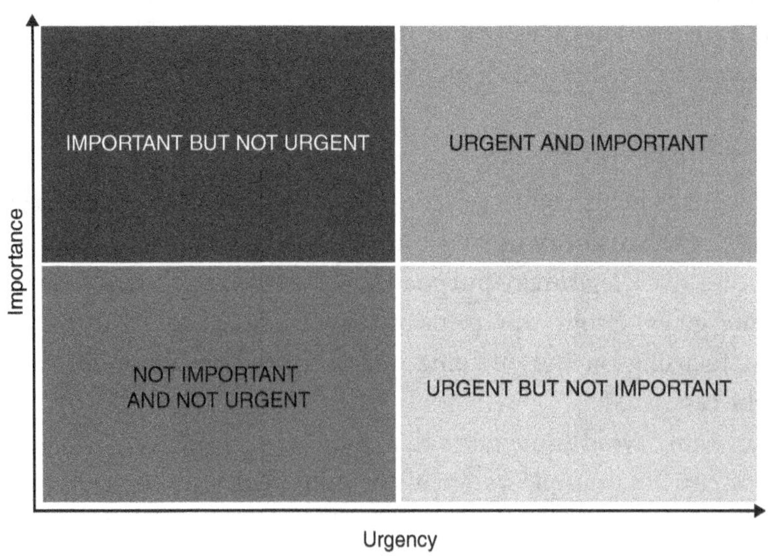

But the activities that Covey calls "important but not urgent" are the tasks that often get carried on a never-ending to-do list. They usually do not have built-in deadlines. And even though they are the activities that are the highest value and that will make the biggest difference to your practice—they'll save you time and money or generate more revenue in the long run—they are often neglected.

FOCUS ON THE ACTIVITIES THAT BRING THE HIGHEST RETURN

High-value activities are those that make the biggest impact, often while using the fewest resources. Many times, these are the very "important but not urgent" tasks that are ignored because you're too wrapped up in the day-to-day activities of the practice or putting out fires to make them a priority. Other times, you just don't know how to identify which activities are high-value activities.

A Note About High-value Activities

While it may seem obvious which activities are high value and which are low value, in our experience, it isn't always that simple. For example, Allison recently worked with a client who had several high-value tasks that needed to be completed, but because his office was so cluttered, he was unable to concentrate on the work he needed to do. In that situation, the best course of action was to take the time to clean up his office to eliminate those distractions. (We'll talk about how to minimize or eliminate distractions in Chapter 2 and how to handle clutter in Chapter 3.)

Some questions to help you identify your high-value activities/tasks (and thus priority) are:

- What is the purpose of this task?
- What will the impact of this task be?
- Is the impact short term or long term?
- How important is this task for my practice or career?
- How important is this task to my client?
- Is it more or less important than the other things that need to be accomplished?
- Will this task help me to advance one of my goals? How?
- Is this task directly related to my personal or the firm's values?
- What will it feel like when this is done? (What will the intangible impact of this task be?)

- What will be the result emotionally, productively, financially, or organizationally?
- Is this a "need" or a "want"?
- How will my firm/practice/clients/employees be affected by this task or its outcome?
- Is this activity something I get paid for?
- Am I truly the only one who can perform this task? Does it require my unique knowledge, skills, and expertise or my personal touch?
- Can this activity help me to strengthen my relationship with an existing client?
- Will this task help me to gain a larger share of my client's business?
- Is this endeavor likely to introduce me to new prospects?
- What will happen if I don't do this task now, or if I delegate it to someone else?

These questions can help you balance your activities. But keep in mind that even if a task wouldn't otherwise be considered a high-value task, it could become a priority because of other factors such as impending deadlines, the age of the task, or the amount of time and energy you have available to devote to it. If the task isn't a high-value task, consider whether it should take precedence over other tasks or can be delegated or deferred, especially if it could be accomplished better, cheaper, or faster.

Prioritizing in this way can help you more easily determine which activities and clients to undertake and which to pass by—at least for now. It will help keep you on track and avoid what some call "Bright Shiny Object Syndrome": being distracted by every new idea or opportunity that comes your way. When you have established goals and priorities, you can decide quickly and easily what deserves your time and attention.

PLANNING

Once you have your goals and priorities in order, you need to make a plan for how to accomplish them. All law firms should have strategic plans, which include big-picture goals. There are many resources available to aid lawyers in creating strategic plans or long-term goals, but these larger plans are beyond the scope of this book. Here, we are focusing more on personal productivity, which requires focus on the day-to-day or week-to-week activities that need to be performed to keep a law firm running, get the work done, and provide excellent service to clients.[4]

Unfortunately, too many lawyers fail to plan their days or weeks in advance. As we have seen, this often causes them to fall into the urgent but not important trap or to allow the priorities of others to supersede their priorities. Do you have a plan for the day, or do you constantly just react to what comes up—emails, telephone calls, or other interruptions? If you're just reacting, you aren't getting the most important things done, and it isn't likely that you're focusing on the task at hand or that you will reach those larger, long-term goals.

Planning is another way to ensure that you are focusing on *your* priorities and getting your most important work done. Before every day, week, or month begins, you should know what you plan to accomplish. When you have a plan, it's much easier to say "no" to interruptions. If those interruptions aren't actually urgent *and* more important than what you already have planned, don't let them distract you. (We'll talk more about interruptions in Chapter 2 and about creating daily and weekly plans in Chapter 6.)

THE POWER OF THREE

Don't let your list of priorities and your plan overwhelm you. Lists can be helpful to keep track of tasks that need to be accomplished, but most typical to-do lists are of limited utility, because they're never ending. No matter how hard you try, instead of getting shorter, your list gets longer—new things crop up, unanticipated client problems arise, or a last-minute emergency that "must" be handled today gets in the way. The typical to-do list gets carried over and repeated from one day to the next. Instead of keeping you focused and making you feel productive, these kinds of to-do lists add to your anxiety, overwhelm, and feelings of helplessness. They're frustrating, exhausting, and ultimately, completely unproductive.

You can focus on only a limited number of priorities at a time. Instead of reviewing your entire to-do list at once, including your wish list of all of the things you would like to accomplish and all of the things that have been left undone, use the Power of Three to help you prioritize.

4. Another excellent resource for a different kind of planning that is also beyond the scope of this book is Pamela H. Woldow and Douglas B. Richardson's book *Legal Project Management in One Hour for Lawyers* (2013) by the ABA Law Practice Division, which addresses management of client matters, fee predictability, and enhanced client communication.

The Power of Three is a concept that has been around for centuries. Humans seem to remember things more easily when they come in threes, and three is a manageable number that can keep you from getting overwhelmed.

The Power of Three can be used for planning on both the macro level (goal setting, big-picture items) and micro level (action steps and daily to-do lists). You should choose only three big goals for your practice at a time. For each of these three goals, there will be numerous objectives to reach and many action steps to perform to get there, so you'll have plenty to do with "only" three goals.

Use the Power of Three to create your daily and weekly plans; identify the three most important tasks that need to be accomplished in a given day and focus on those first. Complete all three of those items before moving on to something else. Your sense of accomplishment that results from completing these three items will motivate you and help to keep you energized in your practice.

By all means, keep a master list of all of your other ideas and your wish list of projects, but use that list as a "brain dump" to simply capture ideas, rather than as a daily working list. It's a good idea to separate this list into short- and long-term goals, priorities, and tasks. Review the larger list only periodically, not daily. When an opportunity, project, or task arises, you can evaluate whether or not it's worth your time and effort by asking yourself whether that particular task will advance you toward one of your three main goals or whether that task "trumps" one or more of the three tasks you've already planned for the day or week. If not, put that item on the master list for the future.

THE POWER OF ONE

Sometimes, even accomplishing three tasks in one day is overly ambitious, particularly in a busy law practice, especially one that typically deals with last-minute emergencies or clients who have immediate needs, such as criminal law. But it can also happen as a result of a real client crisis or simply because some tasks are so time consuming or complicated that they overtake everything else. (For example, if you're working on an appellate brief or preparing for a trial, you may be able to focus on only that one task for an entire day or more.)

To avoid feeling helpless or out of control (or becoming discouraged by even a short to-do list that doesn't get done), ask yourself each day,

> ***"What one thing, if I accomplished it today, would make me feel as if my day had been productive?"***

Focus on that task first. And keep in mind that one task may be only a small part of a larger activity, for example, completing the statement of facts for your brief or gathering the documents and information you need to prepare a contract. If all else fails, at least you'll leave at the end of the day knowing you accomplished something to keep you moving toward your goals.

WRAP UP

The first step to avoiding overwhelm (or what Allison calls "lawyer meltdown") and beginning to be more productive is to develop your own goals and to prioritize your activities based on those goals. Create a plan and make sure you put the big rocks in first. Keep your plans realistic. To avoid being overwhelmed and create laser focus, use the Power of Three and the Power of One. Use your feelings of accomplishment to motivate you to increase productivity.

CHAPTER 1 ACTION STEPS

1. Use the SMART goal framework to develop three main goals you would like to accomplish in your practice in the next six months.
2. Make a list of the main projects on your current to-do list; use the priority questions on pages 9–10 to prioritize your list.
3. Practice using the Power of Three and the Power of One over the next week to identify the high-value tasks you want to complete each day.

Chapter 2 ELIMINATING DISTRACTIONS

As we discussed in Chapter 1, perhaps the biggest enemy of productivity is lack of focus. Despite our best intentions, productivity often falls by the wayside because there are too many distractions, interruptions, or outside demands on our time and attention. These distractions make every task take longer to complete. As a result, a key component to taking back control of your practice and becoming more productive is being able to eliminate (or at least limit) as many of those distractions as possible.

If you're working from home, you may be confronted with even more distractions than you would in the workplace. Demands of other family members, household chores, or even just the call of the refrigerator can all pull your attention away from your work and crush your concentration.

As you saw in the story about the jar of rocks, if you don't ensure that the large rocks (most important tasks) have a place in your day first, the smaller rocks and the sand (less important tasks) will take up all of the available space and time, preventing you from completing important but not urgent tasks. All of those interruptions are like the sand and the water—do they deserve that much of your time? A 2018 study performed by Udemy revealed that reducing workplace distractions helps workers be more productive, increases motivation and confidence in their ability to perform their work well, improves their happiness, and increases their ability to provide a high-quality work product.[1]

1. *Udemy in Depth: 2018 Workplace Distraction Report*, Udemy for Bus., https://research.udemy.com/wp-content/uploads/2018/03/FINAL-Udemy_2018_Workplace_Distraction_Report.pdf.

In this chapter, we'll give you some tools and strategies to help you to eliminate those distractions.

GIVE UP MULTITASKING

Our society has become one in which multitasking is seen as a good practice; people brag about being good multitaskers and wear their attempts to accomplish many different things at once as a badge of honor. Many of those people think that they're productive or getting a lot done because they're multitasking. The truth is probably quite different.

In fact, studies have shown that (with few exceptions) the more you multitask, the less attention and focus you're devoting to any of the tasks you're trying to accomplish. In other words, when you multitask, chances are that you're not performing any of those tasks well. Studies have also shown that multitasking wastes time, rather than saves it.

"Who Multi-Tasks and Why? Multi-Tasking Ability, Perceived Multi-Tasking Ability, Impulsivity, and Sensation Seeking,"[2] a study published in 2013, "examined individual differences in multi-tasking ability by testing participants on multi-tasking activity, perceived multi-tasking ability, impulsivity, and sensation seeking." The findings suggested that *people often multitask not because they are good at it or because it makes them more productive, but because they are simply unable to block out distractions and focus on a single task.*

An earlier study, "Cognitive Control in Media Multitaskers," published in 2009,[3] found that "[h]eavy media multitaskers are more susceptible to interference from irrelevant environmental stimuli and from irrelevant representations in memory."

With the proliferation of devices and additional electronic stimuli in today's society, and the need for lawyers to rely on these tools and devices to practice law effectively, there is a significantly increased risk of media multitasking.

The 2009 study also noted that heavy media multitaskers performed worse on a test of task-switching ability, likely because of their reduced ability to filter out interference from the irrelevant task set. Thus, the authors concluded "that

2. David M. Sanbonmatsu et al., *Who Multi-Tasks and Why? Multi-Tasking Ability, Perceived Multi-Tasking Ability, Impulsivity, and Sensation Seeking*, 8(1) PLoS ONE e54402 (2013), http://www.plosone.org/article/info%3Adoi%2F10.1371%2Fjournal.pone.0054402.
3. Eyal Ophir, Clifford Nass & Anthony D. Wagner, *Cognitive Control in Media Multitaskers*, 106(37) Proc. Nat'l Acad. Scis. U.S.A. 15583, 15583–87 (2009), http://www.ncbi.nlm.nih.gov/pubmed?cmd=Search&doptcmdl=Citation&defaultField=Title%20Word&term=Ophir%5Bauthor%5D%20AND%20Cognitive%20control%20in%20media%20multitaskers.

media multitasking, a rapidly growing societal trend, is associated with a distinct approach to fundamental information processing."[4]

Once again, those most likely to multitask were least able to discern which items most deserved their attention; they were unable to separate relevant from irrelevant stimuli. And according to James Watson, a study team member at the University of Utah, only 2.5 percent of the population (called "supertaskers") can actually process tasks simultaneously.[5]

Considered from a different perspective, based on this study, *for over 97 percent of the population, there's no such thing as multitasking.*[6]

The truth is that you can't simultaneously accomplish two things that require you to expend mental energy. You can only do one at a time. It's how our brains are wired. When you "multitask," what you're really doing is constantly switching back and forth between two or more tasks. In his book *The Myth of Multitasking*, Dave Crenshaw calls this "switch-tasking." Switch-tasking actually *costs* time.[7]

The Cost of Switch-Tasking

If you've ever had the experience of not remembering what you were doing after you've been interrupted, you know that it actually takes more time to get things done when you try to multitask. In his book *Brain Rules*, John Medina contends that people who are interrupted—and therefore have to switch their attention back and forth—take 50 percent longer to accomplish a task. According to Medina, multitasking is nothing more than constantly interrupting the

4. *Id.*
5. *"Supertaskers" That Can Drive and Talk on Phone Rare*, Live Sci. (Mar. 29, 2010), http://www.livescience.com/8186-supertaskers-drive-talk-phone-rare.html.
6. A 2019 study of media multitasking showed that consuming multiple streams of media simultaneously might not be associated with less efficient cognitive processing, as measured with objective tests. (*See* Wisnu Wiradhany & Janneke Koerts, *Everyday Functioning-Related Cognitive Correlates of Media Multitasking: A Mini Meta-Analysis*, 24(2) Media Psych. 276–303 (2019), https://www.tandfonline.com/doi/full/10.1080/15213269.2019.1685393.) However, we do not believe that this kind of media multitasking represents the activities typically undertaken by lawyers during their workday. In addition, these same studies revealed that participants self-reported increasing problems with attention and distractibility, regulating emotions, increased impulsiveness, and memory. A 2016 study (Se-Hoon Jeong & Yoori Hwang, *Media Multitasking Effects on Cognitive vs. Attitudinal Outcomes: A Meta-Analysis*, 42(4) Hum. Commc'n Rsch. 599–618 (2016), https://academic.oup.com/hcr/article-abstract/42/4/599/4064731) indicated that multitasking had more negative effects on users who had less control over the media and where the tasks being performed were unrelated or were physically separate from one another. In our experience, these conditions are more like those most lawyers will encounter when attempting to multitask at work.
7. A study involving four experiments that measured the amount of time lost when young adults repeatedly switched between two tasks showed that multitasking may actually be less efficient—especially for complicated or unfamiliar tasks—because it takes extra time to shift mental gears every time a person switches between the two tasks, resulting in less efficiency for multitaskers. *See* Joshua Rubinstein, David Meyer & Jeffrey Evans, *Executive Control of Cognitive Processes in Task Switching*, 27(4) J. Experimental Psych.: Hum. Perception & Performance 763–97 (2001).

flow of work on one task to replace it with another, supporting the theory that what most people call multitasking is really switch-tasking.

Switch-tasking also costs time because it results in more errors. In *Brain Rules*, Medina confirms that those who attempt to multitask make up to 50 percent more errors. That means those tasks will need to be revisited or repeated. Simply put, fixing mistakes takes time.

Did you get that? *What most people call multitasking actually results in the task taking 50 percent longer to complete, and multitaskers make 50 percent more errors.*

Even within the same projects, multitasking can be a mistake. Consider a brief you are writing. If you stop every time you see a spelling error, you may lose track of what you were writing. Instead, you can ignore the typos and trust that you (or spell check) will catch them later while proofing the document, when you are focused on appearance and not substance.

In general, switch-tasking causes as much as a 40 percent drop in overall productivity. Not only that, but one study[8] performed on behalf of Hewlett Packard showed that switch-tasking can also cause up to a ten-point drop in IQ.[9] That study showed that workers who constantly allowed email and phone calls to distract them reduced their mental sharpness, similar to losing a night of sleep!

The proliferation of technology and ways to communicate, including phone calls, email, text messages, instant messages, and video calls, has created an expectation that lawyers are always available and that responses will come immediately. Let's take some examples:

- You're talking on the phone and a colleague enters your office; you wave them in or hold up a finger for them to wait.
- You're speaking on the phone or with someone in your office and trying to respond to email at the same time.
- You check email during a meeting or video call.
- You take a phone call while a client or colleague is in your office.

In each of these instances, you're not fooling anyone. In fact, when you believe, as even the authors do at times, that you're accomplishing more by multitasking, you're doing just the opposite. Think of how many times you answer an email or text message while on the phone—and then think of how many

8. *"Infomania" Worse Than Marijuana*, BBC News (Apr. 22, 2005), http://news.bbc.co.uk/2/hi/uk_news/4471607.stm.
9. Peter Bregman, *How (and Why) to Stop Multitasking*, Harv. Bus. Rev. (May 20, 2010), http://blogs.hbr.org/2010/05/how-and-why-to-stop-multitaski/.

times you go back to the email or text because you forgot something. And if you don't set all your email messages to delay sending for a few minutes, you end up writing multiple emails to accomplish a result that could have been handled more efficiently if you had focused your energies only on that task and sent only one email.

Not only have you been unproductive, but your switch-tasking behavior may be damaging your relationships as well. You've kept a colleague waiting, giving them the wrong message, that is, that they are not important. You may have sent an email to the wrong party because you weren't paying attention. Or you wasted your client's time or caused confusion because you needed to send multiple messages instead of just one.

Think of a time when you've been on the phone with a colleague and you can tell you've lost their attention; they either stop responding or ask a question about something that, had they been listening, they would already know the answer to. Chances are, that person was trying to multitask. How did that make you feel? How do you think your clients feel in that situation? For example, when Dan meets with clients, his policy is not to take calls during the meeting. This allows him to focus on the clients and assures that a "brief" call doesn't turn into a lengthy interruption that clients will find to be rude.

There are times when you *can* multitask, but only if only one of the tasks requires mental energy and the other is a rote task requiring limited brainpower, or when neither task requires mental focus. Some examples might include folding laundry while watching TV, listening to music while on the treadmill, or putting labels on envelopes while talking on the phone. Crenshaw calls these activities "background tasking"; one task is the main focus while the other occurs in the background, is essentially automatic, and doesn't require your direct attention. But those occasions are rare, especially in the business world.

The next time you're tempted to multitask, think about what it might cost you and how it might negatively affect those around you or even your clients. It's far more productive to focus on only one thing at a time, rather than trying to accomplish two things at once.

INTERRUPTIONS

As you've seen, multitasking is nothing more than allowing yourself to be constantly interrupted, and interruptions are enormous time-wasters. When you commit to giving up multitasking, you'll be faced with a choice when interruptions arise—continue working on your original task or stop, take on the new task, and then return to the original task later. Sometimes you don't have a choice—if a true emergency arises and you need to stop what you're doing, for example, but these instances should be rare for most law practices.

When interruptions are unavoidable, you can help reduce the cost by making a note about what you were doing and where you are and putting that task away so that you can fully focus on the new priority or crisis. As you are working on a task, if something unrelated comes to mind that you need to do or remember, simply make a note and continue working on the original task. Process those notes at specific times during the day to be sure they don't get lost.

Most interruptions don't represent real emergencies or significant priorities that would trump the task you're already working on. In those instances, it's better to avoid the interruption entirely. Resist the urge to permit any interruption at any time. Remember:

- You don't have to answer the telephone just because it's ringing.
- You don't have to check your email every time you hear the tone that announces a new message.
- You don't have to entertain everyone who darkens your doorway and asks, "Got a minute?"

The Cost of Interruptions

Interruptions represent huge productivity losses. According to a 2013 article in the *Wall Street Journal,*[10] frequent interruptions are linked to higher rates of exhaustion and stress-induced ailments and a doubling of error rates. "Employees who experienced frequent interruptions reported 9 percent higher rates of exhaustion—almost as big as the 12 percent increase in fatigue caused by oversize workloads, according to a survey of 252 working adults published recently in the *International Journal of Stress Management*. Interruptions also sparked a 4 percent increase in physical ailments such as migraines or backaches, says the study."[11] And we've already seen how constant interruptions can mimic lack of sleep and reduce productivity.

In a paper entitled *The Cost of Interrupted Work: More Speed and Stress,* Gloria Mark, Daniela Gudith, and Ulrich Klocke reported on a study they conducted on how interruptions affected work performance.[12] The study found

10. *The Biggest Office Interruptions Are . . . ,* Wall St. J. (Sept. 10, 2013), http://online.wsj.com/news/articles/SB1000 1424127887324123004579057212505053076.
11. *Id.*
12. Gloria Mark, Daniela Gudith & Ulrich Klocke, *The Cost of Interrupted Work: More Speed and Stress,* Proceedings of the 2008 Conference on Human Factors in Computing Systems, https://www.ics.uci.edu/~gmark/chi08-mark .pdf.

that it didn't matter whether an interruption was related or unrelated to the task being performed and that many workers were able to compensate for the interruption and complete the task by working faster, but the workers were more stressed, experienced increased frustration and time pressure, and had to expend more effort. These costs are not insignificant. The *Wall Street Journal* article also noted that it can take more than 25 minutes, on average, to resume a task after an interruption, and after resuming complex tasks, it can take an additional 15 minutes to return to the same focus or concentration as before the original interruption.[13] This was confirmed by a study of Microsoft employees reported in the *New York Times*,[14] which revealed that it took an average of 15 minutes for employees to return to full function at complex tasks like writing computer code after checking email. In other words, a single interruption can cost you a total of 40 minutes. Imagine what that can do to your productivity if you allow multiple interruptions throughout the day! These interruptions allow the priorities of others to take precedence over your priorities. But many of these interruptions can be avoided if you set some boundaries and ground rules for how others interact with you.

Interruptions from Colleagues or Staff

Not all lawyers have staff, but those who do often find that staff interruptions can be a major cause of loss of productivity. Busy lawyers can be out of the office frequently: in court, meeting with clients, networking, and more. Or, if they are in the office, they may be busy with client meetings or calls, making them largely unavailable to staff. Solo or small firm lawyers who are involved in just about every matter the office handles may experience even more interruptions.

When you are present or "available," typically when trying to concentrate or get important work accomplished, you can be bombarded with interruptions simply because your staff doesn't know when you will be available next. As a result, staff will take up additional time trying to remember every issue or question they may have because they might not have another chance any time soon. Or they will try to grab you the moment you set foot in the office or as you're walking past. Once they have your attention, they may be afraid to let it go, because it is so difficult to get your attention in the first place.

You can limit or eliminate these problems with a few simple steps.

---

13. *The Biggest Office Interruptions Are . . .*, *supra* note 10.
14. Steve Lohr, *Slow Down, Brave Multitasker, and Don't Read This in Traffic*, N.Y. Times, Mar. 25, 2007, https://www.nytimes.com/2007/03/25/business/25multi.html.

When you want to spend time on focused work, have an assistant screen your calls or use an answering service. Give a definite time when you will return calls and then follow through. Block out "do not disturb" time and instruct others not to interrupt; close your office door or, if all else fails, leave your office to ensure that important work gets done without interruption. In Dan's office, for example, when Dan needs DND time, he puts a blank yellow sticky note on the door and turns on the DND setting on his phone to alert others that he is not to be interrupted.

Train staff to hold all questions for a specific time so you can tackle several issues at once, rather than dealing with multiple interruptions each time a question arises. Give staff a clear time when you'll be available to speak with them, and make sure you are actually available at that time. This will eliminate their urge to grab you every time they see you. Whether you have set office hours or alert your staff to specific times each day when you'll be available, they must know when they can reach you. Some of Allison's clients have had success implementing office hours when they are always available for questions. Staff knows not to interrupt at other times for nonemergencies and to hold their questions for the scheduled office hours.

In Dan's office, he and his small staff meet every morning for a few minutes and go over everything on their agendas to try to avoid multiple additional interruptions during the rest of the day. This is akin to scheduling recurring meetings with those who are accountable to you or have regular questions for you. For example, you could schedule a meeting with your assistant every day at 4 p.m. to resolve any remaining issues from the day and plan for the following day, and a weekly meeting with your associate to report on progress of ongoing projects. Many of Allison's clients have found these recurring meetings to be extremely helpful in boosting their productivity and effectiveness.

Dan's office also explains to clients that he prefers to give every client personal undivided attention, which can be a challenge if he takes a call while with a client or working on matters that require his complete attention. They explain that he will return calls at a time that is convenient for the client but also one when he can provide the client with the same undivided focus he gives to the clients in the office or the matters requiring complete attention. In short, give both clients and staff clear expectations about your availability. As Dave Crenshaw points out, often it isn't unavailability itself that causes the interruptions—it's just the uncertainty about when they might see you again.

Colleagues are another oft-cited source of interruptions. Even solos can experience these interruptions, particularly if they are working in an office suite or shared office arrangement. Colleagues may stop by for feedback or questions, or they may simply want to take a break and chat. This can be incredibly frustrating. Follow the steps we've outlined earlier to deal with colleagues as well: create a "do not disturb" sign, close your office door, or ask them to make an appointment with you to discuss their issue when you have more time and can focus on their problem. Don't be shy about telling a colleague that you'd love to hear about their latest vacation but that you can't do so until you've completed your task; perhaps set a time for coffee, lunch, or a drink with them instead of chatting during your regular work hours.

To further reduce wasted time, remove the chairs from your individual office if you can. While this may not be possible for solos with limited access to conference room space, for many lawyers it is an effective way to limit interruptions. Chairs in your office or by your desk serve as an open invitation for people to take a break in your workspace. If someone needs to ask you a question, she can do it standing up. If you need to have a more in-depth meeting, you can move it to a conference room or other space where there are fewer (guess what?) distractions than in your office.

Moving to a conference room for planned meetings, whether with clients or colleagues, can help you to mentally shift from work mode to meeting mode, and meeting outside of your office proper or away from your desk reduces the temptation to glance at email or answer calls during your meeting, making your meeting more effective.

Another reason to consider removing those guest chairs in your office is that, in Allison's experience, these chairs have a tendency to turn into additional horizontal storage spaces for files, papers, or other miscellaneous clutter, rather than serving their intended purpose. (See Chapter 3 for more on dealing with clutter in your office.)

By answering all of your staff or colleagues' questions, you may be preventing them from learning and growing. When you learn to set expectations and follow through, staff, colleagues, and clients will know when they will have access to you, and they will be more likely to hold their questions for your designated meeting time. Dan has found that it is effective to have a colleague explain the situation and what they propose doing rather than just explaining the problem. By having a solution, even if not the best, they understand their questions better. You may even find that when staff cannot count on your availability, they learn how to resolve some issues on their own.

Keep these same concepts in mind when you are tempted to interrupt others. Respect their time. Ask if you can schedule a time to talk. If you don't want to be interrupted with "quick questions," don't do it to others in your office. Save up questions for those you work with frequently to ask all at once (preferably at a designated time). When leaving messages for others, let them know when you will be available so they can call back at a time that is convenient for both of you (and avoid playing telephone tag).

Technology Interruptions

Some of the most common interruptions are those that result from technology (email, phone calls, text messages, and social media alerts). Just because you have a cell phone doesn't mean you should be always available or that everyone needs to have the number. Being always available doesn't necessarily serve you, your practice, or your clients.

Remember: switch-tasking damages relationships and being always available leads to burnout. Give your full attention to the person in front of you—don't look at the computer screen or cell phone. Don't try to speak on the phone and check your email at the same time. Don't allow yourself to be interrupted by technology when you are in the midst of a conversation with a client, colleague, or staff member.

In the same way that you schedule time for staff, you can schedule time for technology by checking email only at specified times, using the "do not disturb" feature on your phone, and designating time for social media.

As Richard Branson says, "Manage your mobile, don't let it manage you."[15]

Are You Encouraging Interruptions?

Although you'll never eliminate interruptions entirely, taking steps to prevent or limit them can result in a significant increase in productivity. But don't ignore how your own behavior contributes to interruptions or distractions. You may be your own worst enemy if you allow yourself to be distracted or if you cause the distractions yourself.

On her website, http://theproductivitypro.com/, productivity expert Laura Stack highlights the problem of self-sabotage, emphasizing that many distractions are self-imposed. Stack talks about several types of self-imposed distraction, including perfectionism, procrastination, and negative self-talk.

Perfectionism, she explains, "is based on the admirable desire to do the very best job possible; but when taken to extremes, it can distract you from getting the job done." To overcome perfectionism, and avoid the paralysis that can result, she suggests that "once you've made a decision to do something, get

---

15. Richard Branson, *Productivity Hacks: It's All in the Eyes*, LinkedIn (Jan. 21, 2014), https://www.linkedin.com/pulse/20140121000214-204068115-productivity-hacks-it-s-all-in-the-eyes/.

started and work through the details as they arise."[16] (We'll talk more about overcoming perfectionism and "analysis paralysis" in Chapter 5.)

We're all familiar with **procrastination.** Stack suggests that when procrastination rears its head, you need to force yourself to do the work (remember, you won't get paid if it's not done or, worse, you could commit malpractice if it's late): "visualize what you need to do, break it down into smaller tasks that are easier to handle, and then buckle down and get it done."[17] (We'll talk more about procrastination and breaking large tasks into smaller "chunks" in Chapter 5.)

Finally, Stack addresses **negative self-talk,** which is probably more common than any of us wants to admit. Each of us goes through life constantly thinking about and internally commenting on the situations we encounter. Stack notes that "self-talk can be self-defeating" and that "[i]f you convince yourself that something's too difficult or that there's no point in trying, you throw roadblocks in the path of productivity."[18] Her solution is to challenge your negativity by asking:

- Is the situation really as bad as it seems?
- If so, what's the worst thing that could happen?
- How about the best thing?
- What's most likely to occur?
- How would I perceive this situation if I were in a positive mood?

While Stack concedes that it is difficult to eliminate self-sabotage because many of us are our own worst critics, we "have to be realistic and ruthless about facing down [our] subconscious."[19] As mentioned earlier, you may also be sabotaging your efforts by allowing others to interrupt you and not setting good boundaries and limits.

TECHNOLOGY TOOLS TO HELP YOU FOCUS

Instead of allowing technology to be yet another distraction, use it to help you eliminate distractions. There are many software programs, including many designed for children, that will help you to focus by blocking your ability to access specific websites or programs (such as social media sites) for a period

16. Laura Stack, *Dealing with Distractions and Interruptions: Strategies for Staying Focused on Important Tasks,* The Productivity Pro (May 2011), https://theproductivitypro.com/newsletters/num144May2011.htm.
17. *Id.*
18. *Id.*
19. *Id.*

of time. Other programs help you track the time you are spending on different activities on your computer or device so that you can see where you need to make changes.

New apps and programs are being developed every day, while others disappear or become obsolete, so no list of these tools in a print publication can ever be comprehensive or completely up to date, but here are a few tools[20] you might explore to get you started, and if, by the time you read this, some of these tools no longer exist, you can search for these features in other apps or programs:

- RescueTime provides time-tracking capabilities as well as website blocking so you can stay focused and track your time all at once.
- Freedom blocks distractions, including apps, websites, and internet access, on all your devices at once so you can't cheat by using your phone if just your laptop is blocked.
- The Serene app is only available for macOS as of this writing, but a Windows version should be released soon. The app bills itself as good for deep focus sessions—first it directs you to define a goal you want to accomplish, and then you schedule sessions to work on that goal. Once in a session, the app blocks distractions from apps and websites but also provides music, countdown timers, and regular breaks so you can be more productive in each session.
- With the Cold Turkey Blocker, you schedule times in advance and customize what will be unavailable during that block—just specific URLs, entire domains, apps, or your entire system.
- LeechBlock NG is a free browser-based website-blocking app that allows you to specify up to 30 sets of sites to block, with different times and days for each set. You can tell the app when to block the sites or to block after a specified time limit, and you can even block sites immediately for a specified duration.
- Finally, SelfControl, available only for Mac, blocks any internet-based distractions you choose—but beware—once a block is started, you cannot undo it, even if you restart your computer or delete the application. You will be blocked until the timer expires. It is truly the option for those who have no self-control!

20. RescueTime—https://www.rescuetime.com/; Freedom—https://freedom.to/; Serene—https://sereneapp.com/; Cold Turkey Blocker—https://getcoldturkey.com/; LeechBlock NG—https://www.proginosko.com/leechblock/; SelfControl—https://selfcontrolapp.com/.

THE "DON'T DO" LIST

As we discussed in the previous chapter, a long to-do list leads to discouragement and overwhelm. It can be easy to become so preoccupied with how much needs to get done that you constantly rush from one thing to the next to the next without taking time to strategize or look at the big picture. While you're busy doing one thing on your list, ten other things crop up to add to the list. Or you get distracted thinking about what you need to do next before you complete the task at hand.

What You Really Need Is a "Don't Do" List

What's a "don't do" list? It's a list of the things you shouldn't be doing, the things that could be delegated to someone else or outsourced. The "don't do" list also includes all of the things you completely let go—things that can be eliminated entirely (or eliminated for a specified time period).

Creating a "don't do" list doesn't necessarily mean that you need to take time to write an actual list, but it is a conceptual reminder that you need to first take the time to identify habits, behaviors, and tasks that are time-wasters or reduce your productivity and then constantly re-evaluate what you're doing and how you're doing it to make sure that the tasks you undertake are serving you, your firm, and your clients. If you need a physical reminder to stop engaging in those behaviors or taking on those tasks, by all means make a list and refer to it.

Narrow Your Options

Law school trains lawyers to spot issues, but issue-spotting behavior isn't necessarily the most efficient way to run a law practice. In fact, it often leads to "analysis paralysis"—every issue must be at least considered, if not addressed, and this hampers lawyers by creating too many distractions. (See Chapter 5 for more on "analysis paralysis.")

Have you ever been to a restaurant with a huge menu and found it so overwhelming that you ended up just ordering a burger because there were too many choices? The same thing happens with an overwhelming to-do list; it is so massive that it's easier to do the familiar or return to reactive mode, even if the resulting tasks are not priorities. The "don't do" list counteracts this by narrowing your options so that you're not overwhelmed by so many choices every time something new arises.

Having a "don't do" list lets you identify tasks you don't want to do or that you shouldn't be doing because they distract you and prevent you from accomplishing more important tasks; if it's already on the "don't do" list, it's easy to immediately recognize it and move on to more productive endeavors.

How do you decide what goes on the "don't do" list? Anything that distracts you from the main goals that you want to accomplish belongs on the list. The "don't do" list can come into play in a variety of areas in your practice—in the choice of day-to-day activities, your selection of clients or matters, or even what matters you should respond to first.

Take, for example, one of Allison's clients, the managing partner of a four-attorney firm who felt it was her obligation to open the mail every day so she could be on top of what was going on at the firm. But the time it took for her to open and sort the mail was time away from her other, more valuable duties. When she finally used her "don't do" list and gave the job of opening and sorting the mail to her receptionist, she reclaimed a lot of billable time. Now she can breeze through the already opened, date-stamped, and sorted mail and still keep current.

Your "don't do" list may also include certain types of clients. Another lawyer finally fired a client who was difficult from the very first meeting, and she finally drew the line when the client began treating her abusively. She's added abusive clients to her "don't do" list. Now when she sees one coming, she'll just say no. She won't add to her stress level by dealing with clients who don't respect her and don't value her work. The money that client might bring in just isn't worth it. She saved herself endless hours of worry and unproductive activity—because dealing with that abusive client was distracting, even when she was working with other clients. (We'll talk more about eliminating clients later in this chapter.)

Think about your strengths and weaknesses when making your "don't do" list. If you're a great speaker but a poor writer, perhaps writing articles, motions, and briefs should go on your "don't do" list. You can also create a "go to" list, including copywriters, contract lawyers, and others you can rely upon to do the work for you. Or delegate the task to someone else in the firm with excellent writing skills and, if necessary, you can simply provide final approval. Then you can focus your energies on trying cases, giving seminars or presentations, or other activities where you can highlight your speaking skills.

Some marketing activities may belong on your "don't do" list. Consider the solo attorney who belongs to so many networking groups that he's at a networking event every day, sometimes two or three times a day. That means he's at his office late into the night and every single weekend handling his regular work. As a long-term strategy, this might not be the best for him or his family. Marketing and practice building are very high-value activities for a solo to perform. But they're only valuable if they are strategic—if they're putting you in front of potential clients or leads or if the groups or events are ones that you're passionate about.

Saying no is an essential part of your "don't do" list. Being unable to say no to a request when you're already overburdened is a mistake. If you're unable to devote the time and energy necessary to a project or group, your participation can end up working against you by creating a negative impression. Evaluate which groups or activities will be the most beneficial to you (or to the people or causes you're supporting) and then limit your participation to those that are the most valuable. You can get more value for less time, energy, and stress. If the things already on the to-do list are more important or more valuable, these invitations belong on the "don't do" list.

Although lawyers need to be responsive and accessible to clients, a good "don't do" list might include particular days or times when you're "off limits." Dan, for example, does not give his cell phone number to clients, eliminating those calls and texts, but he can retrieve messages at any time from his office phone. He also leaves his phone downstairs after dinner and doesn't take calls until the next morning.

Allowing constant interruptions of family or leisure time—including taking calls at home or on your cell phone—not only robs you of much-needed recharging and rest, but as we've already seen, it is a disservice to clients who are only getting part of your attention. The same goes for interruptions of important business or client-related activities. It's rare that clients have a real emergency that can't wait an hour or two for you to finish preparing your motion in limine or complete a meal with your family.

Your "don't do" list may also highlight where you need to set boundaries with clients and others. As we've seen earlier, technology and remote work have added to our daily interruptions, and smartphones, email, text messages, instant messaging, and the like have contributed to the idea that lawyers are available to clients 24/7. By allowing those interruptions and responding to clients immediately regardless of where you are and what you're doing, you reinforce the client's expectation that you're always available. Instead, train your clients to expect responses within a specific period of time or within a particular time frame, but set boundaries and limits in the same way you would set them for staff or colleagues. For example, you may want to explain to clients that your office policy is to return all calls within one business day or that you only respond to email in the late afternoon. Dan's office explains this in their engagement letters. This is akin to doctors who return all calls after they are done seeing patients or making their rounds.

Practice areas can, and generally should, also be items to add to your "don't do" list. If your practice focuses on family law and a client brings you a medical malpractice case, or if you're a transactional lawyer who has never seen the inside of a courtroom and a client wants you to try a case, turning down the client's request or referring it to a colleague who regularly handles those matters is probably the right decision. It is the right decision not just because you won't be dabbling, but also because you reduce the chances of a malpractice claim against you.

Instead, turn to your "go to" list of referral attorneys (to whom you send these cases and who refer cases in your practice areas to you). If you aren't well versed in the particular area of the law, don't have the time or resources to learn, or don't have someone in your firm to help you, you are asking for more trouble than taking the case is worth. Having a "go to" network of attorneys to whom you can refer cases in other practice areas so you know these clients are well taken care of can assure that you're meeting your clients' needs while still remaining true to your own goals.

Identifying your "don't dos" can be an effective tool for managing your time and reducing your stress. Knowing in advance what things you won't do lets you move on quickly, without wasting additional time analyzing everything that comes to your attention.

The "don't do" list also reminds you to ask for help in the areas that aren't your strengths, so you can focus your efforts on what you do best and what brings the most value to your clients and to your life. It allows you to let go of the idea that you can do everything and be everything to everyone. It's a shorthand way of cutting through all of the clutter of what needs to be done so you can get back to providing great service to your clients.

ELIMINATE CLIENTS!

Some clients may belong on your "don't do" list. Every lawyer has horror stories about bad clients, clients they never should have agreed to represent, or matters they should not have agreed to take on or that got out of control and caused a financial loss.

The 80-20 Rule

You may be familiar with the 80-20 rule, also known as the Pareto Principle, in which 80 percent of your work comes from 20 percent of your clients and 20 percent of your clients will cause 80 percent of your problems.

Focusing on your best clients, rather than on your worst clients, brings a big return. These clients are more likely to be satisfied with the work you perform, pay on time, and refer other good clients. Unfortunately, the reality is that bad clients tend to get more of a lawyer's time and attention than the good clients.

Are there some clients or matters on your current list that you would rather not work with? Do you cringe when you know a particular client is on the telephone or wants to schedule a meeting with you? Make a list of those clients. Then ask yourself why these clients are at the bottom of your list. Are they difficult to deal with? Do they fail to see the value of the work that you do? Are they uncooperative? Do they fail to pay their bills on time? Do they constantly question everything you're doing? Is the work boring or outside of your comfort zone?

Now make a list of those reasons, whether they describe your clients or the matters you're handling for those clients.

Eliminate the Worst Clients

To keep your best clients coming back and referring additional work to you, you must ensure that lower-value clients are not taking the place of or distracting you from higher-value clients. One way to keep the focus on the highest-value clients in your practice is to get rid of the bottom tier of your clients.

Consider firing your nightmare clients, clients who don't pay on time or aren't the proper fit for your practice—your practice will benefit, and so will you. Also, include your staff in this discussion, as they will be glad to tell which clients make their lives the most difficult and which should be jettisoned. Although the idea of firing clients might be scary, allowing bad clients to pull your attention from your highest-value clients can be even more detrimental to your practice.

Bad clients drive out good clients. If your practice is filled with lower-value clients who don't value your work, who are price sensitive, or whose work you just don't feel like doing, you won't have room in your practice to take on the higher-value clients. And you'll shortchange your existing high-value clients because your problem clients will get all of your attention.

You might be afraid that turning away clients isn't a prudent financial move. But not all clients are profitable. Consider the damage that bad clients do to your bottom line, your stress level, your ability to concentrate and to provide quality work not only for the bad client, but for other clients as well.

Bad clients, low-value matters, or matters that are a bad fit for you

- drain your energy;
- make it more difficult to concentrate on the matters you're handling for your best clients;
- prevent you from seeking additional work from your good clients;
- cause you to turn away business from a potentially good client because you're too busy working on lower-value matters or with bad clients;
- sabotage your productivity; and
- increase stress and anxiety for attorneys and staff.

Is it time for you to get rid of some clients? Perhaps there's another lawyer in your area who needs additional work or is a better fit for that client's personality or the type of work that client wants or needs. Now is the time to pull out your "go to" list.

Being busy isn't the same as being successful or profitable. Getting rid of bad clients makes room for you to take on additional, higher-value clients—and chances are that your higher-value clients will be less price sensitive. Often, you can make more money with fewer high-value clients than you can with a high-volume practice filled with lower-value clients.

But getting rid of less desirable clients is only part of the solution. Once your practice is free of bad clients, you'll want to keep it that way by not taking on those problem clients in the first place. You'll need to put some systems in place to help you determine at the outset which clients are good clients and which are bad ones so you can send the bad ones packing before they cause trouble for your practice.

Client Selection: Are You Ignoring Your Gut?

Client selection is one of the most important and most overlooked levers of success. Much attention is paid to marketing and client acquisition, but much less emphasis is placed on determining whether lawyers are attracting and working with the *right kinds of clients*.

As we have seen, not every client is a good client. In fact, some clients are downright awful. If you can eliminate these clients before they shift your focus away from the good, high-value clients who might bring you more business, you'll be ahead of the game.

Intuition (and sometimes fear) provides clues that often get ignored when lawyers first interact with potential clients. Too often, lawyers talk themselves into accepting clients they shouldn't. They ignore the gut feeling and the red flags that almost always are present. Or, they make excuses for a client's bad behavior, inability to listen or follow directions, or other warning signs. But if more lawyers heeded their intuition—that feeling that something just doesn't seem right with the client or the situation—fewer attorneys would be stuck with clients who don't pay or worse. Ignoring your gut can put you and your practice at a disadvantage. Reconnect with that gut feeling in the area of client selection.

Too often, lawyers don't reach out for help until *after* the lawyer has already accepted the client, the retainer has been signed, and the situation has gotten worse. At that point, the lawyer is just trying to find a way to salvage the situation or end the relationship. Frequently, the best thing to do is to get out, and get out fast, even if it means taking a loss on any work that has already been performed. But sometimes it's too late and the circumstances (or the court) require you to continue. That's why identifying and avoiding bad clients early is so crucial.

Allison has had countless conversations with lawyers who have come to her unsure about whether they should take on a potential client. Some red flags have been raised, or they just have a bad feeling about the client. Instead of listening to that feeling, they try to talk themselves out of rejecting the client. They don't trust their gut. Every single time the lawyer has talked themselves into taking the client, they have regretted it. None of the lawyers who decided to forgo the client regretted their decision.

Why Lawyers Take On Bad Clients

Most people who enter the legal profession genuinely want to help people. Sometimes lawyers take on bad clients and ignore their gut instinct simply because they feel bad for the client and want to help them. Sometimes the lawyer thinks they can convince the client to be reasonable or change the client's mind. Other times the lawyer doesn't want to reject the client because they were referred by a friend, a colleague, or someone to whom the lawyer felt they owed a favor.

Often the decision to take on a bad client is made out of fear or uncertainty. This is especially true with young lawyers, lawyers just starting their own practices, or lawyers facing financial difficulties. They fear turning away one client will result in a reduction in inquiries, or they simply don't know where their next case will come from, and they fear that they won't have any work to do if they let the client in front of them go.

But sometimes taking on a bad client puts you in a worse position than having no client at all. When you take on a client who refuses to pay, is unreasonable, drains your energy for others, or worse—files a complaint or grievance against you—you're worse off than if you had rejected the work from the beginning.

Dan has what is called the "manure" rule. Manure doesn't smell better the longer it's in your office. If a client is a bad client, or a case goes from good to bad, it's better to cut your losses than to let them continue to grow. Your gut is often the best judge of bad clients. And there is a difference between bad clients and bad cases, but you need to evaluate both. Don't ignore that gut feeling that signals that a client is not telling you the truth or isn't the right fit for you. Take the time to process what you hear, how you feel, and how clients react to you during your initial interactions with them, whether those interactions are by telephone or in person. Does this person seem more like your best clients or your worst clients? Does something seem off? Are you questioning whether you should agree to represent them? If so, pay attention.

Identify Bad Clients Early and Avoid or Disengage from Them

Lawyers who have found themselves in a difficult situation in the past can often look back and identify warning signs or clues that the client would be trouble. Most times, these warning signs appeared at the time of the initial consultation or first telephone call. For example, if you and the client have difficulty agreeing on a fee, it's likely that you'll have difficulty agreeing on just about everything else that happens throughout the course of the engagement. Attorneys will often admit that they considered not taking a case but talked themselves into it because it was referred by someone they didn't want to disappoint, or because they were simply afraid to turn away any work. But operating from a place of fear puts you at a disadvantage from the outset. The client learns that if they press, you will back down, and that can lead to the client taking more advantage as time goes on.

The feeling that something is wrong is itself a warning signal. Everything else is just a way of explaining the feeling. But you may be so used to second-guessing your intuition that you no longer recognize or trust the feeling. If that is the case, creating some objective systems or measures can help until you can trust those feelings again.

Look for patterns in past client relationships. Look at the lists you made earlier of your bad clients and the reasons you identified them as such. How did prior bad client relationships begin? What were the warning signs or red flags? What do they have in common? If you examine several of those relationships together, patterns will begin to emerge. For example, the clients may have said similar things at the beginning of the engagement or had a similar (poor) attitude. They may have given you the feeling that they weren't telling you the whole story, or the objective evidence and documents did not back up the client's version of events. Perhaps you felt that you were on the defensive with these clients and felt as if you had to justify your decisions or actions you wanted to take on the client's behalf.

Ten Bad Client Warning Signs

If you can recognize the warning signs, you can stop bad clients before they enter your practice. Here are some warning signs we have observed or gleaned from the lawyers we've worked with. Bad clients

1. are overly concerned about the fee, ask about the fee before you discuss their legal problem, won't talk to you about their budget or don't know what it is, or simply cannot agree with you about the fee (remember, if clients cannot agree with you about fees, they probably won't agree with you about much else either);
2. have tunnel vision about the matter and don't want to listen to new ideas, aren't interested in other options, or can't face reality about their role in creating the situation;
3. have overexaggerated expectations, particularly for their budget or time limitations;
4. need everything in a rush;
5. don't keep the initial appointment, show up late, or fail to call when they say they will (particularly in combination with the previous warning sign);
6. don't listen or don't understand simple initial instructions;
7. take a long time to return your retainer agreement or to provide requested documents or materials;
8. have fired (or been fired by) several lawyers before you;
9. don't exhibit an understanding of the issues involved, even after you explain them; and/or
10. bully or disrespect you or your staff.

Use this information when screening potential new clients so that you can identify potential problems before they start.

Educate Your Referral Sources

Some lawyers find it difficult to turn clients away because they've been referred by a friend, colleague, or client that they do not want to disappoint. But if a client is not right for you, it probably is not worth the headache for you, and if you aren't invested in the client's matter, you may not provide the client with the level of service they deserve. Both you and the client will likely be more frustrated and disappointed if the attorney–client relationship breaks down later in the engagement, if the client is dissatisfied and/or stops paying, or if you are forced to withdraw. That could harm your relationship not only with the client, but with your referral source as well. A better approach might be to take the time to explain to the referral source why the client is not the right fit and help the client find a lawyer who can better serve their needs.

Some referral sources aren't clear about what you do and who you want to work with. Others understand that not every client may be the right fit, but they'd rather that you made that decision. Be open with referral sources about whether you want all referrals or only targeted ones (being a hub, or the first person people think of or refer to, has its advantages), and make sure that your referral sources understand that not every client may be right for you but that you appreciate they thought of you and that you would appreciate it if they continue to do so.

Be polite if you need to reject a potential client. Then contact your referral source, tell them you could not take the client, and thank them for the referral. Offer an alternative or referral to another lawyer who may be better suited for the client or matter where possible. Use the conversation as an opportunity to educate the referral source about what kinds of clients you're seeking.

The attorney–client relationship is a two-way street. Sometimes bad clients are created because of the interaction between lawyer and client. If you continually encounter the same warning signs or find that every potential client exhibits some of them, the problem may be with your prescreening or prequalifying procedures or your inability to communicate properly with potential clients or referral sources. Take a good hard look at how you (or your staff) interact with potential clients to see where you can improve. Manage expectations to help ensure your client interactions are positive.

If you're confident that the problem is not you, listen to your gut, pay heed to the warning signs, and turn away those clients who don't fit into your practice. You'll be glad you did.

WRAP UP

Interruptions, whether they come in the form of phone calls, email messages, colleague and staff questions, or other sources, account for much of the time wasted during most lawyers' workdays. If you can learn to limit those distractions, your productivity will improve dramatically. Giving up multitasking; setting aside "do not disturb" time to concentrate on important work; and training colleagues, staff, and clients on how to interact with you more effectively can go a long way toward providing productive time to work and reducing errors. Eliminating other kinds of distractions, including unproductive tasks and bad clients, can help you hone your prioritizing skills even further, allowing you to focus on the highest-value tasks and clients.

CHAPTER 2 ACTION STEPS

1. Resolve to limit multitasking. When you catch yourself doing it, *stop*! Enlist others to help you. Ask them to point it out to you if they see you doing it.
2. Set boundaries and create rules that help limit interruptions. When you're working on an important project, turn off your email notifications, turn down the ringer on your phone, or ask your assistant to hold your calls. If all else fails, move to a different location to eliminate distractions.
3. Set expectations and boundaries with both staff and clients about communication and response time. Schedule regular meetings with the people you work with most, and let your staff find their own answers to questions. Be clear about when you are and are not available.
4. Create your own list of warning signs or red flags for problem clients. Look at your past client relationships and think back to the first interaction—are there certain questions, attitudes, or other things all of those clients have in common? Did you have the same gut reaction to all of them? Using a list of warning signs can take the emotion out of saying no to a potentially problematic new client.

Chapter 3 ELIMINATING THE CLUTTER OBSTACLE

Managing your activities well requires organizing not only your tasks, but also your environment. But we've seen that many attorneys don't manage their environments well, which causes additional stress, overwhelm, lack of productivity, or potentially even malpractice.

Even the design of your office has an impact on your productivity. One study suggests that factors such as furniture, lighting, spatial arrangement, privacy, temperature, noise, lighting, outside view, presence of plants, and color can have a significant impact on productivity in the workplace.[1] Clutter can also affect your performance.

It is almost, if not completely, impossible to be efficient and effective while being disorganized and surrounded by clutter.

Many (if not all) of the top time-wasters are related to clutter of one or more types:

- Physical clutter
- Mental clutter
- Technological clutter
- Clutter related to old or outdated priorities
- A cluttered to-do list
- Clutter created as a result of rushing from one task to the next

1. Rasha Mahmoud Ali El-Zeiny, *The Interior Design of Workplace and Its Impact on Employees' Performance: A Case Study of the Private Sector Corporations in Egypt*, 35 Procedia Soc. & Behav. Scis. 746–56 (2012), https://www.sciencedirect.com/science/article/pii/S1877042812004570.

Clutter includes all things unfinished, unused, unresolved, tolerated, or disorganized. Clutter bogs you down, suppresses energy, and disrupts growth. Clutter obscures what is most important.

Clearing away the clutter means getting rid of anything and everything that is outdated or no longer useful.

THE IMPACT OF CLUTTER

With a busy law practice, it's difficult to keep control of the clutter. If you're like most lawyers, your office is a clutter collector—catalogs, CLE fliers, bar association announcements, periodicals, office supplies, and paperwork just keep piling up. Technology hasn't reduced this clutter, either. Instead, technology has multiplied or, at a minimum, electronically duplicated physical clutter, with email, social media notifications, and all sorts of other digital detritus to deal with.

Why should you care about clutter in the first place? After all, is it really important to have a clutter-free office when you've got important client work to do?

Clutter wastes time—How much time have you spent over the past week looking for paper or electronic files, notes on tiny pieces of paper, the contact information of the person you met last week at a networking event, or a document on your computer?

Clutter wastes money—If you bill by the hour, anything that wastes time wastes money. But clutter wastes money in other ways as well; you may purchase duplicates or reinvent the wheel by duplicating work if you can't easily find what you're looking for. If your email inbox is so cluttered that you miss a new client inquiry or a request from an existing client that could have led to more work, clutter has just detracted from your bottom line, too.

Clutter creates distractions—Piles of paper, files, periodicals to be read, and other miscellaneous clutter are distracting. It's difficult to focus on the task at hand when the "stuff" that represents unfinished projects or work to be done is literally looming over you. The physical reminder of all of the other tasks that need to be accomplished can lead to the urge to attempt to multitask.

Clutter wastes energy—Physically, you've got to work around or climb over it. Mentally, it zaps your energy by overwhelming or paralyzing you. Clutter causes you to postpone making decisions, and the longer an item (or a decision) stays on your to-do list, the more it drains your energy.

Clutter is scary—Just look at the piles of paper on your desk or your email inbox that seems to go on forever. You can't possibly know what is in each pile or what deadlines or other traps are hidden within them. As a result, clutter should not only scare you but also be a red flag that a malpractice claim could lie within. Why? If you don't have good organizational, filing, and naming systems so that you can find files easily, or if you leave messages languishing in your inbox instead of moving them into the client's file or taking action on them, clutter can lead to missed deadlines.

Based on our experience as both lawyers and consultants, here are some common causes of missed deadlines, all of which are exacerbated by clutter:

- The client supplies misinformation about the time and date of underlying events.
- You miscalculate the deadline or expiration of the statute of limitations.
- You apply the incorrect statute.
- You lose interest in the case.
- The file "falls through the cracks."
- No one is specifically assigned to work on the file.
- No one is working on the file.
- You wait until the last moment and then do not have time to complete the task.
- You are unsure how to proceed.

Clutter prevents you from working efficiently by distracting you, covering up important documents or files, and adding to anxiety and stress.

Mastering some of the skills discussed in this book will help you to get rid of clutter, eliminate missed deadlines, and better meet your client commitments.

WHAT'S YOUR ORGANIZATIONAL STYLE?

If past attempts at organization have failed, it may be because you haven't taken your personality and your approach to work into account when designing your organizational systems.

Do any of these sound like you?

- You don't know when good enough is good enough, or you fail to delegate because you think you're the only one who can do it right: You may be a **perfectionist**.
- You can't do anything until the very last minute, or tasks don't get completed because you just never "get around" to it: You're a **procrastinator**.

- You constantly rush from one thing to the next, focusing on the big issues but allowing the details to fall through the cracks: You could be a **multitasker**.
- You keep track of all of the details but hold onto everything just in case you might need it sometime in the future: You're probably a **packrat.**[2]

There's nothing necessarily "bad" about any of these styles, but if you want to stay organized, you need to understand your own style so that you can work with it. If you consistently operate the same way, there must be some benefit or payoff for you, or you wouldn't continue to behave in that way. For example, maybe clutter is your excuse for not meeting deadlines. Remove the clutter and you remove the excuse.

Whatever that payoff is, you have to be willing to give it up if you want to be more productive. For example, if you're a perfectionist, can you give up the idea that you're the only one who can get it done right and admit that others are competent, too? Can you give up control and accept when something is good enough? If you're a multitasker and being busy and rushing from one thing to the next makes you feel important, you must be willing to let that go and find something else that makes you feel important.

If you're a procrastinator, you may work better under pressure or thrive on the adrenaline rush that comes with trying to beat the clock. You may need to give up that rush or find some other way to get it. If you avoid tasks that you find unpleasant or are outside of your comfort zone, you may need to give up the notion that you should know everything and be willing to find someone who is an expert to perform that task. And if you're a packrat, you may need to give up the security blanket of "stuff" and recognize that it is an obstacle to getting your work done.

Once you understand your individual style and the unique challenges it presents, you can address those challenges. Any work style can be helped by any of the strategies that follow, but they address the specific issues associated with distinctive styles and therefore will be most helpful to the work style that corresponds with that strategy. We'll address strategies for each of these styles throughout the book, but no matter what your style, to reach peak productivity, you may need to give up the idea that you don't need outside help to get organized.

2. Adapted in part from Office Depot's "Put Your Work Style to Work" organizational plan: http://www.officedepot.com/promo.do?file=/promo/makeover/getorganized.jsp.

One of the most important strategies the **perfectionist** can learn is delegation. Start small and delegate less important or less valuable tasks, particularly those that do not require your expertise. Try delegating tasks you've been avoiding. Talk to your staff and help them to understand how you like things done and why they're important to you. Create checklists or procedures that will help you to follow up and feel comfortable that tasks are being completed to your liking. Delegating is a skill that can be learned and perfected over time, as we'll see in Chapter 4. Or break unpleasant tasks into smaller increments, tackling one small bit at a time, as described in Chapter 5.

The **multitasker** can benefit from good, solid systems, defined deadlines, and reminders, to ensure that details don't get lost and deadlines aren't missed. If you are a multitasker, rely on your calendar and schedule specific appointments to get the important, but not urgent tasks done, as described in more detail in Chapter 6 on using your calendar effectively. As a multitasker, you will be tempted to try to do too many things at once, have difficulty keeping track of it all, and only respond to the urgent items on your list. Creating deadlines with consequences will create urgency where it otherwise might not exist, which will help both the multitasker and the procrastinator. (See Chapter 6 to learn how to create these deadlines.)

The **procrastinator** can also benefit from the "doing the worst first" strategy described in Chapter 5. Procrastinators tend to avoid the most important tasks or tasks that require the most attention. Getting those tasks out of the way will keep them from cluttering up your thinking and pulling focus from the other things you're working on.

If you're a **packrat**, you'll need some guidelines to help you determine what you really must keep and what can be tossed. (Pay special attention to the Quick Sort and Purge described in the next section.) In this electronic age, almost any kind of information can be found on the internet, and electronic documents, PDFs, scans, etc., can really cut down on the amount of paper you need to retain. (We'll talk more about reducing paper later in this chapter.) But ridding yourself of unnecessary paper isn't the only challenge for the packrat.

Relying on electronic storage can exacerbate the problem, since packrats will be tempted to just save everything. While it is best practice to save everything related to clients and business, saving all of those newsletters and other attachments isn't necessary. And, of course, you'll need to make sure that you've got backups in place and that sensitive client information is encrypted.

Whether your documents are paper or electronic, a good filing system is essential for staying organized and working effectively. Whenever you convert paper files to electronic ones or access documents and information electronically instead of getting up to find something, you save time, increase your productivity, and avoid having to search for what turns out to be a "lost" document. Your filing system and other procedures and systems must also be easy, and applied uniformly, for everyone in your office to understand to ensure that you maintain your organization. The simpler your filing system, the better. Don't file things just to get them off of your desk or out of your email; first decide whether you need to retain them. If the item is part of a client's file and needs to be retained, scan it immediately and save it electronically (see Chapter 10 for more on working with electronic files). Electronic storage space is cheap, and even the packrat will be relieved to know that the documents and information you need will be quickly and easily available if you have a good electronic filing system with appropriate search functionality.

Although all lawyers need good filing systems, this is especially important for the packrat, since reference materials are valuable only if you can access them easily. (We'll talk more about filing systems and the need to have an easy-to-understand and consistent file naming protocol in Chapter 8.)

HOW TO GET RID OF THE CLUTTER

The television show "Clean Sweep" on The Learning Channel took two incredibly cluttered rooms in someone's home (you wouldn't believe the *mountains* of stuff that some people have hiding behind closed doors!) and transformed them by showing the homeowners how to eliminate their clutter and make room for what was really important to them. We'll try to do the same with your office clutter in this chapter.

Perhaps the worst thing we do is save every piece of paper or electronic document. Why do we do it? Because we're accustomed to doing so (and this is even more true for the packrat). It's not efficient—in fact, it's terribly inefficient. Why? Because it takes time to search for the information you need, and the more information you have to search through (and the less organized it is), the more time it takes to find. And if you have to get up from your desk to go and look for it, you lose even more time.

One solution to paper clutter is to convert it to electronic format: scan it, save it with a name you'll remember, and use programs with good search functionality to easily locate what you need quickly. But that is only a partial solution that may lead to a different kind of clutter. We'll tackle working with electronic documents in Chapter 8, but for now, here is a simple five-step process to get rid of your physical clutter.

Step 1: Clear Out

The first step in decluttering is to determine what you have. What's hiding in those piles? The best way to do that is to clear everything out. Ideally, that would mean taking *everything* out of the space. But it may not be possible or practical for you to tackle your whole office at once. If that's the case, you can begin decluttering on a smaller scale by doing one area (such as one shelf, one desk drawer, or your desktop) at a time.

One of the enemies of organization is duplication. Clutter breeds duplicates because if you don't know what you have or you can't find it, you tend to collect multiples. If you're not doing your entire office at once, you'll have to be even more aware of duplicates.

Once you've gotten everything out of the space, take a look around. Take note of how the space feels when it's empty. (And take advantage of the opportunity to give your office a good, thorough cleaning—banish the dust bunnies!)

Step 2: Quick Sort and Purge

Now your space is empty, but you've got a big pile of "stuff" to deal with. The next step is to sort it out.

The initial sort is done on a "one touch" basis—pick something up and make an immediate decision about which pile it belongs in. During this initial sort, don't give yourself time to think too much about it; go with your original gut feeling, especially if that gut feeling is telling you that an item belongs in the toss pile. You usually won't miss it if it's gone, especially since you probably didn't even remember you had it in the first place.

Sort into these piles:

- Toss (goes directly in the circular file)
- File in space (for any filing that needs to remain in the space you're working on)
- File elsewhere (includes items to be scanned by others and electronically filed)
- To do (actual client or administrative work to be done or delegated)
- To read
- In space (items such as mementos, books, office supplies, etc., that will stay in the space)
- Elsewhere (anything other than filing that belongs somewhere other than the space you're working on)

Your office should contain only files and paperwork that you're *currently* working on, supplies and files that you need on a *regular basis,* and a limited number of meaningful mementos or personal items. The rest is trash or should find another home. Keep only those items in your office that you need to take action on or that you need to refer to when doing your work. Not only does this keep clutter at a minimum, but it also reduces distractions.

As you go through the decluttering process, take note of which items cause the most clutter. Often, these items represent decisions that need to be made. What decisions are you putting off by keeping the clutter that represents the decision? Is there another way that you can remind yourself to make that decision, such as by putting a note on your calendar to follow up and then tossing the document?

While you're sorting, remember David Allen's two-minute rule from *Getting Things Done*—

> If an action will take less than two minutes to accomplish (like making a quick phone call or entering something on your calendar) you should do it right away while you're going through your sort. If it takes less than two minutes, you're better off getting it out of the way immediately rather than wasting time making a note and coming back to it later.[3]

This two-minute rule may not work for you if you're going to try to get your whole office organized at once. In that case, you may want to create a two-minute pile for all of the two-minute items and then tackle that pile all at once as soon as you've completed your sort.

Decluttering also is important with email, and the two-minute rule can come into play there as well. When possible, read email and act. If it can be read and deleted without action, do it immediately. Then respond to emails that are easy to handle (two minutes or less) and triage the rest. If your email inbox contains too many messages, it is easy for important communications to get lost or overlooked, so deal with it as quickly as possible.

One of the most important parts of the initial sort is the purge—getting rid of what you don't need. This includes everything from old telephone messages, flyers for CLE programs that have already passed, and old periodicals to files that should go to archives or be destroyed. Eliminate drafts of old documents that are no longer needed and notes or working files that are not part of the

---

3. David Allen, *Episode #79: David Allen with a Two-Minute Tip—The Two-Minute Rule*, Getting Things Done (May 29, 2020), https://gettingthingsdone.com/2020/05/the-two-minute-rule-2/.

client's file. Purge anything that you can easily find later on the internet; do you need to keep a copy of that case if you can access it just as quickly online?

Purging is important for electronic clutter as well. Don't forget to archive or purge old client files, unneeded documents, and outdated reference materials.

If you're feeling stuck in your practice, you might be surprised at the effect that a good purge can have. Getting rid of the old or outdated makes room for the new and frees up your energy.

After this first round of sorting, you'll probably still have more stuff than you really need to keep. That's where Step 3—Organize—comes in.

Step 3: Organize

First, take everything that doesn't belong in your office and put it where it belongs—the file room, your staff's desks, etc. Then you'll be organizing only what needs to go back in your space.

Before you put anything back, make absolutely sure that each item belongs in the space. Ask yourself these questions:

- When was the last time I used or referred to this?
- Is this something I need to use or access frequently?
- Is this information I can easily find elsewhere (like the internet)?
- Does it fit my current practice and my goals?

If you work from a home office, you may find that your workspace attracts a lot of items that are not related to work. Find another home for those items. The answers to these questions will make it clear whether you need to keep the item.

Categorize

Now that you have determined what you need to keep in the space, separating it into categories will help you decide where each item belongs and how much space you should allocate to each category. Create broad categories. Too many categories or categories that are too specific or narrow may be difficult to remember and may make organization more difficult.

Some categories you might consider when decluttering your office:

- Marketing/promotional materials
- Client files
- Personal files

- Personal items (photos, mementos)
- Office supplies
- Books
- Reference materials
- Work to be done immediately
- Archive
- Delegate

As you categorize, you may find more items that can be removed from your workspace (such as items that can be archived or work to be delegated to others). Get those things out of your workspace as soon as possible.

Give Everything a Home

Next, you'll need to create a home for everything that's left. You might consider organizing by

- proximity (put things that you use together near each other);
- space (place things where you have room for them—use space to your advantage); or
- frequency of use (how often you need to access something—the more you need it, the more accessible it should be).

Ensure that

- high-traffic areas are free from congestion (don't put boxes or files on the floor!);
- storage space and necessary materials are accessible; and
- you can easily see memo boards and vital information that is accessed daily.

TIP — Get Help

It can be tough to tackle a project like this on your own and to be objective with your "stuff." Asking a friend, colleague, or staff person to help you out can give you a different perspective. If you don't have a colleague or staff member present who can help, you can also do this virtually by clueing a friend in to what you want to do. Check in with each other at a predetermined time. Report what you completed and what you will do in the following hour or day. Working with a friend also helps improve your productivity by providing accountability. It's embarrassing to tell someone what you intend to do and then have to tell them you didn't do it.

Step 4: Schedule

Regardless of your style, your calendar—whether paper or electronic—is one of the best tools you have for organizing both your activities *and* your space. We'll talk more about using your calendar in Chapter 6, but for now, we'll focus just on scheduling time to organize and clutter-bust your office on a regular basis. This is a vital part of keeping clutter at bay. It won't get done unless you block out the time on your calendar now.

You'll want to schedule frequent, short blocks of time for the 15-minute pickup discussed in the next step and to review your immediate tasks and your weekly schedule, as well as a larger block of time for more thorough decluttering every few months. Use this larger block of time for not only decluttering your space and electronic files but also getting rid of bad clients; planning for the future; reviewing your goals, priorities, and project lists; and creating schedules and procedures that work for your office.

Schedule time regularly to sort through your email inbox and get rid of anything you don't need, following the steps we outline in Chapter 10.

Step 5: Maintain

To keep your environment clutter free, you need to maintain it regularly. Daily maintenance may be too ambitious, but weekly or monthly maintenance is essential. This is the hardest part of conquering clutter. It's easy to fall into the clutter trap as daily life (and law practice) gets in the way, but don't let that make you give up on organization and clutter-busting.

One of the keys to keeping clutter to a minimum is to ensure that everything that you keep has a purpose and a "home," or a place where it's always kept, so that you don't waste time looking for things (whether it's your stapler or a client's file). The time spent thinking about where that home will be is well worth it.

Conduct a periodic review and purge during those larger time blocks we discussed in Step 4, especially if you are a packrat or a multitasker. These styles tend to hold on to unnecessary items or paperwork either because they are afraid to get rid of things (packrat) or because they're constantly moving from one task to the next and not taking the time to evaluate whether items should stay or go (multitasker).

15-Minute Pickup

Performing a brief sort and purge weekly can go a long way to keeping clutter at bay. Before you leave the office at the end of the week, take 15 minutes to do a quick pickup of your office—move out files and paperwork that don't belong, get rid of any unnecessary mail or junk flyers, etc. Take a few minutes to review your calendar and tasks for the following week and make a plan.

When you use the weekly 15-minute pickup strategy, Monday mornings will be much easier. You'll arrive to a neat, organized office and a plan. Rather than spending precious time at the beginning of the week trying to figure out where you left off and what you have to do, you'll be able to get right down to work.

DESIGNING YOUR OFFICE FOR MAXIMUM PRODUCTIVITY

It is not uncommon for us to hear from lawyers that once they've moved to a new office, things started opening up in their practice; they started getting the clients they wanted, inquiries increased, and other positive changes occurred. These changes happened in part because the move forced them to get rid of clutter, to rethink their office setup, or to make other positive changes. Even if you aren't moving, you can achieve some of the same results in your existing office, whether you work from a home office or a more traditional office environment.

Clutter in Nontraditional Offices

While there were certainly some lawyers working in nontraditional offices prior to the Covid-19 pandemic, more lawyers have joined those ranks since 2020 than ever before. Having experienced working from home and practicing in a virtual environment for the first time as a result of the pandemic, many lawyers have decided that they prefer to have a largely virtual practice, and more law firms have decided to allow their employees to work from home—many reducing their physical office space and taking advantage of cost savings in the process.

Some lawyers have decided to move to a hybrid environment; rather than working full-time from home or the office, they split their time, working a few days in each space. Still others take advantage of flexible spaces like Regus or WeWork, which provide some services for professionals in addition to office or conference space when needed.

Each of these nontraditional office spaces can pose challenges when it comes to clutter (and client confidentiality). If your home office does double duty as a kids' homework space, corner in your living room, or guest bedroom, having work files scattered about in open view or in a space where others may inadvertently interfere with work or move it around is certainly not ideal. Lawyers who work in these environments need to be extremely vigilant about clutter.

Similarly, lawyers who have a hybrid work schedule need to ensure that they have all of their necessary paperwork, information, and electronics available to them regardless of which space they are working in. Frequently, lawyers working on a hybrid schedule are sharing physical office space with other lawyers who work the opposite schedule. Keeping each attorney's work files separate and ensuring that the workspace is ready for the next user will be of paramount importance. If you are sharing an office, it is a good idea to have a conversation with your office partner to discuss how you will each use the space and how it can be configured to support both of you, as well as how and where you will leave unfinished projects and tasks so that they will be ready for your return.

REDUCING FUTURE CLUTTER

Sometimes the best strategy for eliminating clutter is to start where you are now and work forward, rather than trying to deal with the backlog first. The strategies outlined in this section can help you to keep clutter from building up in the future and help you maintain your reduced-clutter existence once you've tackled the backlog.

Cure "I Need to See It" Syndrome

What is "I need to see it" syndrome? It's that habit—common to many lawyers—of keeping files, paperwork, and notes in piles on their desk, floor, or office chairs, or a pile of sticky notes on their computers, as a "reminder" that they need to accomplish a particular task or work on a particular file. These lawyers are afraid that if they can't see it, they will forget about it, and the task will never get done. They have become dependent on a physical reminder of what they need to accomplish. But this strategy creates clutter and hampers productivity.

Once the pile, file, or note stays in one place for too long, it no longer serves as a good reminder. Instead, it becomes part of the furniture—you become so used to seeing it in the same place day after day that you stop noticing it. Its utility as a reminder or a trigger to act disappears over time. If there are many of these so-called reminders present, it is likely that priority items get buried under less important tasks or items, and you will likely have to go through the entire pile or all of the sticky notes to determine what has to be done and which items are most important.

Using the item itself as a reminder also reduces efficiency and effectiveness instead of increasing them because it is more difficult to focus on the task at hand with a pile of reminders physically looming over your head; you're literally getting buried under your to-dos! The more of those reminders you have, the more difficult it is to distinguish the truly important from the unimportant. Eventually, those piles blend into the background and you don't see them anymore—thus defeating the purpose of having them there in the first place.

In our experience, the pile of files or documents that accumulate on the desks or in the offices of the lawyers we've worked with aren't the most urgent or important items you need to address, but just seeing them there makes you *think* you need to address them first. Thinking back to our jar of rocks example from Chapter 1, tackling that pile first is like filling the jar with sand and keeping out the big rocks.

Lawyers aren't the only ones afflicted by "I need to see it" syndrome. Paralegals and other legal staff can fall victim to it as well, reducing productivity further if the supervising lawyer has to periodically review not only their own piles, but also those that accumulate on the desks of those they work with, in order to establish priorities and ensure that deadlines aren't missed.

You can break the habit by putting good systems in place to ensure that important tasks get done. "I need to see it" syndrome is based on insecurity; if you suffer from it, you don't trust your systems to appropriately capture what needs to be done. The key to changing this is to rely on your calendar and reminder systems. Instead of using the files, paperwork, or sticky notes as a physical reminder of what needs to be done, use your calendar and your action folders or master project list as the trigger to take action. Schedule an appointment with yourself to do the work. Then put the file away until the appointment date and time arrive.

If the file or note represents a task that needs to be done at some point but is not currently urgent, doesn't have a specific deadline, and you can't fit it into your calendar now, put a reminder on your calendar with the name of the file or task and a short description of what needs to be done. When the reminder date arrives, you'll decide whether it is important enough to schedule or whether you should push the reminder into the future.

We'll talk more about how to do all of this in Chapter 6.

If you really can't do without the physical reminder, consider using David Allen's system of folders.[4] Instead of keeping a big bulky file in your office, you'll have only an item on your list or one piece of paper noting what you need to do. Use a "tickler" system with folders for each month and number diary items 1 to 31 for more efficient follow-up. You can do something similar with an electronic

4. David Allen, *The Tickler File*, GTD, https://gettingthingsdone.com/wp-content/uploads/2014/10/2016-Tickler-File-.pdf (last visited Aug. 11, 2022).

system. For example, you could create weekly and monthly calendar entries for review and add tasks to those lists as they arise. Or use a project management program such as Asana, Trello, or another to manage all of these tasks.

Your Desk

Your desk is *prime* real estate—the most prime real estate in your office. Anything that's kept on your desk should be something that you use daily. Move nonwork items off of your desk. Keep office supplies in drawers or on shelves where they're within reach but not cluttering up your desk. Make use of vertical space—hang shelves, wall pockets, or bulletin boards to keep control of paperwork that regularly piles up on your desk. These methods keep the important reference information or reminders in view without interfering with your work.

Don't keep shuffling paper around on your desk. Make a decision about what to do with it; if it needs action, *schedule* it. (We'll talk more about this in Chapter 6.)

Paper

Reducing your reliance on paper can exponentially improve your productivity, and in light of need to work remotely, it may be ethically necessary to always digitize (scan and save electronically) every item so it is available no matter where you are working. Like email, eliminate paper as soon as possible after it arrives. But first scan every important piece of paper. Paper can get lost or have coffee spilled on it, and relying on paper limits when and where you can work. One study found that workers spent an average of three hours per week searching for paper that had been misfiled, mislabeled, or lost.[5] That's why it is so important to open your mail over the trash and immediately toss anything that you don't need. Scan everything else and file it appropriately. Don't let paper clutter up your workspace.[6]

Business Cards

Lawyers collect business cards whether they want to or not. Adversaries give you a card in court, and cards are exchanged at bar events, when networking, and even at social events. Don't let these cards create clutter. Scan the information into your contact system and toss all of those business cards! If you're an

---

5. K.J. McCorry, *The Cost of Managing Paper: A Great Incentive to Go Paperless!*, InformIT (Sept. 16, 2009), https://www.informit.com/articles/article.aspx?p=1393497.
6. For more tips on eliminating paper, read Sheila M. Blackford and Donna S. Neff's *Paperless in One Hour for Lawyers* (2014) from the ABA Law Practice Division.

Evernote user, consider their Premium account, which will let you scan business cards and enter all of the information into your address book and into LinkedIn, making following up and connecting with new acquaintances even easier.

Periodicals

If you are like many lawyers we know, you've probably got all kinds of periodicals and other materials that you'd like to read but that you just haven't had time to go through. Newspapers, trade magazines, bar journals, and other periodicals multiply quickly. They might contain valuable articles or information, but if you've got a pile of periodicals three feet high or months of electronic bar journals to go through, the more time that passes, the less likely it is that you will ever read them. One way to combat this is to begin where you are; toss the old ones and start anew. Almost every piece of information can be found online, more quickly and easily than by wading through a stack of periodicals because you think you might have seen an article somewhere on the issue—assuming you remember that you saw the article in the first place.

To keep periodicals from piling up, when you receive one, skim through the table of contents and pull out, bookmark, or move only those articles that you want to read to a reading file and toss the rest. Review the reading file while waiting in the doctor's office, between court appearances, or riding on the train. Or have a secretary or assistant prescreen your periodicals and pull articles for you.

We all love paper articles. We were raised on them, and nothing replaces the feeling of reading that nice original publication. But the reality is that we can't schlep all of those magazines around. That's why, despite our love of paper, scanning the materials or converting them to an electronic document and saving them is much more effective. You can read the articles anywhere and then delete them from your device once they have been read.

If you see an article that you think might be helpful to archive, scan it (desktop scanners scan quickly and can scan both sides of a document at the same time) and save the resulting PDF file to your computer or to the cloud. The Fujitsu Scansnap desktop scanner is a popular scanner, and it comes with Adobe Acrobat software. You'll feel lighter without all of that paper!

If you find the articles online, use a tool built into your browser or Evernote, Microsoft OneNote, Pocket, or similar apps that will clip the article and allow you to read it later on. Allison saves scanned articles in a subfolder of her "My Documents" folder, labeled "My Library," or uses Evernote or Microsoft OneNote to save and tag articles.

Dan sorts his articles by topic and even numbers them (starting at 01) so that he knows which articles are most recent and deletes the material after review. If he needs to save it for the long term, he'll store it in OneDrive, use the Remarkable tablet, or email it to himself and then store it in his office's electronic filing system, whichever makes more sense. And it's there if he needs it again.

Evernote (https://evernote.com/) is online archiving and notetaking software with desktop versions as well as apps that will work with any operating system, in addition to the web-based version. You can create notes directly within Evernote or capture web pages (or emails) and then add annotations, tag for easy categorizing, sync across multiple devices, and easily search—the program even lets you search text within a photo.

Microsoft 365 offers OneNote, which includes a notetaking feature as well as OneNote WebClipper,[7] which captures, edits, annotates, and shares information.

Diigo (https://www.diigo.com/) is a cloud-based knowledge management program that archives the webpages for the links you save and makes them fully searchable; even if the link is broken or disappears, you'll still have the information you need. Instapaper (http://www.instapaper.com/), Delicious (https://delicious.com/), Reeder (http://reederapp.com/ios/), and Pocket (http://getpocket.com/) are other popular options.

When all of this information is in one central location, it is easy to find when you have downtime.

Paper Files

An efficient filing system is crucial to being productive. Since most law practices will be unable to eliminate paper entirely, your filing systems should mimic one another, that is, your paper file folders should be named the same as your electronic ones. When creating a filing system, the simpler, the better. Don't file anything just to get it off of your desk. Only file what you'll actually need or are required to maintain. Statistics show that 80 percent of what you file will never get used or referenced again anyway,[8] so be selective.

7. *Getting Started with the OneNote Web Clipper*, MICROSOFT, https://support.microsoft.com/en-us/office/getting-started-with-the-onenote-web-clipper-5696609d-c5ae-4591-b3af-1f897cb6eda6 (last visited July 22, 2022).
8. Britney Pay, *Piping Down on Paper: Why 80 Percent of Files Stored Once Are Never Looked At or Used Again*, EFILECABINET (Jan. 15, 2016), https://www.efilecabinet.com/piping-down-on-paper-why-80-percent-of-files-stored-once-are-never-looked-at-or-used-again/.

To reduce "reference" files—ask yourself these questions:

- Can this information be found elsewhere (such as on the internet, with a simple search)?
- Do I need the whole thing (for example, do I need the entire case, or will retaining the citation be sufficient)?
- Will it be outdated by the time I need it again?
- Can I scan it and save it electronically?
- How would I find this if I needed it again?

Paper Filing Systems

There is no one best way to maintain your office files. The "best" filing system is the one that is easily understood by everyone in the office, that is followed consistently, and that makes it easy for you to find the information you need when you need it. Your practice area and jurisdictional rules may impact how you maintain your files and how long you keep them. Many lawyers use Redweld files with internal file folders separated by category, but this method might not work for everyone in every practice area. Some lawyers find it easier to work with binders with dividers instead of files and folders. And sometimes a combination of both works best (for example, using Redwelds with internal folders for litigation files but creating trial notebook binders specifically for trial). You may want to experiment to find what works the best for you.

Whatever method you choose, you'll want to keep your filing system as simple as possible and keep a master index or database of all of the files in your office and their names and/or numbers. In Chapter 8 we'll talk more about systems and protocols related to documents and files.

Use shelves or file cabinets to keep files neat and organized or leave the files in the file room. It's far better to walk to the file room or file cabinet to get a file than to have files piled all over the floor and furniture in your office. But of course, as we'll explain later on, you save a ton of time if your files are on your computer or office server, and you never have to get up from your desk to view a file or anything in the file.

Move closed files to an out-of-the-way or offsite storage area. Don't let them use prime space in your office. Even better, scan them and save them electronically, use cloud or other backup storage solutions, and then dispose of the physical files. Make sure, however, that you return original documents to clients and that you disclose in advance that you intend to dispose of their paper files. If the client wants the hard copy, you can send it on after it is converted to electronic format and eliminate the time and cost of shredding the file.

Mail (Snail Mail)

Open your mail over the trash and immediately toss anything that you don't need. Don't let junk mail sit around and clutter up your workspace. Divide the rest into the following piles:

- **Do** (items that require action)
    - *Scan everything* that needs to be retained. If you need to keep the paper version because there is a legal requirement to retain it or because it will need to be returned to the client in the future, mark the original to confirm that it has been scanned.
    - Your highest priority should be items with dates or deadlines, such as hearing notices, trial scheduling orders, and briefing schedules. As noted earlier, the best practice is to *immediately* scan them and then enter these items into whatever calendars, to-do lists, and case management and other systems your office uses. That way, if someone gets sidetracked, the event or deadline is recorded. You should also attach a copy of the scan to the calendar or reminder so that you can instantly see it. For hearings, this provides a quick way to confirm where and when the hearing is, without the need to run around searching for the original notice.
    - Finally, address any other client-related items and be sure they are noted in the client files.
- **Decide**
    - Some mail represents decisions that need to be made that are not related to a client file. These items might include CLE programs, invitations to events, or offers from vendors. These items can also be scanned, particularly if there are dates or deadlines that will impact your decision.
    - It can be helpful to make a note of the event and schedule a specific time on your calendar to make a decision.
    - Alternatively, you may want to create a "decide" folder that you review as part of your weekly plan.
- **File**
    - Any items that you need to save, either for a client's file or for your records, but that don't require other action go into this pile.
    - Or, if you are paperless, place the nonoriginal items in your shredding piles. Make sure, however, that you never shred anything until it is docketed, scanned, and backed up. There's no rush to shred—but

remember, don't just throw out items with client or confidential information. Those items should be securely disposed of (which, in most cases, means shredding).

- **Pay** (bills to be paid)
- **Read** (handle like periodicals earlier)

In some offices, the scanned items are still given to attorneys (Dan likes that method). This is fine, as long as the attorney knows that he can't keep everything on his desk and should dispose of the item once it is reviewed. Don't let your staff or attorneys circumvent the scanning process.

Once the mail has been sorted, your work is not done. Add to-do items to your calendar or task list. Delegate filing and bill paying where necessary or create homes for those items and designate a specific time for those tasks to be performed.

Email

Most lawyers have email clutter. Many have inboxes with thousands of messages in them. Because email is such a major clutter and productivity obstacle, we've dedicated an entire chapter to it later in the book. See Chapter 10 for our email tips.

Faxes

Tip — Electronic Faxes

You should switch to an electronic fax service or ask your IT staff about converting internally to all electronic faxes to cut down on paper (and get your faxes by email even when you're not in the office).

Anything named "e-something," such as email or e-fax, was created and designed to be electronic. Thus, electronic mail (email) is an alternative to paper mail. Similarly, e-faxing was created so that attorneys (and others) would stop having to wade through piles of paper faxes and could, instead, have faxes delivered to their inboxes as another form of email. By using e-faxes, recipients no longer have to go through every paper fax, including all the junk advertising CLEs, vacation packages, etc.

Most faxes are junk or don't need to be kept in hard copy. As a result, there is no reason to send or receive faxes in the traditional paper form. Instead, use one of the many services such as Ring Central (ringcentral.com) or eFax (efax.com) that allow you to send and receive faxes by email. With these services, you email faxes to a specified email address from a list of approved email addresses you specify, and they will be faxed to the recipient, many of whom use the same type of service. When you receive a fax, it will be emailed to you at the fax number registered with the service, and then you can (only if necessary) print it. Or you can save it electronically as well.

E-faxing can help to reduce paper and improve efficiency. First, you don't need to have a dedicated phone line for faxes. Most services will designate one. If you do so, you will eliminate your monthly fee for the fax line. You'll also eliminate long-distance charges for sending faxes because they will now be sent as email attachments. And you'll eliminate the time and expense associated with printing something, faxing it, and then discarding the printed document.

Second, your faxes will be delivered to your email and the email of anyone else in your office who should be receiving them. This means that there are no more piles of paper to wade through, and if the fax isn't for you, just hit the delete button.

Third, e-faxing eliminates all fax machine expenses, including paper, toner, and maintenance/repairs. These costs add up and, just like reducing your reliance on paper is good for the environment, so is eliminating your use of paper fax machines.

Fourth, most electronic fax services are inexpensive and require no setup (unless you have a larger firm and want every staff person to have a dedicated fax number).

Fifth, you can send an e-fax from anywhere, provided you have internet service (so you can email the fax to the service).

Finally, because the services are online, you can send and receive multiple faxes at once, and the quality is generally better than that of most fax machines. Plus, if you accidentally delete a fax, most services store the faxes and allow you to log in and retrieve them, even months later.

Electronic Clutter

Electronic clutter can be just as distracting and unproductive as paper clutter. Don't waste the same time searching for electronic files and documents as you did searching for their paper counterparts.

Although saving items in electronic rather than paper form can reduce paper clutter and help you to keep better track of documents and information, beware of creating electronic clutter. Don't save everything simply because the information is stored electronically. Use the strategies you've learned to eliminate unnecessary electronic files or move them to archives. And don't save everything in your email inbox—having 1,000 items in the inbox is not a badge of honor, it's merely turning that overcrowded inbox on your desk into one on your computer. There are ways to tame this inbox beast, including using Rules, which we'll discuss in Chapter 10.

To avoid creating electronic clutter, you will need firm rules on what paper documents should be converted to electronic format and how and where those documents will be maintained. That said, every client-related document and all firm-related financial documents should be digitized (scanned and saved electronically). Electronic documents are generally easier to find than hardcopy documents, even if they are misfiled, because of the search features available on electronic systems, but time can still be wasted on such searches. And if you are viewing a file and a document is missing from that file because it was saved in the wrong location, the search feature won't help you.

We'll talk more about filing systems and electronic clutter in Part II (Chapter 10).

WRAP UP

The battle against clutter is ongoing, even in this age of electronic media. Lawyers still create, receive, and exchange copious amounts of paper, and lawyers who have been practicing for some time may have difficulty letting go of old habits and reducing their reliance on physical files, folders, and documents. But creating good habits around paper and clutter can help reduce anxiety and improve organization and productivity within your office.

CHAPTER 3 ACTION STEPS

1. Determine your clutter style and choose the clutter-busting strategies that will work best for you.
2. Take one area at a time, whether it's a desk drawer, file cabinet, or your desk itself, and follow the five steps to decluttering.
3. Don't try to tackle everything at once; get in the habit of using the strategies outlined in this chapter to deal with new items coming into your office so that you don't contribute to clutter in the future.

Chapter 4
ELIMINATE BY DELEGATION

When you manage your activities effectively, you enjoy your work more and have more time to devote to those things that are important to you, whether they're related to your practice or not. One of the best ways to manage your activities is delegating. Just because a task or item on your to-do list is a priority doesn't mean you are the only one (or even the best one) who can do it. And if the task is a billable one, you can improve your bottom line by delegating that task to someone else while you focus on other billable work.

But in our experience, many lawyers have difficulty delegating or do not delegate effectively.

As we discussed in Chapter 1, your time is best utilized by focusing on tasks that are high value—those tasks that require your personal touch or your specific expertise. And in Chapter 2, we saw how eliminating unnecessary tasks can be an effective way to increase your productivity. In Chapter 3, you eliminated a lot of clutter so that you could create more breathing space within which to work, and by doing so, you may have identified additional tasks or to-do items that need to be completed.

In this chapter, we'll tackle the tasks that cannot be eliminated and don't fit in your schedule, tasks that are priorities but that you can't focus on, and tasks that do not fit into your strengths. Many—if not most—of those tasks can be delegated, either with or without your direct supervision.

Delegation not only helps you to get more accomplished in less time, but it also helps you to develop your skills as a manager. Giving work to others provides you with an outside perspective on the tasks being performed. You may even get suggestions to improve how you perform those tasks and how you serve your clients.

Delegation is important both for you and for the people you delegate to, whether they are associates, staff, or even people outside of your firm or organization. By delegating, you allow others to contribute to the firm and to accomplishing the firm's goals. It gives them an opportunity to grow and to gain new skills and gives them a sense of pride and accomplishment, especially if they understand how their work is important to reaching those goals or contributes to your clients' matters.

WHY YOU DON'T DELEGATE

Lawyers tend to be perfectionists. But perfectionism can be an enemy of productivity, as we'll see in Chapter 5. It is also an enemy of delegation. Although most lawyers acknowledge that delegating is generally a beneficial strategy, those same lawyers have multiple excuses for why they themselves don't delegate. These excuses include:

- "I can do it better (and faster) than anyone else. It will take longer to explain it to someone else, and then I will have to spend too much time making corrections later." (Remember the perfectionist from the previous chapter?)
- "I have no one to delegate to." (This is often the excuse of the true solo who thinks that since they don't have staff, they can't delegate.)

If you're not delegating, you must be getting some payoff for not doing so. For some lawyers, that payoff is being seen as the one person who can do it all or who is always on the go. Many lawyers see being busy or being the "only one" who can perform certain tasks as a badge of honor. But the downside is that failing to delegate could result in more staff turnover because others aren't getting the opportunities they feel they deserve.

Here's the truth about delegation:

- Although it may require an investment of time to train someone else, if the task is one that truly should be delegated, the overall return on your time is well worth it. It will pay dividends in the long run.
- Delegation may be even more important for true solos than it is for lawyers in a firm or larger organization because solos have to wear so many hats that they need to choose their activities even more wisely if they want to be effective.

Despite the clear benefits of delegation, some still persist in their belief that the payoff just isn't worth it. Ask yourself what you're gaining by not delegating. What is your payoff? Do you secretly like being too busy, bragging about how much work you have to do? Are you proud of how late you stay at the office every night? What is the *real reason* you don't delegate? In most cases, that reason is not more important than improving your bottom line, spending more time with your family, or truly providing excellent service to your clients.

In some cases, lawyers don't delegate because when they've tried to delegate in the past, it hasn't worked as well as they'd hoped or it didn't work right away, so they gave up. But many delegation failures can be solved by following a few simple steps.

If you're truly sick and tired of killing yourself, you can learn to delegate effectively.

WHAT SHOULD YOU DELEGATE?

Knowing your strengths and weaknesses can help you to decide what you should delegate. But even if you happen to be great at a particular task, it might not be effective to spend your time on it. Anything that you avoid doing, hate doing, or just don't do well is a potential candidate for delegation. If someone else can do it faster, cheaper (without sacrificing quality), better, or more consistently, delegate it. If someone else will get it done well enough and it isn't your highest priority or doesn't require your personal touch, delegate it.

Here are some questions to help you determine which tasks you should delegate. As you can see, some of these questions are similar to the questions we used in Chapter 1 when deciding which tasks should be prioritized.

- Is this task the highest or best use of my time?
- Does this task play to my strengths?
- Is this task at the core of what I get paid for?
- Is it one of my highest priorities?
- Does it serve my goals?
- Does it require my individual participation, personal touch, skills, or expertise?
- Is this task something I can teach others to do?
- Is it something that is done repeatedly in my practice?
- Do I enjoy doing it? (If so, why? Is there a higher-value activity that gives the same payoff?)

- Does this task go to the heart of how I bring in business?
- Do I have the requisite expertise to complete this task effectively? Do I know someone else who has more expertise in this area?
- Will it cost less (for me or the client) if someone else does it?
- Will someone else do a comparable job as, or possibly a better job than, you?

Use these questions to delegate effectively by learning how to balance what needs to be accomplished and when with how important that work is and whether it requires a specific individual (namely you) to complete it. Repetitive tasks may be good candidates to create systems and procedures around (see Chapter 8), which might make them easier to delegate to someone else or to automate completely.

Focus your energy on the tasks that

- advance your core values,
- are the most profitable, and/or
- require your personal participation or expertise

and delegate the rest.

TO WHOM SHOULD YOU DELEGATE?

Once you've decided which tasks you want to delegate, you need to determine those to whom you should delegate them. One way to do so is to determine the strengths and weaknesses of those individuals available to delegate to. Some of those individuals may already be working in your office, but you may need to seek out external help. That help might come in the form of experts, virtual assistants, or other lawyers with whom you can collaborate.

If you're like most lawyers we know, you lament about clients who try to handle their legal matters on their own, often making the situation worse instead of better. Don't be a DIY lawyer! Know when to hire a professional. A professional can be anyone who is specifically trained or has detailed knowledge about a certain project or task that needs to be accomplished. Your training is in law. Know when to hire someone who has training in marketing, spreadsheets, bookkeeping, etc. Focus on what you've been trained to do and let others focus on what they've been trained to do.

Solos are often concerned about the cost of delegating because they don't have sufficient staff, which usually means outsourcing. But delegating doesn't mean that you have to spend a lot of money. In addition, consider that the cost of doing something yourself is often higher than the cost of hiring someone else to do it, especially if that person can do it better or faster or if you are freed up to do the tasks that contribute directly to the bottom line. For example, many solos we know try to be their own webmasters, maintaining and updating their own websites. But most lawyers don't have the time to learn all they need to know to ensure that their website is running properly and complies with search engine algorithm updates, etc. It would be far better for them to employ an expert to perform routine website maintenance; the expert will know what needs to be done and how to do it and can likely accomplish it much more efficiently and effectively than the lawyer, averting a host of potential problems in the process.

You don't have to actually hire an employee or make a long-term commitment to start delegating. One advantage of delegating by outsourcing is that it can be a short-term, temporary arrangement with individuals who don't require a lot of supervision or extra benefits.

New apps and programs are being developed every day, particularly with recent advances in artificial intelligence. As a result, many tasks can be delegated to technology. For example, digital dictation services can get your typing done while you sleep; case management software can automatically track deadlines and tasks; and chatbots can be employed to take basic information from visitors to your firm's website, streamlining your intake process. Take some time to think about what tasks might be automated or made simpler, easier, or faster by employing technology.

WHEN DELEGATION DOESN'T WORK

There are many reasons why delegation may not work. Some of these reasons include:

- Poor hiring
- Choosing the incorrect person (or program) to delegate to
- Lack of training
- Absence of incentives or motivation of employee
- Fear or risk aversion

- Ill-defined job duties or unclear task assignment
- Constant criticism of task results and techniques
- Unrealistic goals
- Ambiguous objectives
- Micromanaging

Some of these reasons are the fault of the employee/delegatee, and some are the fault of the supervisor/delegator. Even if you have no control over hiring and firing and don't have the opportunity to choose the individual to whom you will be delegating, you *can* work on becoming a better delegator.

LEVELS OF DELEGATION AUTHORITY

When you delegate, you can either eliminate the task from your list entirely, handing over all of the responsibility to someone else, or delegate only a portion of a task, project, or activity and retain a portion for yourself. For example, you might delegate someone just to gather information for you and then use that information to complete the task yourself.

The person you are delegating to must understand how much authority they have to make decisions with respect to the task or project you're giving them. When you are unclear about how much authority is being delegated, it can not only cause confusion, but it can also foster mistrust, resentment, and other problems.

One example is a client of Allison's, the managing attorney in a midsized law firm who had begun to delegate some managerial responsibilities to some of the senior lawyers in the firm, over and above their client and case work. These responsibilities included tasks such as reviewing and revising client bills, dealing with vendors, and supervising staff. But the managing attorney was unclear about the level of responsibility he was delegating. The young partners thought he was turning these tasks entirely over to them, but the managing partner apparently still wanted some level of involvement or at least final approval. As a result, the managing partner felt that the younger partners were overstepping their boundaries, while the younger partners felt that the managing attorney was micromanaging them, leading to frustration for all involved.

Figure 4.1 illustrates the different levels of delegation. Keep this in mind and be sure to communicate which level of authority you are providing when you delegate a task or project.

In this illustration, "me" refers to the person who is doing the delegating.

Figure 4.1 Levels of Delegation Authority

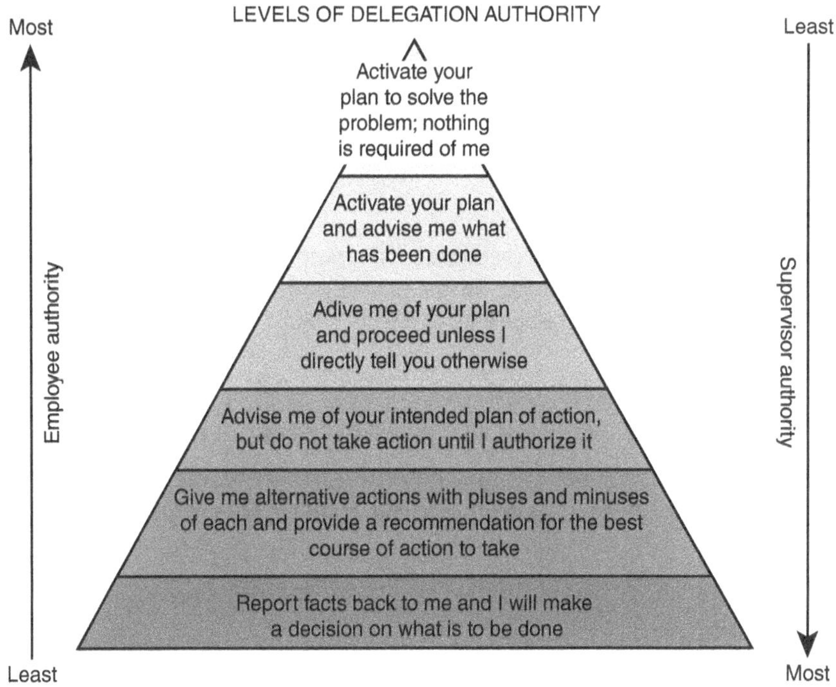

FIVE STEPS TO EFFECTIVE DELEGATION

Haphazard delegation—delegation done with little thought or planning, usually done on the fly—is bound to fail. To delegate successfully, follow these five steps:

1. Give clear, comprehensive instructions.
2. Ensure that you have been understood.
3. Set expectations and priorities.
4. Establish benchmarks and check-ins.
5. Evaluate and share the outcome.

Step 1: Give Clear, Comprehensive Instructions

This is the single most crucial component of effective delegation. It's harder than it sounds, particularly because it may require some trial and error. One of the most common reasons why delegation fails is that the person who is delegating gives up too easily instead of adjusting their communication to provide better instruction. What makes this element so difficult is that when you are an expert or have been doing something for a long time, you often assume that others know as much as you do; you forget that what is obvious to you may not be obvious to someone else, especially someone who is new to the task or to your expectations or way of working. As a result, initial instructions are often lacking simply because you forget that the person you are delegating to often doesn't know what you know.

Tip — Use Checklists

To make delegating easier, try creating checklists or other written instructions, particularly for tasks that will be performed repeatedly, for jobs where turnover is likely, or for tasks that are performed by more than one person. A great resource for checklists is Dan's *Checklists for Lawyers* published by the Law Practice Division.[1]

Be specific about the scope of the project. Provide an estimate of the length of time you anticipate that it should take to complete the task or give guidelines for how many pages the end product should be. If the employee/delegatee is spending more time on it than you anticipate, they can check back with you to determine whether they should keep going, cut the project short, or go in another direction.

Tip — Check-Ins and Time Limits

Create check-in times or designate maximum time limits (see step 4 later). For example, indicate that the project should take no longer than three hours or designate a time limit at which the person must stop working and check in with you. For example, ask your employee to report back on their progress after two hours of working on the task before going further. This can help you to spot problems or get the project back on track if there has been a miscommunication.

Another essential element to communicate when you delegate a task or project is why this assignment is important and how it fits into the overall work of the firm:

- How does this project or task affect clients?
- How does it help the firm function?
- How does this project or task fit into the overall strategy of a particular case?

When the person you delegate to knows that their role is important and how their work affects the role you play for your clients, they will be more invested in the project—and more likely to get it right.

1. Dan's book *Checklists for Lawyers* highlights how the use of checklists can improve efficiency, eliminate errors, and reduce the potential for malpractice claims (https://www.americanbar.org/products/inv/book/174675660/).

Step 2: Ensure That You Have Been Understood

Miscommunication is inevitable, no matter how good you think your instructions are. A memo might mean a short, one-page, bulleted document setting forth the current state of the law to one lawyer. But to a newly minted associate, a memo may mean a full-length legal brief complete with case citations.

Encourage questions, even when using written instructions and checklists to delegate. Too often delegation fails because the employee or delegatee is afraid to ask questions or to let their boss or supervisor know that they don't understand. Instead, thinking they "should" know, they decide to figure it out for themselves or to ask someone else who may or may not be aware of what you want done or how you want it done. Foster an atmosphere that encourages communication; it is better to find out that your employee doesn't understand the assignment *before* they get started on the project than it is to find out after they've already wasted hours or days on the wrong task.

When delegating, ask the delegatee to repeat back to you their understanding of the project *in their own words*. This process eliminates misunderstandings, reduces omissions (oops, I forgot to include that step in the instructions), and creates greater accountability. Don't just ask, "Do you understand?" The answer will invariably be "Yes," whether they understand or not. Let them tell you what they think you want them to do. This is your opportunity to ensure that your instructions were clear and that you've properly defined both the scope of the project *and* the ultimate goal. Let the employee tell you their understanding of the project before they begin. This will also increase their buy-in to the project.

Another strategy is to have the delegatee write down the assignment. This can reinforce it for them and give them something to refer back to later.

Step 3: Set Expectations and Priorities

Delegation can also fail if deadlines for completion are not set or the employee/delegatee is not informed of the priority of the project or doesn't understand the expected outcome.

Communicate goals, deadlines, and priority whenever you delegate so that your delegatee knows when the project must be completed and how important it is in relation to other work they have to do. That way, if they receive another assignment and they're not sure what should be done first, they can ask you or decline the other assignment. If you delegate several projects to the same employee, make sure you establish the priority of each project in relation to the other work you have already assigned. Human nature dictates that work that is urgent gets attended to first. If there are no deadlines, there is no urgency, and the work may never be completed.

Step 4: Establish Benchmarks and Check-Ins

Keep track of project deadlines on your calendar or in your reminder system, but don't wait until the deadline to determine whether the task or project is on track. By then it may be too late. This is especially important if you're new to delegation or to working with this particular person.

Schedule a time to check in when you think enough time has passed to have uncovered some questions but not so much that you can't get the project back on track if something has gone wrong. Even when you encourage questions, some people will still be afraid to ask. To combat this problem, establish specific benchmarks or milestones or specify a check-in date. Add the check-in date to your calendar along with the deadline for completion.

When you're first delegating to someone, you'll probably want to be a bit more vigilant, but checking in does not mean micromanaging. You must develop confidence in your employees/delegatees, particularly professionals, and allow them to do their jobs. Micromanaging stifles learning and discourages people from continuing to progress to higher levels of authority.

The need to check in will depend on the nature of the project and how well you know the person's work and level of experience. If you've been delegating to someone for a while and they are meeting your expectations, the need to check in should be reduced drastically and perhaps eliminated, especially once you are satisfied that the employee will ask questions if necessary.

Step 5: Evaluate and Share the Outcome

Completion of the task isn't the end of the delegation process.

Feedback is an important part of good delegation. Lawyers who have to delegate but insist that delegation doesn't work or isn't productive complain that the tasks they delegate are never completed properly (perfectionists) and they end up having to do it over themselves, wasting more time and adding more pressure and stress to their day. But when those lawyers are asked whether they ever shared these complaints, disappointments, or deficiencies with the individual to whom the task was given, many respond that they never bothered. If you can't take the time to teach your employees and let them know where they've gone wrong, you can't expect them to grow and improve.

Give praise for a job well done. Positive feedback can be even more important than negative feedback, particularly for those who are new to a task.[2] Positive feedback fosters loyalty, both to you and to your clients, and it helps

2. Ayelet Fishbach, Tal Eyal & Stacey R. Finkelstein, *How Positive and Negative Feedback Motivate Goal Pursuit*, 4(8) Soc. & Personality Psych. Compass 517–30 (2010), https://compass.onlinelibrary.wiley.com/doi/10.1111/j.1751-9004.2010.00285.x.

motivate employees/delegatees to continue to improve. Let your employees know what you think of their work and especially what they've done right.

Share the outcome of the overall case or project with those who worked on it. Sharing the outcome signals to your employees that their work is an important part of what you do and that they are an integral part of your success. Bring it full circle.

Delegation is a two-way street. The delegatee has a task to complete, but you have an obligation to hold the employee accountable and to provide feedback so that they can improve. Failure to follow through with accountability causes associates and staff members to lose respect for the process; question the partner or firm's commitment to them, to their work, and to their clients; and may even result in the employee failing to follow through with future assignments.

Feedback can go both ways. In addition to giving feedback to employees, ask for feedback from them so you can continue to improve your delegation skills.

WRAP UP

Delegation is an important leadership skill that too few lawyers take the time to master. Not only will delegation help you leverage your employees and get more done in less time, but it will also empower your employees and help them to grow.

To be an effective delegator, you must master all five steps to effective delegation. Your instructions must be clear and establish the level of authority for the task or project that is being handed over. But no matter how clear you think your instructions are, don't take it for granted that your employee understands; let them tell you what they think the assignment is. Set expectations and priorities so that your employee/delegatee knows what they should focus on first. Establish benchmarks and check in to ensure that the project does not go off track. And remember to evaluate your performance and share the outcome of the task so that your employee knows the value of their contribution to the team.

CHAPTER 4 ACTION STEPS

1. Make a list of the tasks you can delegate, using the questions on pages 63–64 as a guide.
2. Make a checklist or list of instructions for tasks that you often delegate.
3. Delegate your next assignment using the five steps you learned in this chapter.

Chapter 5
STRATEGIES FOR GETTING IT ALL DONE

So far, you've learned to prioritize; to eliminate unnecessary tasks, clients, and clutter; and to delegate important tasks that you do not need or want to do yourself. Now it's time to take care of what is left.

This chapter and Chapter 6 will provide you with tips and tools to help you manage the many activities that make up a typical lawyer's day. We'll talk about how to determine what actions to take to pursue the goals you set and the priorities you established in Chapter 1, as well as how to combat procrastination and get down to the business of getting that work done.

GET EVERYTHING OUT OF YOUR HEAD

Lawyers often have too many demands on their time and not enough resources to meet those demands, leading to increased stress and poor productivity. David Allen's book *Getting Things Done* describes his process of organizing all of your stuff and reducing anxiety about it at the same time.

Allen's basic premise is that you are not as productive when your mind is busy trying to collect, process, and keep track of all of your commitments, or "open loops," as Allen calls them, pulling focus and concentration from what you're doing right now. His process centers on managing commitments so you can free your mind to concentrate on the task at hand—and be more productive in the process.

The first step in this process is what Allen calls "get everything out of your head." When you don't have faith that the systems you have created will ensure that all of your important tasks will get accomplished, you rely on your brain to remember all of the things you have to do. But expending all of that mental energy trying to remember makes it difficult to concentrate on anything else.

When Dan was a true solo, he relied on his memory—and a great case management system—to get things done. As his firm grew and he added staff, he assumed his new employees knew all the rules and procedures Dan kept in his head. They didn't. They came to him all the time with questions, and his office seemed to stop moving forward. Dan needed to do a brain dump—to take what was in his brain and get it into the brains of his staff. He did the next best thing—he created checklists and started saving things into a "Law Firm Training & Procedure" file in his case management system. Efficiency improved, everyone's tempers calmed, and his office was a much better place to work.

Essentially, "get everything out of your head" is an information dump. Write down *every single thing* you can think of that you need to do, whether those items are short term or long term, large or small, priorities or not. One of the things that you will notice as you do this exercise is that some of the items on your list will be single tasks that need to be accomplished. Others will be projects that consist of multiple tasks. Don't worry about that too much during the initial exercise—just try to get everything down on paper first.

When you are confident that you have collected everything you can possibly think of and you aren't missing anything important, your mind will be a bit clearer, and you will be better able to focus on your priorities. Your mind (and your thinking) won't be cluttered up with trying to remember things and instead can be used to solve problems for your clients. As Allen says, you'll be using your mind to think *about* things, instead of thinking *of* things.

IDENTIFY NEXT ACTIONS

After your brain dump, you'll have a list of projects and tasks to be accomplished. But how do you move forward? Looking at the big picture all of the time can get overwhelming, as we have already seen with our to-do lists in Chapter 2. Instead, break large projects down into small, concrete steps to make the project much more manageable. You've probably heard the old joke:

> What's the best way to eat an elephant?
> One bite at a time.

Or you've heard one of our favorite sayings:

Yard by yard, life is hard, but inch by inch, life's a cinch.

Simply put, taking things one step at a time instead of being overwhelmed by the entire project or the totality of work that needs to be accomplished makes any task or project much more manageable. As David Allen says, instead of thinking about the impossibility of completing the entire project, just identify the *very next action* that needs to be done—the smallest possible task you can undertake to move the project forward.

For example, let's say you have to write a legal brief. Instead of thinking of the entire brief-writing project, break it down into more manageable pieces and then concentrate on the first small step that you need to do. In this case, it might be gathering the documents for the record on appeal or doing some research to determine if there are more updated cases that address the legal issue in question. An even smaller first step might entail simply putting the briefing deadlines on your calendar and scheduling a time to begin the work.

Let's take another example: improving your online presence. It's easy to get overwhelmed by all of the potential places you could participate online and the time it might take to do so. Your first step might be a telephone call with a savvy colleague to see what is working for them or scheduling a brainstorming meeting with your staff. Or it might simply be reviewing your existing online presence to see if there are any glaring gaps or mistakes that need to be corrected. Maybe it is researching reputable marketing agencies or experts that you can enlist to help you.

Once you have identified the very next step that needs to be taken, schedule a time to complete that step using the techniques you'll learn in Chapter 6 or, if it is a small enough task, consider doing it right away (see the two-minute rule discussed in Chapter 3 and reiterated later in this chapter).

A series of tiny steps will take you further than you could have imagined.

TIME YOURSELF

Whether you bill by the hour or not, you have only so many hours each day to accomplish productive work. Estimating the length of time it takes you to perform regular tasks can be invaluable in helping you to plan your days (which will help you when you get to Chapter 6), but it can also provide you with insight about how well you manage your activities now. If you consistently put more tasks on your to-do list than you have hours in the day, you will always be frustrated and exhausted.

Try this exercise:

1. Make a list of the activities you perform on a daily, weekly, or monthly basis and then separate those tasks into categories.
2. Estimate the amount of time you spend on each category per day, week, or month.
3. For one month, keep track of your activities and the amount of time you actually spend on each.
4. Take note of activities you perform during that month that you failed to include in your original list.
5. Be aware of "time hogs" and interruptions and how they affect your day.
6. At the end of the month, compare your original estimates with reality.
7. Adjust your task list, your schedule, and your expectations accordingly.

In today's hectic world, many of us are unrealistic with our expectations or routinely try to accomplish too much. This exercise can be a real eye-opener and can help you see why you may be feeling overwhelmed and where you may need to adjust. It will also help you to plan better in the future and avoid, eliminate—or, if that's not possible, make room for—the "time hogs."

BEATING PROCRASTINATION

Even when we know exactly what we need to accomplish, sometimes we avoid doing it. As we saw in Chapter 2, procrastination can be a form of self-sabotage or self-interruption. Sometimes you need to force yourself to just do the work. Here are a few strategies for doing so.

15-Minute Timer

Using a timer can be an effective method to combat procrastination. Perhaps you've got a project or task that you are avoiding or that seems so overwhelming that you don't know where to start. You may be wasting more time worrying about what to do or how to begin than it would take to complete (or make significant progress on) the task!

Try setting a timer for 15 minutes and committing only to that amount of time to work on that task. Anyone can stand almost anything for 15 minutes. You'd be surprised how much you can accomplish in 15 minutes. When 15 minutes is up, feel free to move on to the next task. But you may find that once you've gotten started, you're able to keep going and bring that matter to completion. Sometimes getting started is the hardest part, and once you get going, you realize that the task wasn't as bad or as difficult as you thought it would be.

Another version of this strategy is known as the Pomodoro Technique®,[1] pioneered by Francesco Cirillo. This technique uses a timer to break work into short intervals, punctuated by short breaks. One of the main tenets of the technique is that each designated work interval should represent uninterrupted working time—no answering the telephone, checking email, or otherwise moving away from the task at hand during that interval.

This technique works even better if you have completed the previous exercise and kept track of the length of time it generally takes you to accomplish specific tasks, because you'll have a better idea of what can be completed within your 15- (or 25-) minute window.

Two-Minute Actions

We mentioned the two-minute rule in Chapter 3 on eliminating clutter. But it's one of the more helpful tips in David Allen's *Getting Things Done*, so it bears repeating here: when you're going through the stack of things that you have to do, if something can be done in two minutes or less, *do it* right away. Don't put it aside or make a note or anything else. By the time you put it down and pick it up again, or make the note, you could have completed the task.

This can be a helpful technique for processing your email; if the email requires a response or represents a task that can be completed in two minutes or less, do it right away. This reduces time wasted by returning to your inbox to complete the task later—and ensures that the task or response isn't forgotten.

Do the Worst First

Sometimes the best way to beat procrastination is to do the worst task, the one you are avoiding like the plague or that you hate, first thing in the morning when you arrive at work. Let's face it—not everything you do as a lawyer is enjoyable; not every case is interesting and not every client is a joy to work with. But the more you avoid the tasks, clients, and cases that you dislike, the less productive you're likely to be—even in other areas.

If you have a file that has been sitting around because no one wants to deal with it or an important project that you know will be time consuming or uncomfortable, these may be precisely the tasks you should prioritize as

1. The technique was named after a tomato-shaped kitchen timer; "pomodoro" is the Italian word for tomato.

important but not urgent. Do those tasks first. Get them out of the way and keep them from cluttering up your thinking and pulling focus from the other things you're working on.

Once you get started, you may realize that the offending task isn't as bad as you thought it would be. But even if it is terrible or uncomfortable, you'll feel better when it has been completed. You'll be free to focus on everything else that needs to be done—and you'll find it is much easier to do so when your mind is clear of thoughts about that nasty task or file.

And if the task is one you are avoiding but not one that *must* be accomplished by you, find someone who actually likes performing that particular task (or someone who is lower on the totem pole than you but can still get the job done) and delegate it to them, as we discussed in Chapter 4.

Make Procrastination Work for You

As we've seen, procrastination is often an obstacle to productivity. Even if it isn't your main style, everyone has a bit of the procrastinator in them. Procrastination is usually a bad thing—it usually means you are avoiding something, and procrastinating can make you feel guilty and unproductive. But sometimes procrastination can work *for* you if you examine the reasons behind your procrastination.

If you are procrastinating because the task isn't one you enjoy or one that you are proficient at, it may signal that the task in question is a good candidate for delegation. If the task isn't a necessity or a priority, your procrastination may actually be your way of choosing not to undertake that particular project. Perhaps you felt obligated to agree to do something that, with hindsight, doesn't serve your goals. If that's the case, release the guilt associated with your choice, fess up, and remove the item from your to-do list.

Procrastination can also result from an emotional response to a particular project or task. Can you get an objective viewpoint or otherwise remove the emotion from the situation?

Finally, you may be procrastinating for no reason—perhaps you're just afraid of something new, or you think the task will be worse than it actually is. Use reverse psychology on yourself and employ a version of the 15-minute timer. Put the task or a representation of the task in front of you. Then force yourself to do absolutely nothing. Stare at the task. Do not allow yourself to be distracted or to do anything else for at least 15 minutes. Chances are that you'll be so sick of staring at it that you'll get started—and it's likely that the task won't be as bad as you think once you do.

GOOD ENOUGH IS GOOD ENOUGH— OR THE 70 PERCENT SOLUTION

Here come the perfectionists again. One of the reasons why some important, strategic tasks never get accomplished, or why more work isn't delegated, is that too many lawyers wait until they have time to devote to "doing it right." They never complete the project because it isn't perfect. Or they fall into the trap of analysis paralysis, wanting to be 100 percent sure they are making the right decision before they proceed. This perfectionism can be another form of procrastination.

Waiting for perfection isn't an excuse. Nobody is perfect. Of course, you shouldn't put out work product or business development materials that are sloppy or unprofessional. But most of the time, good enough is good enough. Allison sometimes calls this the 70 percent solution; sometimes it's better to call a project complete at 70 percent and move on than to never complete it at all. You will never be 100 percent sure if a decision is the correct one until you take action.

Success is measured by the actions we take.

Analysis paralysis prevents action. For many lawyers, wasted time is wasted money. If you never take action, you never find out what works. It's the action that's the key to breaking the pattern.

You have to be willing to take risks and accept that some actions may have to be changed or discarded over time. But action is what will determine whether your firm is thriving or just surviving.

The success formula that every lawyer needs to remember and look at daily is

Information + Implementation = Transformation

Lawyers have the information part down. They're natural researchers and information-gatherers, searching for precedent and what has worked in the past. But often they don't know when to stop researching. They fail on the implementation component of the equation. The irony is, of course, that the implementation is what will yield the results lawyers want. Without implementation, all of the time spent gathering information is merely wasted time.

Lawyers need to remember that every decision isn't going to be perfect and that an important part of this process is to discover what doesn't work and go from there. Just because you go down one road now doesn't mean that you can't change course later if it doesn't work out.

To avoid getting stuck in that endless loop of continuing to tweak or improve before rolling out a new procedure, plan, fee structure, or service, follow the 70 percent rule. Attaining perfection is unlikely, if not impossible. Focus instead on getting your project to 70 percent. Then introduce it, accepting its imperfection and recognizing that the best way to improve it is to expose and test it in the real world. *Then* you can tweak the parts that aren't working.

Think like software or technology companies: they roll out the product in beta form; allow some testing, feedback, and tweaking; and then release version 1.0. The beta version always has bugs or is missing something, but the company rolls out the product anyway, knowing that it will perform some functions well and that other functions need improvement. They may even learn of some features that they were unaware were important to their customers. If these companies had simply kept the product in-house without real-world testing, two things might have happened. First, another company might have introduced a similar product and beat them to the market, and second, they would have missed the opportunity to engage with their customers and learn what features, benefits, or results their customers desired.

Instead of waiting until you think your website is 100 percent perfect or your plan for alternative fees is guaranteed to make you more money than your current hourly system, get your project to 70 percent, take action, and start getting feedback. Then you can improve from there, with the help of your clients. Maybe you will even be able to put that project behind you and move on to something new.

GET A BUDDY

As we've already seen with goal setting, any time you really want to accomplish anything, it can be helpful to let someone else in on what you're doing and ask them for help. Even if you don't need help accomplishing the task itself, the buddy system can provide accountability. It's easy to break commitments to yourself—who would know the difference? But it's much more difficult to admit to someone else that you didn't do what you promised. Most people are embarrassed to admit if they haven't done something. That kind of friendly peer pressure can be a powerful motivator, particularly if you schedule regular appointments or progress reports.

Often, having an appointment with yourself or, even better, with a buddy, coach, or consultant is the only thing that makes you actually take action, even if it's at the last minute right before your scheduled appointment or progress report. A buddy can also provide support and encouragement when you're having trouble and will be someone with whom you can celebrate your successes. You may be surprised how much you learn by supporting and teaching another person.

GET OUT OF THE OFFICE/TAKE REGULAR BREAKS

Looking at the same four walls or sitting behind a desk for hours at a time, particularly if you practice on your own, isn't exactly conducive to creative thinking. To perform your best, your mind and your body have to breathe. This is another of the principles behind the Pomodoro Technique; taking regular breaks helps you to be more productive during your working times. In fact, Dan requires his staff to take a lunch break and not eat lunch at their desks. Getting out from behind the desk is helpful by itself.

A change of scenery is sometimes all you need to get going on a particular project or to get yourself out of a slump.

Getting away from your office or even just away from your desk is particularly helpful when you're working on planning and strategy. When you take a walk or work in another location, you're less likely to be distracted by the telephone or the piles of paper that call out to you. Your attention is less likely to be divided between what you're working on now and the other things that you could or should be doing.

REWARD YOURSELF

Rewards are great motivators. If you are avoiding a particular project, devise a reward that you can give yourself when you've accomplished it, or when you've completed each step or stage. Your reward can be some time relaxing, a meal at a favorite restaurant, or a piece of chocolate—anything that will help motivate you to complete the project.

REPURPOSE

Repurposing is one of our favorite strategies. Everything you do can be used more than once or for more than one purpose. Why reinvent the wheel if you don't have to? Try to use everything you do more than once.

For example, when you give a speech or presentation, record it and use the audio or video on your website. Turn your notes or outline into an article and publish it in a trade publication, on your LinkedIn profile, or on your firm's website or blog. Turn your slides into a video you can send to your clients.

Create one seminar or presentation and give it in many different venues, for different audiences.

Create case studies or testimonials out of your experiences working with clients (be sure to get clients' consent if you will include their name or other identifying information). Write articles or blog posts or give seminars on a new twist in the law or new case law that affects your practice. When you write an explanation of a legal concept or process for one client, turn it into a flowchart or handout to give other clients. Turn the questions you get repeatedly from clients into FAQs on your website and capture them as Quick Parts to insert into email messages when another client asks the same question in the future. (We'll talk more about Quick Parts in Chapter 10.) Develop templates for documents you use frequently.

WRAP UP

It's easy to get overwhelmed by the sheer enormity of the volume of tasks you need to complete. Trying to remember it all can be paralyzing and prevent you from taking action and moving forward. When you are not certain that your systems have captured all of the tasks you need to perform, it can be distracting. Bad habits like procrastination and perfectionism can be extremely demotivating.

By documenting everything that needs to be done; breaking it down into smaller pieces; and using some of the other techniques described in this chapter, such as taking regular breaks or working with a buddy, you can reduce stress and improve your motivation.

CHAPTER 5 ACTION STEPS

1. Make some time on a regular basis to do a brain dump and get everything out of your head—all of the projects you'd like to accomplish and the tasks you need to complete.
2. Next, choose three of the items on your list and determine the next action for each.
3. Find a buddy, share those projects and actions with them, and schedule time to follow up.
4. Set a timer for a short interval of time to get started on your action steps.
5. Reward yourself when your action steps have been completed.

Chapter 6
ORGANIZE AND SCHEDULE TASKS WISELY

In the last chapter, we talked about some specific ways to ensure that your day-to-day work gets done, from identifying next actions on a project to working around the tendency to procrastinate. In this chapter, we'll talk about how to organize all of those projects and tasks and fit them all into your schedule.

GROUPING LIKE TASKS TOGETHER

Sometimes it is easier to accomplish tasks in groups, rather than as stand-alone actions. Tasks can be grouped in several different ways, including by

- Location (post office, law library, out of the office/errands)
- Tool (all tasks that require the computer, scanner, telephone)
- Type of work (all files to be closed, all complaints to draft, all bills to review)
- Category (administrative, planning, marketing, writing, etc.)

When organizing by category, don't create too many categories; a large number of categories can be difficult to keep track of and can result in wasted time trying to determine which category a task belongs in. Make the categories relatively broad. For example:

- Administrative tasks
- Networking

- Planning
- Writing
- Family
- Social
- Clients
- Working
- Exercise
- Alone time

KNOW YOUR OWN PEAKS AND VALLEYS: ORGANIZING BY ENERGY

Each person has their own conditions under which they operate optimally. Some people have more energy first thing in the morning, and others do their best thinking in the evening. Some people are more energized by doing research and writing, and others are energized by interacting with people. Get to know what times of the day are your peak energy times. If you don't already know, find out which activities energize you and which ones exhaust you. Plan accordingly.

USE YOUR CALENDAR: BLOCK YOUR TIME

Your calendar is one of the greatest activity management tools in your arsenal. Use it wisely. One way to do so is time blocking. Time blocking is simple: it's all about planning. Instead of haphazardly choosing tasks with no rhyme or reason, you reserve a specific block of time on your calendar to complete a task or series of tasks.

To use time blocking effectively, it is helpful to be good at estimating time. If you know how much time a task or series of tasks will take to accomplish, you can determine how much time (or how many different blocks of time) you need to reserve on your calendar for that task.

Before you undertake an activity, estimate the time you think it will take you, and write down your estimate. Once the activity is complete, compare your estimate with the actual amount of time it took you to complete. Adjust your future estimates accordingly. You may be wasting a lot of time or putting additional, unnecessary pressure on yourself by over- or underestimating the time it will take you to complete a particular endeavor. When you are better at estimating how long tasks will take to complete, you'll make better use of your calendar.

There are several ways that you can block your time.

For example, the Success Calendar system[1] run by Allison's friend, Wayne Cotton, uses full days as blocks of time and assigns each day a color as follows:

> **Blue Sky days:** Strategy and Planning (one or two days per quarter, if you're alone or have little staff; four or five days if you're working with a team or larger staff)
> **Red Tape days:** Education and Administration (one day per week—this is what I'd call your "non-billable" workdays)
> **Green Machine days:** Productive days (working on client projects)
> **Mellow Yellow days:** Personal/vacation time (one week at the end of each quarter)

You can adjust this system to add more categories, such as marketing and business development or volunteer/pro bono time. Wayne suggests making every single day have only one color theme, recognizing that some of the other colors may creep into those days but that most of the day will be devoted to one type of activity.

This one-purpose-per-day system might not work for everyone, especially if you're an associate and don't have as much control over your own schedule, but it's worth trying. You could also try to use half days, or at least blocks of several hours. Having one full day devoted to something like planning can make a big difference in your focus and productivity.

SET DEADLINES

A goal isn't worth much unless there's a deadline. The same is true for a task. When you have a scheduled meeting with a client or a hearing date for a motion, you make sure the work gets done on time. The deadline creates urgency and provides a framework within which to structure your activities. But what about those activities that Stephen Covey calls important but not urgent that we discussed in Chapter 1? Those are the tasks that often get carried on a never-ending to-do list simply because they have no built-in urgency.

1. Success Calendars, https://nobrowndays.com/ (last visited July 26, 2022).

Without a deadline, chances are you won't get around to accomplishing your goal. When there's no deadline, it's far too easy to keep putting important but not urgent tasks on the back burner.

For important but not urgent tasks, you must *create your own deadlines.* Dan's office assigns a deadline to every project, without exception, even if there is none. They have learned that work never gets done without a deadline.

Assigning a deadline creates urgency for otherwise nonurgent goals or tasks. For larger goals, choose a deadline that is a bit of a stretch for you or that will take a concerted effort on your part to reach. Don't make the deadline too short so that it's impossible to meet, but don't make it so long that you put the activity or goal right back on the back burner again.

List the steps you'll need to accomplish to reach the goal or complete the project, set a deadline for each step (or at least for the first step), and then put the deadline on your calendar. For example, if one of your goals is to get a website up and running, steps could include things like choosing a web designer, deciding on a style, creating the content for the home page and other pages, choosing a web host, etc. Even those steps can be broken up into smaller actions. Each of those actions should be turned into tasks and assigned a date and time on your calendar.

MAKE DEADLINES EXTERNAL

Assigning a deadline is only the first step. Just because you've created a deadline doesn't mean you'll actually meet it. Indeed, some of you may be thinking that you've tried this before, and setting deadlines, or even putting them on your calendar, has never worked for you. But perhaps that is because you've missed the most important aspect of setting deadlines—they work better when the deadline is *external.* Deadlines and to-do lists that remain private are easy to ignore. If you are the only one who knows about them, there is no one to hold you accountable. The most important aspect of setting external deadlines is making those deadlines have meaning outside of your own personal wish list or calendar. To improve your chances of meeting the deadline, make it external by publicizing the deadline or sharing it with others to make it real.

As we've already seen with goals and action steps, by sharing your deadline with someone else and asking them to hold you accountable for accomplishing your goals, you'll increase your odds of reaching those goals.

The nature of your goal will determine who to share both the goal and the deadline with. In some cases, it will be another lawyer or staff member within your office. Other times, a consultant or colleague is a more appropriate accountability partner. Whenever it is appropriate, share your goals and deadlines with clients; this is the most effective, since clients are the ones you'd least like to disappoint.

Why External Deadlines Work

External deadlines use the power of peer pressure. They work because they act like commitments to other people, even if the only one who really benefits is you. Most of us are okay with shortchanging ourselves or putting our own priorities aside, but we are much more reluctant to break promises or fail to follow through when we've made a commitment to someone else. Nobody likes to break their word or fail to fulfill a promise or look like a failure.

External deadlines also work because they create a support system for your efforts where you wouldn't normally have support. When you share your deadlines with others and ask them to keep you accountable, you've created a cheering section—and perhaps even an offer of help. At the very least, you'll have moral support.

Here are some examples of how this might work:

Goal	Accountability and External Deadline
Go through the publications piled on your office floor.	Share the deadline with your assistant. Most likely, your assistant will be just as happy as you are to see the clutter disappear. And they can help you, either by actively going through the publications with you or by helping to clear your schedule and reduce or eliminate interruptions while you complete the task.
Ramp up your business development efforts by doing a seminar.	Choose a topic. Set an external deadline by publicizing the date on your website, sending out a press release, and/or notifying your clients about the seminar.
Finally get your new website up and running.	Choose a launch date for the new site. Send postcards to clients and strategic alliances announcing the launch date or tease the new site in your social media posts.

One of the advantages of external deadlines is that they force you to get over your perfectionism by letting good enough be good enough, as we saw in Chapter 5. The article, website, or seminar presentation may not be perfect, but at least you've taken the first step. You can always refine it the next time.

SCHEDULING TIME TO GET WORK DONE

Now that you've set a deadline, put the deadline on your calendar, and committed to someone else to complete the task or project by that date, it's time to actually do the work. Your calendar can help again. Pull out that list of actions you need to take to complete the project or reach your goal and schedule the activities on your calendar.

You may find that using the time-blocking technique alone isn't enough to allow you to reach peak productivity. That may be because although you've blocked out the time on your calendar, within each block of time you revert to reactive mode.

For example, perhaps you've blocked out a specific day to work on your marketing. But if you do not have specific tasks planned to execute during that time, you may jump from task to task, checking on social media, then remembering you wanted to write an article, and finally deciding you want to create a follow-up letter for clients. At the end of the day you finally realize that what you should have done was work on your website. You blocked the time, but you didn't use it wisely. You did not complete any of the tasks you started during that block, and your main marketing task—your website—received no attention at all. That's where your calendar and those external deadlines can help.

If something is important enough to put on a to-do list, it's important enough to be an appointment in your calendar just like a court appearance, a closing, a client meeting, or a doctor's appointment. Your regular deadlines, like court dates or client meetings, are noted on your calendar. Your nonurgent deadlines need to be recorded on your calendar, too. But tracking the deadlines alone isn't enough. To avoid doing everything at the last minute, schedule the time to get the tasks done. Make appointments with yourself and block the time on your calendar to write the motion papers, review your website copy, or develop a plan for the client's case, and have a plan to follow when the time arrives.

When scheduling tasks on your calendar, leave room for what Allison calls the chaos factor, otherwise known as Murphy's Law; whatever can go wrong will go wrong. Emergencies, crises, and unforeseen circumstances are sure to arise. Priorities get shifted. You never know when it's going to hit or how long you'll be sidetracked. The only thing that's a definite is that it will come, probably when you least expect it, so you might as well be prepared.

Don't schedule every minute of every day. Leave some room in your schedule between tasks or just for downtime. Build a cushion into your deadlines, whether they are deadlines for clients, colleagues, family, or just yourself. If you think you can get the document to the client within a week, give the client a date two weeks ahead. If you know the presentation is next month, put the deadline on your calendar two weeks in advance. That way, if the unexpected happens, you can still deliver on time. And if the chaos factor doesn't hit, you'll have impressed the client with your exceptional response time—or you can actually take some time to enjoy yourself.

The advantage to setting specific times to accomplish important tasks and leaving some flexibility in the schedule is that as soon as the crisis or emergency has passed, you can return to your schedule without missing a beat. Simply reschedule the tasks that were displaced by the emergency to a new date and time on your calendar, and they won't fall through the cracks. But if those tasks were never on your schedule in the first place, when the emergency arose, those tasks would have fallen off of your radar, and they would be much less likely to get done.

Scheduling gives you a blueprint or plan for every day. If it needs to change, so be it—but at least you'll be choosing another specific time to get it done and it won't languish on a to-do list.

If it isn't on your calendar, it doesn't get done. Urgent gets done—things that have deadlines get done. But setting the deadline isn't enough. Use your calendar to *schedule appointments to get the work done.*

WRAP UP: CREATE DAILY AND WEEKLY PLANS OF ACTION

Don't let yourself be overwhelmed or paralyzed by the amount of work you need to accomplish. Let's recap what we've learned from the past few chapters and then create a plan of action:

- Determine every day which actions or tasks are the most important and make sure those take center stage in your day. Don't let smaller, urgent but not important activities get in the way. Put the big rocks in first! If you're a perfectionist, don't let your obsession with getting everything right overwhelm you or prevent you from accomplishing your goals. Delegate tasks that don't require your full participation.
- Create your Power of Three list every evening for the next day's work so that you start your day with action, rather than with figuring out what you should do first.

- Eliminate distractions; say no to interruptions and bad clients. Multi-taskers, use the timing techniques and create do-not-disturb time. Give each task your full attention.
- Clear the clutter so you can focus on what's important. Packrats, resist the urge to save everything, and make use of electronic filing!
- Next, determine the amount of time each activity you've prioritized will take to accomplish. Don't be stingy with your estimate; estimating too little time will add stress and confusion to your schedule.
- Finally, determine when you will perform that activity and put the activity on your calendar. Make sure you leave some empty space or downtime on your calendar in addition to the personal and family time that you schedule. And leave room for the chaos factor.
- Use your calendar to plan not only deadlines but also time to complete work. When unforeseen circumstances arise, revise the plan as necessary, moving your appointments to complete work the same way you would reschedule any other appointment.
- Choose a time each week to review the work you need to accomplish and create a plan for the upcoming week. Many of Allison's clients have more success doing their weekly planning on Thursday, rather than on Friday, when they are trying to get out the door for the weekend. Mondays work for some, too, but waiting until the week has already begun is not the best strategy for most. It's easier to enjoy the weekend when you know you can hit the ground running and get right to work with a preset plan on Monday morning.
- Be flexible: recognize that the schedule is not entirely set in stone. It is likely that there will be last-minute emergencies, unforeseen circumstances, or client crises that must be addressed. As part of your weekly review, ensure that your plans cover all aspects of your practice, including marketing, management, administration, business development, and client work.

More often than not, you probably react to whatever is in front of you, rather than determining in advance what you want to accomplish. Instead, schedule time on your calendar for important tasks. If this allows you to complete them even half of the time, it's probably a lot more than you're doing right now.

Don't leave your schedule to chance. Schedule and block time to create a purpose or plan for every day.

CHAPTER 6 ACTION STEPS

1. Notice your work habits—when and where are you most productive?
2. Instead of simply creating a to-do list, place tasks or work to be done on your calendar for a specific date and time.
3. Block some time for important tasks over the next week. Make sure you're putting the big rocks in first.
4. Get into the habit of setting external deadlines by telling someone else when they should expect work to be completed.
5. When you encounter a new task that needs to be done, set a deadline, publicize it, and schedule time to complete the work.

Chapter 7

EFFECTIVE MEETINGS

Lawyers attend (and host) a lot of meetings. Even solos are involved in bar association committee meetings, networking meetings, and client meetings, just to name a few. Technology has made scheduling meetings even easier. For example, we can share calendars and send electronic appointments that automatically get added to the recipient's calendar. As a result, you may find your days and weeks clogged with more and more meetings, whether in-person meetings or virtual. Some of those meetings are entirely unnecessary and can be eliminated completely. Others may require only a few participants.

Meetings can be huge time-wasters. In addition to the studies we discussed at the beginning of this book, one *Harvard Business Review* survey cited in a 2017 article[1] found that 71 percent of senior managers from different industries said that meetings are unproductive and inefficient. Only 17 percent reported that their meetings were productive uses of group and individual time. Sixty-four percent said deep thinking suffered because of meetings.

In a study conducted by Korn Ferry in 2019,[2] more than two-thirds (67 percent) of respondents said that spending too much time in meetings and on calls distracted them from making an impact at work.

According to the *Harvard Business Review* article, "Many organizations we have worked with endure the triple whammy of meetings that are (1) too

1. Leslie A. Perlow, Constance Noonan Hadley & Eunice Eun, *Stop the Meeting Madness*, HARV. BUS. REV., July–Aug. 2017, https://hbr.org/2017/07/stop-the-meeting-madness.
2. *Working or Wasting Time?*, KORN FERRY (Nov. 13, 2019), https://www.kornferry.com/about-us//press/working-or-wasting-time.

frequent, (2) poorly timed, and (3) badly run, leading to losses in productivity, collaboration, and well-being for both groups and individuals. This is the worst-case scenario—and, unfortunately, the most prevalent. The majority of our survey respondents—54 percent—put their meetings in this category."

If a meeting is unproductive, your practice is losing productivity overall. Meetings require you to make decisions about how and when you will accomplish your individual tasks. Some may not get done at all or get done ineffectively. Other tasks will take over what otherwise would be personal time, leading to turnover or burnout.

Because scheduling meetings is so much easier, it seems that less and less thought is put into determining who needs to attend and why. Many meetings are unproductive because they lack a specific objective, have an unclear agenda, or fail to identify next steps. When the wrong people attend or when meetings are unfocused, participants lose interest.[3] When people don't contribute to the discussion or pay attention to what is being said, the meeting loses purpose and becomes simply a waste of time.

Meetings can be invaluable tools for brainstorming, collaboration, getting input from a number of people at once, developing goals or strategies, discussing a problem, or choosing an action or outcome. But just as email isn't the best tool for all purposes, meetings aren't the best tool for all communications. If you're tempted to schedule a meeting just to provide an update to a number of people, unless the update is significant or is tied to an event or celebration, it may be more appropriate to provide that update using another method, such as a project management tool, an email, or a note in the client or project file. Meetings should have a specific goal or intended action outcome.

If you can't eliminate the necessity for the meeting, make it more effective by avoiding the most common meeting time-wasters and developing a meeting system.

BE MINDFUL OF POTENTIAL MEETING PITFALLS

Meetings can fail or be unproductive for a whole host of reasons, including:

Lack of preparation: Nothing gets accomplished during the meeting because participants did not know what the purpose or intended outcome of the meeting was, because they did not receive an agenda or necessary documents,

3. Michael Mankins, Chris Brahm & Greg Caimi, *Your Scarcest Resource*, Harv. Bus. Rev., May 2014, http://hbr.org/2014/05/your-scarcest-resource/.

or because they failed to prepare by familiarizing themselves with topics of discussion or documents before the meeting.

Lack of engagement: It is difficult to keep meetings on track even when only a few participants are disengaged. Disengaged participants distract other participants, especially if the disengaged participants are engrossed in other activities such as surfing the net, texting, or checking email during the meeting. When meeting participants get frustrated, have a bad attitude, or feel they are wasting their time or are not needed to achieve the meeting's intended outcome, they can bring down the energy of the rest of the participants.

Failure to follow through or implement: Even meetings that seem productive can ultimately be a waste of time if there is no follow-up to ensure that results of the meeting are documented and communicated, next steps are identified, and decisions are implemented.

Lack of accountability: We've seen a failure to implement (often resulting in additional meetings and wasted time) even where action steps have been identified if accountability for those action steps has not been established. When clear responsibility for action steps has not been established, everyone can leave the meeting thinking that someone else will be performing those tasks or action steps. And when no deadlines, check-in dates, or follow-up plans have been confirmed, meeting action items often end up taking a back seat to other tasks.

As you read through our suggestions to make your meetings more effective, think about these potential pitfalls and how you can anticipate and circumvent them.

DETERMINE YOUR PURPOSE

First, decide the purpose and goal for the meeting. What outcome do you want to see from the meeting? Is this a brainstorming meeting to generate ideas, a meeting to identify and/or resolve issues, an action-based meeting to identify next steps and responsibilities, a task-based meeting to accomplish a particular assignment, or a meeting to make a decision?

Once you know what you are trying to accomplish, you can decide on the meeting structure that will work best: will it be a free-flowing discussion (good for brainstorming or generating ideas) or will participants have a set time to speak (perhaps better for check-in or status-based meetings)? Does the meeting address a time-sensitive issue that must be tackled right away, or is it a future-oriented, planning meeting?

DECIDE WHO SHOULD PARTICIPATE

Attendance can make or break your meeting: inviting too many people can unnecessarily complicate it, but inviting too few (or the wrong people) can hinder progress.

Your knee-jerk reaction might be to invite everyone in the firm or everyone in a particular category (all associates, all legal support staff, all members of a specific practice group, etc.) to participate in every meeting, but we recommend that you give a little further thought to who should participate in your meetings.

The meeting's purpose should also drive the attendance. Whose experience or expertise will be necessary to accomplish the meeting's purpose? If the meeting is a decision-making meeting, it makes sense that the decision-makers must be present in order to accomplish the goal of the meeting. But be sure to include other stakeholders and those who might be significantly impacted by the decision so that they may provide their input or perspective on what factors should be considered.

You may also want to consider whether some participants should be present only for a portion of the meeting, rather than for the entire meeting.

SET THE AGENDA AND COMMUNICATE IN ADVANCE

Create a meeting agenda with topics to be discussed and persons responsible. Show that you respect the time of all involved and set limits for discussion, with a concrete beginning and ending time for the meeting.

Some executives have found that adding questions to be answered under each agenda topic is a helpful technique to direct meeting discussion.[4]

Give attendees advance notice of the date and time of the meeting. Communicate the purpose and expected outcome of the meeting, goals, and agenda to all participants far enough in advance of the meeting so they can prepare. Include any supporting documents needed for the meeting or that you expect participants to have reviewed or to be familiar with for the meeting. Advise participants of their expected role at the meeting. Request that participants respond to confirm their attendance. Send out a meeting reminder the day before the meeting to confirm.

4. Lucy Handley, *The Rise of the 15-Minute Meeting—and How to Run One*, CNBC Work (Jan. 25, 2022), https://www.cnbc.com/2022/01/25/the-rise-of-the-15-minute-meeting-and-how-to-run-one.html.

HIGHLY EFFECTIVE MEETINGS

Start on time and stick to your agenda. Make sure introductions are made if you are not certain that everyone participating knows one another or if some participants are attending the meeting remotely. Have each person indicate who they are and why they are there or what their role in the firm or group is.

Begin the substance of the meeting by repeating the goal or purpose. Advise participants of the format of the meeting. If there is a projected (or firm) end time for the meeting, announce it in the beginning so that everyone is aware of it.

If issues arise that are unrelated but must be discussed during the meeting, request agreement of the participants to continue the meeting beyond the originally agreed-upon end time and establish that only those individuals involved in that particular project or issue are required to stay. If nonurgent issues arise, table them for a meeting to be held at another time specifically for that purpose.

Designate one person to be the meeting facilitator to keep the meeting on point and on time or assign a timekeeper to keep an eye on the clock and remind the facilitator.

To obtain maximum participation, make the meeting a safe place for people to express their opinions without judgment or ridicule. Allow each person the opportunity to speak, but don't let one person take over the meeting. Obtain different perspectives by asking open-ended questions. Increase participant engagement in the meeting by assigning different people to lead the discussion on each agenda item.

When controversy arises, look for points of agreement. ("Can we all agree that the goal is . . ." or "If I'm hearing correctly, everyone seems to think there is a problem with Y, but we haven't come up with the best way to solve the problem yet. Let's see what we can come up with.")

Before concluding the meeting, always summarize the meeting and create a future plan. You should develop an action plan based upon your initial agenda. If necessary, recap the decisions that were made, lessons learned, or options identified during the meeting. Reiterate any goals that have been set, identify next steps, establish milestones, set deadlines for the tasks identified, and assign responsibility for those tasks to specific groups or individuals. Agree on how progress will be monitored. Decide whether additional or follow-up meetings will be required and, if possible, schedule them immediately.

POSTMEETING ACTIONS

Even if you don't take formal minutes of each meeting, make sure that the main goals and decisions, deadlines, action steps, and responsibilities that were determined during the meeting are communicated afterwards—in writing, if necessary. Consider whether they need to also be disseminated to those who were not present at the meeting to make follow-up and future meetings more productive, even for those who were unable to attend. Follow up individually with those who have action steps to complete. If follow-up meetings are necessary, add the tasks and responsibilities that were established to the agenda for the follow-up meeting, or request that responsible parties submit a report of their progress to be attached to the agenda for the next meeting.

You may also find it useful to send meeting participants a short questionnaire[5] to rate the effectiveness of your meetings and help you improve meeting efficiency in the future. Ask participants to rate the meeting in each of the following categories:

- The meeting's **purpose** was clearly defined and was important to me.
- The **information** shared in the meeting was valuable to me.
- The **issue** being discussed was clearly defined and was important or significant to me.
- **Decisions** were made as a result of the meeting, there was clear **responsibility** defined for carrying out those decisions, and it was clear **who was responsible** for carrying them out.
- The meeting resulted in clearly defined **plans, next steps, and deadlines.**
- How valuable were the **outcomes** of the meeting compared with the **time spent** in the meeting? Use a scale of 1–5 as follows:

  1 No value, a total waste of my time
  2 Some value, but not really worth the time
  3 Not great, but not horrible either
  4 Valuable, one of the better uses of my time
  5 Absolutely valuable, one of the best things I could have done with my time

  Multiply each participant's total score by 4 to get a score out of 100, and see whether your meetings rate an A, B, C, or worse.

5. Adapted in part from Russell Bishop, Workarounds That Work: How to Conquer Anything That Stands in Your Way at Work (McGraw-Hill 2011).

DIFFERENT MEETING FORMATS

Some kinds of meetings Allison's clients have found useful include the following:

Stand-Up Meetings

A stand-up meeting is a meeting conducted with all participants standing up to reinforce the brief nature of the meeting and ensure that participants don't settle in. Stand-up meetings are meant to be extremely brief, often held simply to alert everyone in the firm or on the team of the status of projects or the activities undertaken by each member.

An example might be a weekly stand-up briefing in which each member is given a brief opportunity to report on what they did in the past week, what they are working on this week (or intend to accomplish this week), what potential obstacles they anticipate, and where they might need help. These meetings can help supervisors and managers to quickly determine whether resources (time/energy/staff) are being allocated appropriately or if projects are off track.

Given the time it takes to create and review reports or email messages, stand-up meetings may be a more efficient and effective way to manage some teams.

Departmental or Practice Group Meetings

Sometimes it's important to convene all of the individuals working in a particular practice group or service area to talk about changes, coordinate the handling of different matters for the same client, discuss changes in procedure that affect only that department, or even catch up on the status of matters. It isn't necessary for everyone in the firm to attend these meetings, but it can be helpful to hold them periodically to ensure consistency within a service or practice area. When conducting these meetings, consider whether it may make sense to include not just the lawyers working in that practice area but also other staff who may interact with those clients.

Partner Meetings

Many small firms don't have regular partner meetings, which can result in inconsistent decision-making or lack of communication. It is often beneficial to conduct meetings with partners when firm-wide decisions will be made so that all partners can provide their input and perspective. In our experience, when this isn't done, there are often unintended consequences, as decision-makers may not always realize the impact of their decisions on other partners or practice areas until it is too late.

Staff Meetings

Particularly in small-firm settings, it can be extremely beneficial to conduct meetings solely with staff or to include staff in larger meetings. In-person meetings foster communication and collaboration among staff members and between attorneys and staff, but if done well, virtual meetings can have a similar effect.

Consistent meetings between attorneys and the staff who regularly work with them can help reduce interruptions, as we saw in Chapter 2, and may be useful for effective delegation, as we saw in Chapter 4. But don't overlook including staff in meetings about policy or procedure changes, either; as front-line workers, staff often have valuable contributions to make that can aid the overall efficiency of the firm.

Interest Group or Committee Meetings

Small-group meetings are often more effective than large-group meetings in part because it's more difficult to hide in a small-group meeting, and small groups can be more interactive. As we've already seen, in larger groups, it is almost impossible to keep everyone engaged the entire time, particularly if every item on the meeting agenda is not important to every participant present. Small-group meetings by interest or practice group, or committee meetings to accomplish specific non-client-related work, can be particularly effective.

CREATE TEMPLATES

Do you routinely repeat meetings in your office? For example, does your firm have regular weekly or monthly partner or staff meetings that cover the same topics? If so, don't reinvent the wheel for every meeting. Create a template agenda that covers all of the items you routinely cover in the meeting and adjust only when special issues arise. This will not only help to keep your meetings focused and on track but will also let meeting participants know what to expect and how to plan for these regular meetings.

VIRTUAL MEETINGS[6]

Since we wrote the first edition of this book, virtual meetings have exploded, thanks in no small part to the Covid-19 pandemic. From internal office meetings to client consultations to bar association meetings, family dinners, and

6. A version of this section on virtual meetings was previously published (June 5, 2020) on Allison's blog at https://www.legaleaseconsulting.com/legal_ease_blog/2020/06/10-tips-for-better-zoom-meetings.html.

virtual happy hours, Zoom has become the go-to platform for many who had never attended a videoconference before 2020.

Having attended far too many Zoom meetings ourselves, we've found that many lawyers—as well as our nonlawyer friends and colleagues—are making simple Zoom meeting mistakes that can be distracting to other attendees or even hurting their professional reputations.

Stories of Zoom fails have circulated on the internet, including the admonition by one Florida judge who complained about what lawyers were—or weren't—wearing to court video calls; the reporter from *Good Morning America* who got caught with a shirt, jacket, and tie but no pants on camera; and "Jennifer," who took her laptop to the bathroom with her during a Zoom meeting. There was even a flush heard during one of the first-ever livestreamed virtual Supreme Court arguments. Although it was not a Zoom call (thankfully), it was clear that proper etiquette of muting when not speaking wasn't followed in this virtual argument.

There have already been several articles written about "best practices" for Zoom meetings, including two on Above the Law: from Bob Ambrogi on ten blunders to avoid on Zoom,[7] and from Niki Black of MyCase on Zoom videoconferencing tips and tricks.[8] There are also several articles out there about Zoom security.[9]

Here are a few of our favorite tips from those articles, along with some of our own comments.

1. **Consider a virtual background—or not**—Both Bob and Niki talk about adding a virtual background to enhance your Zoom meeting presence, but in my experience, they don't work all that well for most people. You need a device that's relatively new, and even then, they can be glitchy if you move around a lot when you're speaking. Also, some of your body parts can disappear or can reveal your green screen, which is more distracting than having a boring background, so use virtual backgrounds with caution.

And that brings us to:

2. **Be aware of your surroundings**—What can others see around you on camera? If you're attending a Zoom meeting from your bedroom, for example, you might want to sit in a place where the bed can't be seen. If that's not possible,

7. Robert Ambrogi, *10 Blunders to Avoid on Zoom*, Above the Law (Mar. 30, 2020), https://abovethelaw.com/2020/03/10-blunders-to-avoid-on-zoom/.
8. Nicole Black, *Zoom Videoconferencing Tips and Tricks*, Above the Law (Apr. 2, 2020), https://abovethelaw.com/2020/04/zoom-videoconferencing-tips-and-tricks/.
9. Here is an article written specifically about Zoom security for lawyers: Juda Strawczynski, *Security Tips for Lawyers Hosting a Zoom Meeting*, AvoidAClaim (Apr. 23, 2020), https://avoidaclaim.com/2020/security-tips-for-lawyers-hosting-a-zoom-meeting/.

at least make the bed. And keep in mind who else might be in or enter the room during your meeting—it's probably not a good idea for the judge in your virtual court conference to see your scantily dressed spouse walking through the bedroom.

3. **Watch your camera angle**—How many Zoom meetings have you attended where at least one participant can only be partially seen? If you're one of them, please check out what your video looks like when you join a meeting. You can tilt your laptop, tablet, or smartphone to an angle that allows participants to see your entire face, not just the top of your head. And you can prop up your device so that the camera is at eye level. If it's too low, the camera angle will frequently show a lot of ceiling and an upward view of your face (which sometimes is unflattering and often feels like attendees are looking up your nose). Another option is to buy a camera like the Dell UltraSharp 4K Webcam, which uses advanced AI auto framing so that you always stay focused (in other words, centered) on on the picture no matter where you move. You can also control the sensitivity and how quickly the camera tracks you, and how tight the framing is. Cameras like this can make a tremendous difference.

4. Speaking of appearances, Zoom has a "**touch up my appearance**" setting that can help you put your best foot forward in any Zoom meeting you attend. You can find this setting by clicking the up arrow next to the video camera icon in Zoom.

5. **Pay attention to your lighting**—Backlit is bad because usually it makes it extremely difficult to see your face. Not all of us have professional lighting, and yours doesn't have to be, but we would like to see your face. Often, if you are in a room with a window, it is best to have the window and natural light to the side, or even in front of you, rather than behind you. Overhead lighting can be harsh—if you can place a light in front of you, that is often better. Ring lights, for example, are generally inexpensive, and they can make an enormous difference in a person's appearance. Sometimes it helps just to make your computer screen brighter so that it shines on your face. If you wear glasses, you have double trouble, because lighting can wreak havoc—in the form of glare—on your glasses.

6. **Use an appropriate screen name**—It's probably not the best idea to log into a Zoom meeting with the court, a client, or other professionals with a screen name like "ballbusteresq."

Your name will be displayed in the bottom corner of your video block when hovering over you in Zoom and in the participants list, including Chat and Q&A lists of participants even if you don't type anything into the chat or Q&A boxes, and it will appear in bold white letters if you turn off your video and don't have a Zoom profile photo. You can add a profile photo or update your Zoom screen name from your Profile settings, or you can rename yourself while in a Zoom meeting by clicking on the participants icon, finding your name, and clicking on "rename" (unless the host has disabled this feature).

7. **Mute yourself when you're not speaking**—Zoom is no different from any other conference-calling platform. It's common courtesy to mute yourself if you aren't speaking so that attendees can focus on the speaker. Even if you think you're in a quiet place, moving around, shuffling papers, or typing on your keyboard during a meeting can all potentially be heard and distract others—not to mention your cell or office phone ringing, dogs barking, etc.

8. **Review your Zoom settings**—As with any other program, the default settings in Zoom are not necessarily the ideal settings for you. One example is your microphone settings. In most cases, I've found that turning off the "automatically adjust" setting and manually setting your microphone level is best, because the "automatically adjust" setting can sometimes kill your sound entirely. Also, if you're using an external mike, rather than the one built into your device, you may need to make adjustments there separately. You can find these and other audio settings by hitting the up arrow next to the microphone in Zoom.

Another setting you may not be aware of is your **view options**—when in a Zoom meeting, you have a number of options to change the view. Most people know about gallery view (the "Brady Bunch" view, as some like to call it), where you can see many participants at once, instead of just the speaker, but you can also hit the view options button during a meeting to change the view from "100 percent" to "fit to window," which is especially helpful during screen sharing, when some of the slide or screen being shown is cut off or blocked by the video view.

As a **meeting host**, Zoom provides you with some additional settings to help make your meeting more effective and productive. For example, meeting hosts can turn on attention tracking so they can see when a participant does not have Zoom in focus for more than 30 seconds while a screen is being shared (presumably, when screen sharing is off, it's easy to tell who's paying attention just by looking at them).

The meeting host also has the option to put security measures in place when they schedule a meeting. For example, meeting hosts can set a password for the meeting or otherwise restrict access, and they can mute participants automatically upon entry to the meeting. Zoom also allows hosts to enable the waiting room, so the meeting host has to manually admit each participant into the meeting, reducing the likelihood of unauthorized entry. We recommend locking meetings once all participants have arrived to prevent unauthorized people from entering.

Hosts can also manage meeting participants during the meeting, such as muting someone who is disrupting the meeting or preventing participants from unmuting themselves or sharing their screens.

With the ever-changing nature of technology, including Zoom, Teams, and others, a quick search of sites such as ZDNet, Cnet, PCWorld, and others will often provide access to the latest tips and tricks for using Zoom and other platforms.

9. **Get more out of the Chat feature**—If you don't have Chat open in Zoom, you'll get a popup when someone has added something to the chat, but I've personally found that it's easier to keep it open at all times during a Zoom meeting.

This feature allows you to send private (just to one individual) or public (to everyone) messages during the meeting. You can also save the chat (if the host hasn't disabled this feature),[10] which is helpful if people post links or other info in the chat. We save chats from webinars to have a record of questions people have asked to improve webinars in the future (or to create other content responsive to them). If you save your chat, it will save both your public and private chat messages.

10. **Record the meeting**—Zoom and other similar programs have recording capability, which can come in handy for a number of reasons. There is a simple record button that will allow you to record a Zoom meeting and save it to your local computer, as long as the host has not disabled this feature. There are also options to store a Zoom meeting recording in the cloud.

Bonus: **Explore breakout rooms for large meetings**—Large Zoom meetings can get unwieldy and become unproductive. I've attended a few large meetings lately that incorporated Zoom's breakout rooms feature, which allowed participants to break into smaller groups for targeted discussions or problem solving and then rejoin the larger group to report their findings.[11]

Although Zoom became a very popular platform during the pandemic, there are other virtual meeting platforms that are also commonly used by lawyers and other legal professionals, including Microsoft Teams, which is integrated into the most recent versions of the Microsoft Office Suite and Microsoft 365. Many of the same or similar features can be found on these other platforms, and most of the practices discussed earlier can be translated into the

10. *Enabling or Disabling In-Meeting Chat*, Zoom Support, https://support.zoom.us/hc/en-us/articles/115004809306-Controlling-and-Disabling-In-Meeting-Chat (last updated July 17, 2022).
11. An interesting set of tutorials on Zoom for lawyers can be found here: *Zoom Tutorials for Lawyers*, Knoxville Bar Ass'n, https://www.knoxbar.org/index.cfm?pg=ZoomTutorialsforLawyers (last visited July 29, 2022).

other platforms as well. For more information on this topic, see the Work from Home Edition of *The Lawyer's Guide to Collaboration Tools and Technologies*, by Dennis Kennedy and Tom Mighell, from the ABA Law Practice Division.

MEETING TECHNOLOGY

Technology can help with some of the most onerous meeting planning and execution tasks. For example, one of the biggest meeting-related time-wasters is attempting to schedule meetings with a series of telephone calls and emails. Using scheduling programs such as Doodle.com or Calendly.com can allow meeting organizers to find the time that works for the most participants and to notify everyone quickly and easily of the scheduled date. Used in conjunction with Microsoft Outlook to send a final calendar appointment with meeting details, these tools can take a lot of the pain out of meeting planning.

Firms and organizations using Microsoft Exchange can use the Scheduling Assistant built into the app to see attendees' calendars and choose the time that works best for all participants.

Other programs or apps can also be helpful for creating meeting agendas and minutes or for following up on postmeeting tasks. For example, Beesy[12] allows you to take notes on your iPad, create professional meeting minutes, and automatically follow up on meeting notes tasks in Beesy's To-Do manager. Meeting Result[13] is a software program that helps you with meeting planning, execution, and follow-up. You can develop an agenda based on defined objectives, invite participants, distribute the agenda, keep track of attendance, capture meeting notes, develop next steps, and prepare a meeting summary. Otter.ai is a program that can take real-time notes and transcribe meetings.

WRAP UP

Meetings don't have to be a black hole of wasted time if they are utilized properly. First, you must determine whether conducting a meeting is the correct way to accomplish your objectives. If it is, you'll want to define your purpose, develop a meeting agenda based upon your objectives, and invite only those people who are required to meet those objectives or make decisions necessary

12. Beesy, https://itunes.apple.com/us/app/beesy-take-meeting-notes-automated/id499578384?mt=8 (last visited July 29, 2022).
13. MeetingResult, http://www.meetingresult.com/ (last visited July 29, 2022).

to move the project forward. Communicate the objective and agenda in advance to allow participants to fully prepare. Then use meeting facilitation techniques to keep the meeting on task and on time. And don't forget to summarize what was accomplished and document next steps, deadlines, and responsibility. Consider creating templates for agendas and minutes and using available software programs or apps to make scheduling, note-taking, and follow-up easier.

CHAPTER 7 ACTION STEPS

1. The next time you're planning a meeting, give some thought to the purpose of the meeting, the objectives to be accomplished, the type of meeting best suited to meet those objectives, and the people who will need to participate.
2. Consider using meeting scheduling software to eliminate time-consuming email chains.
3. Create an agenda for your next meeting and disseminate it, with the meeting objectives, well in advance. Communicate to all participants that you expect them to be prepared. Send calendar reminders to ensure that the meeting appears on participants' calendars.
4. Develop templates for agendas and minutes for repetitive meetings and use software to make preparation and follow-up easier and faster.
5. Don't forget to assign deadlines and responsibilities and decide how you will follow up to ensure implementation of action items identified during the meeting.

Chapter 8
CREATING SYSTEMS FOR YOUR PRACTICE

The practice of law uses a lot of mental energy, and anything that depletes mental energy unnecessarily or causes additional anxiety is a hindrance. As we've seen already, although the practice of law requires you to think like a lawyer, it's tough to do substantive legal work or to focus if you're distracted by piles of clutter in your office, if you waste precious time in unnecessary meetings, or if you're overcome with anxiety about how you're going to get it all done.

Developing systems and procedures for your practice helps you focus your mental energy on practicing law. You can concentrate on serving your clients when you know important tasks are being done consistently and effectively.

Although innovation, individual judgment, and creation of legal arguments and strategies on individual matters cannot be systematized, there are many things in a law practice that can and should be. In this chapter, we'll discuss how you can create systems and procedures for your practice to help reduce anxiety, increase consistency, and create loyal clients.

SYSTEMS CREATE LOYAL CLIENTS

Clients want to know what they can expect when dealing with their lawyer. Clients want to know their lawyer is watching out for their best interests and doing all they can to bring their matter to resolution. Systems make it less likely that things will fall through the cracks. Your staff will be more comfortable because they will know what is expected of them. Outsourcing and delegating become much easier.

Clients like stability and reliability. When everyone in the office follows the same procedures every time, you create a consistent experience for your clients.

Systems allow you to set clients' expectations more accurately at the outset of the engagement, thereby reducing complaints and questions about bills.

Systems that provide for periodic follow-ups with current and former clients increase the trust clients place in you and improve your chances of receiving referrals or new business from those clients.

SYSTEMS FOR SOLOS AND SMALL FIRMS

Firms of all sizes can benefit from systems and consistent procedures. Most large firms develop either firm-wide or practice group systems and procedures out of necessity; the volume of work and the number of people working is too large to allow everyone to develop their own way of working. But in our experience, solo and small-firm lawyers frequently operate with few or inconsistent systems, which results in wasted time, inefficiencies, loss of revenue, poor client experience, or even malpractice claims. For these reasons, we'll focus on systems for small firms and solo practitioners, but the principles apply regardless of the size of your firm.

In addition, we recognize that not everyone reading a book on personal productivity for lawyers will have the ability to implement—or even suggest—firm-wide systems. But individual lawyers can create their own systems for consistency in dealing with their clients and matters that will stand them in good stead for the duration of their careers.

As a solo practitioner or small-firm lawyer, it's likely that you're wearing many hats at once. You already have far too many things to think about during the course of the day. The better and more automated your systems are, the more you can focus your time on high-level, revenue-generating tasks.

For a solo or small-firm lawyer, spending too much time on tasks that don't generate revenue can be disastrous. That's why documenting your practices for others is so important. If the practice grows and you need to hire an associate or legal assistant, or even outsource work on a temporary basis, having documented procedures will make training much easier, quicker, and more effective.

Good documentation is also helpful if you want to take a vacation or need to hire a backup in the event of an emergency, illness, or scheduling conflict. Systems will also make for a smoother transition for clients in the event that you decide to retire or sell the practice.

When everyone knows who is responsible for what, and when and how tasks should be performed, your office will run much more smoothly, and your clients will have a much more consistent and enjoyable experience with your firm. And you can focus on bringing in more business and serving your clients well.

Tip — Checklists

Look for Dan's *Checklists for Lawyers* book from the ABA Law Practice Division, which contains procedures for creating checklists and checklists already started for you. These will give you a good foundation for creating your own procedures and checklists in your firm. Other good resources include the ABA Law Practice Division's *Law Office Policies, Procedures, and Operations Manual*[1] (as of this writing, now in its seventh edition).

Once you know why you need systems, you can determine what kinds of systems you need and how to create them, regardless of the size of your firm.

WHAT TO SYSTEMATIZE

Anything that is done repetitively can be systematized, at least in part. Systems can include checklists, procedures, automated tasks, templates, and forms. Examples of tasks or processes that can be systematized within a law firm include:

- Potential client interviews
- Conflicts checking
- Client intake
- Opening files
- File naming
- Reporting and notes on files
- Depositions
- Obtaining medical records and/or other evidence
- Standard due diligence
- Public records searches

1. Marcia Watson Wasserman & Cynthia Thomas, Law Office Policies, Procedures, and Operations Manual (7th ed. 2022), https://www.americanbar.org/products/inv/book/419978900/.

- Day-to-day file handling
- Billing and accounts receivable
- Closing files
- Client contact
- Client feedback
- Marketing and business development

HOW TO CREATE SYSTEMS

Once you determine what tasks or functions you'd like to systematize, document the steps and the timing in real time as you're performing them. Although this may take some time and energy up front that isn't billable per se, the time and mental energy saved in the long run is well worth the investment.

Here are some things to consider when creating a system or procedure:

- What is the purpose of or strategy behind performing this particular task or set of tasks?
- How does this activity or set of tasks provide value for clients?
- What can you do differently, or how can you perform this task in the most effective manner?
- Who should be assigned to perform the task? Are we leveraging correctly here?
- Does this task require more than one person? If so, how will they work together?
- If there is a series of tasks, is there a particular timeline that must be followed?
- What is the order the tasks should be performed in?
- Is there a way that we can perform this task differently than our competitors to make it a selling point or point of differentiation that will entice clients to hire us over our competition?
- Can we simplify this task or set of tasks?
- Is this activity really necessary?
- How can we use our existing office technology?
- Do we need additional training?

Think strategically about the best way to accomplish tasks within your practice and document the process. If necessary, use the recording feature on your phone and explain what you're doing as you do it. You can have someone transcribe the recording later to begin creating your procedure manual. Or have someone take notes while you perform a task that you want to document.

Example: Case Handling Systems

To create a system for day-to-day matter handling in your office, you might want to ask:

- What steps does each matter of the same type need to progress through from intake to conclusion?
- How will these steps be accomplished?
- Who is responsible for accomplishing each step?
- When do these steps need to be completed?
- How often do we need to communicate with clients?
- How should communication with clients be handled?
- What systems can be put into place for consistent client communication and follow-up?

Example: Client Intake System

You may need to create smaller systems within larger systems. For example, your system for client intake might be a subsystem of your file handling system. A client intake system might be developed as follows:

- Determine what information you need to obtain from every client (or every client in a particular practice area). Although every matter is different, you should know at least the categories of information you need to obtain from clients during an initial interview or consultation, the documents you'll need to obtain, etc.
- Create a checklist or questionnaire for use with every client so you don't forget anything.
- Create templates, scripts, or form letters to follow up with potential clients.
- Create templates or forms for your retainer agreement and engagement letter.

- Create a timeline or list of items to follow up on after the initial intake and enter any deadlines or follow-up dates into your calendar system for follow-up. Part of your system will include *who* will do *what* (i.e., perhaps the lawyer does the initial consultation, but a staff member enters the information into the computer, or perhaps the first part of your intake can be performed by a chatbot on your firm's website and then the client can be directed to a page where they can schedule the initial consultation themselves, etc.).

Even if you don't know all of the dates at the outset, you should be aware of the general steps or stages the matter will progress through. Document the steps and the deadlines for completing them. For example, if you're a personal injury lawyer, enter the statute of limitations date and the date you anticipate filing the complaint, as well as dates to follow up for the defendant's answer or to prepare default motions, etc.

One easy way to get started is by working on your systems and procedures as you're working on an individual case or matter; as the case progresses, keep track of the steps you (and others) take on the matter and the things you need to remember.

Put It in Writing

Don't forget one of the most important rules we've discussed in this book: **Put it in writing. Virtual plans are virtually useless.** Documenting your systems not only makes it easier to share them with others, but it also removes the burden of needing to remember every step in the process. Just follow the written procedure or checklist and it's more likely to be done right.

Don't let the idea of creating systems and procedures for your practice overwhelm you. Instead of thinking about creating a checklist, procedure, or template as a separate activity, develop it as you perform that underlying activity itself. For example, document the steps you take the next time you perform a client intake. Include the list of documents you request that the client bring to the initial meeting. If it's easier for you to dictate as you're working, dictate the steps and have it transcribed into a written procedure.

Circulate the first draft of your system or procedure to others in your office for their input and to ensure that you haven't missed any steps or other important items. Then add or revise as necessary as you perform that task or use the system over time. Test and revisit your systems to ensure that they remain valuable to both you and your clients.

Over time, having the systems and procedures documented will create a more effective practice and will allow you to focus your attention on the legal issues and the client's needs. You'll be more motivated to act.

Don't give up because there are too many procedures and systems that need to be created in your practice. Take them one at a time. Assign systems and procedures to the people who perform them most often. Making and following the rules will help you play the game to win and pave the way toward great lawyering and excellent client service.

CASE AND FILE MANAGEMENT

Practice, case, matter, and document management systems are crucial systems for any law firm. Many solos still have not implemented software to help them with these systems. Some lawyers contend that these kinds of software programs are unnecessary, but we disagree. Those who believe document and practice management software is a waste of money miss some of the most important reasons for using these programs in their practice.

But before we discuss the software programs themselves, it is important to understand that no software program will be valuable if there are no systems or procedures put into place to ensure consistent use of that software. It's the old "garbage in, garbage out" theory. If you spend the money and take the time to install practice/case or document management software but do not develop and implement protocols for using it, this software will be of limited utility. A directory/folder structure and good naming conventions will be important whether or not you use practice or document management software; the difference is that with document management software, these protocols will be programmed into the software. Essentially, you'll be able to "set it and forget it."

We'll talk more about the available kinds of software programs and platforms a bit later in this chapter, but since it is unlikely that law firms will be able to entirely eliminate paper anytime soon, and since many firms will need to maintain paper files alongside of or in addition to their electronic files, let's begin by talking about file systems and organization in general.

File Organization

Before computers and electronic files became commonplace in law firms, all legal files were kept solely on paper. Generally, law firms would create files for each client or matter, often with subfolders for various categories of documents and information. For the most part, this system of organization has remained today, only it has become more complicated because now lawyers need to contend with electronic files, folders, documents, and information in addition to paper ones.

Although there is no single best way to organize files and folders, and each practice area or type of service you provide may require slightly different protocols, there are some general guidelines you should keep in mind when organizing both paper and electronic files.

We recommend that you create a separate file for each client or matter. If it is likely that you will represent the same client in more than one matter, creating files by matter, rather than client, is preferable to avoid confusion and misfiling of documents. You can, however, cross-reference those matters or create file names that indicate that there are other existing matters for the same client. This can be done in several different ways.

Some lawyers develop not only names but also numbers for their files. Sometimes, these numbers show how many new files have been opened in a given year. You could use colors or create file numbers that also help identify different clients or practice areas easily. For example, if a firm has a client, ABC Corp., for whom they will be handling several matters, the firm might decide that ABC Corp.'s files will be green and that all of their file numbers will begin with a prefix, such as 01. If the firm also wants to keep track of files that are opened by year, the file number might also include the year. Let's assume the firm receives two different matters for ABC Corp. in 2022: Smith v. ABC Corp. and Jones v. ABC Corp. Both files will be green. But since they are two separate matters, they will not simply be called ABC Corp. Instead, the file names and numbers might be as follows:

Smith v. ABC Corp., 2022-01-001

Jones v. ABC Corp., 2022-01-002

In these examples, the file name is the matter name (Smith v. ABC Corp.), 2022 is the year the file was opened, 01 is the client code, and the final number represents the order in which the files were opened in 2022.

For multidisciplinary firms, numbers and/or color coding can be used to differentiate files in different practice areas as well. For example, instead of color coding by client, the firm might choose to color code by practice area, say red for personal injury and yellow for contracts. In the previous example, if the Smith matter is a personal injury case and the Jones matter is a contract dispute, the file numbers might be the same, but the Smith file would be red and the Jones file would be yellow. You would still be able to tell from the number code (01) that both files involved the same client. Alternatively, you could assign additional number or letter codes to the file number to differentiate by file type—for example, RE for Real Estate, PI for personal injury, etc. In this case, the file name and number might look like this:

Smith v. ABC Corp., PI 2022-01-001

Your electronic and paper file systems should mirror one another to avoid confusion, so the file name and number on the paper file must match those on the electronic files. Whatever method you choose, keep it consistent and as simple as possible.

The next question is whether you need to keep paper files, and if so, how much information should be kept in hard copy and how much should be retained in electronic form.

Electronic vs. Paper Files

Perhaps the worst thing lawyers do is save every piece of paper they receive and rely on the paper file as the "official" version of their file, even if they maintain some documents electronically. Why do they do it? And it is a question worth thinking about. The answer may be as simple as they were trained that way or they are just accustomed to doing so. But it is a terribly inefficient habit, because every time you need to find something in a file somewhere else, you have to get up, go look for it, hope it's there, and then come back to your desk. This is simply a waste of time.

For example, if you store files in a file room, it could take you one minute to get up from your desk and go to the room, another 30 seconds to find the file, and then another minute to go back to your desk. That's 2.5 minutes, and if you do it ten times a day, that's two hours a week, or 100 hours (2.5 weeks) a year, doing nothing but getting up to find a file. If your computer system is set up correctly, you could do the same thing in a few seconds and save $20,000 per year in billable time (100 hours @ $200). And we haven't even factored in the time to find what you're looking for *in* the file.

On the other hand, if every file-related item is scanned immediately when received and named with a name you'll remember, you will be able to locate it quickly and easily on your computer, whether it is stored locally, on a file server, or in the cloud.

Having more information available electronically will not only help you clear the clutter but will also help you provide better service to your clients. The more information you have available at your fingertips as you're speaking to the client (rather than having to find the paper file itself), the fewer times you'll have to put people on hold or call them back; in other words, you'll be far more responsive.

Be aware that scanning and saving may eliminate or reduce paper clutter, but it's not the end of the clutter battle. Storing more information electronically leads to creating electronic clutter, which can have similar consequences to physical clutter—poor organization of electronic files wastes time and money.

DEVELOPING A GOOD ELECTRONIC FILING SYSTEM

The keys to a good electronic filing system are first creating a directory structure that works, that is, having directories (folders on your computer) that are similar to the names you would have on file folders. A good case management system can make this part of the process even easier and more efficient. Second, use a logical and consistent file and document naming convention/protocol so that you always know where to find what you're looking for.

Begin with broad categories and name documents accordingly. For example, to keep templates on your computer, you might create a folder called Templates with subfolders for Pleadings and a sub-subfolder for Complaints, etc. Client files could be named for the matter (e.g., Jones v. Smith MVA Claim) with subfolders/directories for Memos, Correspondence, Pleadings, Discovery, Trial, etc.

As we discussed in Chapter 3, paper clutter comes in many forms, including clutter not related to client files. Law firms have forms, templates, checklists, periodicals, reference materials, and other types of paper that represent information the firm may want to save, share, store, and reference, but developing scanning and saving systems will help organize every type of file or document, including business files. For example, scanning and storing all of your financial records will permit you to provide them in electronic format to your accountant, making it far easier for them to prepare your taxes (and reduce the time it takes to do so, thereby reducing the fee). In each instance, you are taking far greater advantage of your computer system.

Documents and files must be named and saved consistently for easy sort and search, using the tips that follow.

Save Consistently

Most law firms will have a server, whether locally in their office, offsite, or in the cloud, where all of the firm's documents and information will be stored. However, if you don't have a server or if you are using a laptop, save all documents only in the My Documents folder and nowhere else. Whether it's a spreadsheet, a letter, or a PowerPoint presentation, it should be saved into the My Documents folder. This will make it easier to find your files and backing up the My Documents folder will automatically back up all of your documents.

Create Subfolders in My Documents

Treat electronic files the same way you treat paper ones. Every client, matter, or topic should have its own folder. Use plain language to name your folders and avoid novel abbreviations so that you can easily locate information in the future. If you share files with others, they won't have to guess what your file names mean.

Your My Documents folder should mirror the way you would name and store physical documents and folders. Within each client or topic, create subfolders. For example, you might have a folder called Office Memos, which may contain folders called 2021, 2020, and 2019 or folders titled by the subject matter of the memo. Client folders might include Pleadings and Correspondence subfolders. The goal is to have every file in a folder rather than having a list of orphan files.

Use File Naming Conventions

File names should be logical, specific, and consistent. There is no need for document or folder names to be all one word. Use spaces in file names. For example, a client file could be "Jackson, Michael," not "JacksonMichael." It's easier to read file names when they look more like normal words.

If you file documents in client subfolders, it is also not necessary to include the name of the client in the file name—the document is already stored in that client's folder. The longer the file name, the more confusing it is and the less likely it is that you'll be able to see the entire name on your screen in some formats. Easy and simple but descriptive should be the order of the day. Name documents in a way that allows you to tell at a glance what the document contains so that you don't have to open multiple documents to find what you are looking for. While it is true that each operating system has its own search function, many of these search functions are not as robust as those that are made a part of practice management software packages.

The goal when naming documents, files, and folders is to be able to tell what the document or folder contains without having to open it. For example, if the document is a letter to a client reminding them about an upcoming hearing, name it something like "Ltr to client re hearing 2022-02-15" rather than just "letter." But don't go overboard—file names that are too lengthy or complicated will simply create additional confusion and inconsistency. If the letter is in a correspondence folder, perhaps you don't need "ltr" at all. Your naming convention might specify naming all correspondence in that folder to contain the recipient's last name and subject.

Using Dates in File Names

Lawyers often want to find files based on when they were created or modified. Dan believes that one of the easiest ways to do so is to include the date the file was created or modified in the name, and his firm uses a specific naming protocol with dates for every electronic file. The system has worked superbly for him for nearly 20 years. But you need to do it in a specific way if you want it to sort properly in Windows.

Don't include a date format such as 01012022 or 112022 for a January 1, 2022, file. Instead, use the year-month-day format and use consistent naming conventions. Dan's office requires that every file name include the date it was created—or the date of the hearing or other event. For example, a letter to a client dated January 1, 2022, might be named "Ltr to Client 2022-01-01." While this date format seems cumbersome, it makes it easy to review file dates, it's clear, and most importantly, it ensures that all files of a similar type will sort in order by date. Following these rules allows Dan's office to easily search for the date in the file name and know that the date is accurate. They find it to be essential to their case and document management systems.

On the other hand, Allison does not recommend including dates in document names unless absolutely necessary. She believes the simpler your system and the simpler your names, the easier it will be to maintain consistency. Operating systems allow you to *sort* documents by date created or modified regardless of how they are named. Naming them using the date is not only redundant but, because of the complexity involved in keeping those naming conventions consistent, it also creates an avenue for additional errors. Including dates in file names makes them unnecessarily long and complicated and makes scanning through a document list for a particular document type or name difficult.

If you're scanning documents received from opposing counsel, your client, etc., the date of the document in your operating system won't be the same as the date the document was created; instead, it will be the date it was saved to your system. But is the date the document was created important? There may be occasions when that is the case, but it will most likely be the exception, rather than the rule. Often, the more important date (at least in terms of searching for the document) will be the date that the document was received by your office. On the rare occasion that there is some special reason the date of the document itself is important, that date can be included in the document name, but as a general rule, Allison believes it is unnecessary.

Filing documents by file type also isn't necessarily productive or helpful—should it matter whether a document is a PDF or a Word file in most instances? When you are searching for a particular document, is its format most important? Consider naming documents using criteria that you would use most often to search for them, or names that give you some idea of the substance of the document itself, to make the document easier to identify during your search.

In short, while your naming convention is important and needs to be consistent, it needs to be user-friendly. What works for one law firm may not work in another. Create a system that works for you.

Create a Junk Drawer on Your Computer

Every computer Dan owns has a folder in the C drive known as Temp, and there is always a shortcut on the desktop to C:\Temp. That's the place to store temporary files or things he wants to look at but doesn't need to keep; in other words, it's his electronic junk drawer. Periodically, he deletes the files in the folder without having to worry whether he deleted something important.

USING SOFTWARE TO MANAGE DOCUMENTS AND FILES

Software programs can help to solve the consistency problem with file and document organization, naming, and storage by taking away the ability of individuals within the firm to create their own naming and filing conventions, rather than follow those established by the firm. These systems can also make storage and search easier with features like full text searching and more.

There are two main types of software that can help in this regard: case or practice management software and document management software. For purposes of our discussion, we use case management and practice management software interchangeably. Although different programs have different features, most practice management software allows attorneys to effectively manage client, contact, calendar, and matter information. Essentially, your practice management system is a universal database of the files in your office. It organizes and stores not just documents but all of the information related to a client's matter. By contrast, a document management system is a system specifically for managing documents generated or received by the firm.

Keep in mind that each type of software program can be server based (accessed locally on your server or individual computer) or cloud based (accessed through the internet).

Although many solo and small firms have what they call practice management or document management systems, many of these are homegrown systems that are usually document, rather than database, driven (i.e., the firm keeps a "master list" of all of their files in a Word document, rather than in a searchable database). While these homegrown systems sound logical and can work for a while, as a practical matter, they have a number of pitfalls that we have, unfortunately, witnessed firsthand both in the law firms we've worked in and in the law firms we work with as consultants. One of the main problems with these systems, as we've already discussed, is consistency.

Practice or Case Management Software

Case management programs create a centralized database of client and matter information, resulting in easier searching, indexing, conflicts checking, and more. These programs also offer to-do lists, reminders, management of fee and billing information, time tracking, and other features. Some programs come with integrated billing modules that generate client invoices and create billing reports; others will link to third-party billing and accounting programs. Some case management programs also offer document assembly features, aiding in drafting documents and linking to word processing programs. The calendar features of these programs generally allow staff to view and schedule deadlines and appointments, set reminders, and calculate important dates.

Document Management

Many lawyers manage their documents *without* using fully functional document management software, and this is the default position for many solos and small-firm lawyers: the individual creating the document determines on their own where the document will be stored and what it will be called. This presents a number of problems, particularly when more than one person needs to access files and documents. Time is often wasted trying to locate documents (or determine if they exist at all) due to inconsistent naming and storage conventions. Effort can be duplicated if documents are generated more than once. Files can be inconsistent without consistent scanning procedures, and others (such as emails) may be lost entirely due to improper storage.

Of course, firms can develop naming and storage conventions and attempt to enforce them across the firm, but this depends on the cooperation of all attorneys and staff within the office. Similarly, some case management programs have a cross-reference system that will allow the user to note in the case management system where the document is stored, but again, this requires compliance with firm procedures.

Using a fully featured document management system will limit or eliminate many of these problems.

Fully featured document management systems do not allow users to circumvent or ignore the document management policy, which is integrated into the system itself. In other words, users cannot create or store documents in the system without answering certain questions that will allow the system to properly store the document. In addition, document management programs have more fully functioning search features, added security, and the ability to integrate into scanning and email systems to properly store documents created outside of the system. Document management programs can even keep track of different versions of documents so that users are certain they are viewing the correct version of documents and automatically archive older documents.

Some objectors opine that a special program for document management isn't necessary. These lawyers extol the virtues of storing documents using your regular computer operating system, which is the default method for most solos and small law firms (and even some midsized firms). These systems use folders for each client and subfolders for individual document types, along with a naming system for those folders. On the other hand, a good case management system will eliminate the need for the Save As > Drive Letter > Clients > Doc > File Name > Doc Type steps and still allow you to find any document in seconds.

Another plus of practice management software is its ability to link clients with matters and documents with clients or matters. You can easily see what work has been done for a particular client across multiple files, and any document created on a particular file is also linked to that client and contact—along with to-dos or tasks for that client and upcoming dates or calendar entries. This is a big advantage when communicating with clients, because you have all of the information at your fingertips without having to search several different applications (Word processing, email, calendar, etc.) and individual client matters for information—you can get it all through the client interface.

Practice management software also is a huge time-saver when a client's information changes. Instead of having to go into each file separately to note an address change, a contact name change, telephone number change, etc., the change can be made once in the client's information screen, and it will automatically be applied to each of that client's matters. Over and over, we have seen law firms struggle with address, telephone number, or contact name changes where files and information are stored in individual file folders because lawyers and staff either are not informed of the change or forget to make the change in each individual file.

Conflicts are another area of concern that can be addressed with practice management software. While it may be easy to determine whether you've ever represented a particular party before, it may not be as easy to determine whether you represented another party (such as a codefendant) with adverse interests without a robust database of information. Many lawyers have gotten into a case only to realize some time later that a conflict or potential conflict existed. You could develop your own conflict checking system, but is it worth the time and effort to do so when you can use one already created with lawyers in mind? If a grievance arises or your malpractice insurer inquires about what you're using to do conflicts checks, are you comfortable saying that you rely on memory or a local search on your system?

Practice management programs integrated with time and billing programs can not only help you create and assemble documents using information stored in the system (rather than constantly typing the same information over and over) but also help you track and bill your time for those activities as they're being performed (if you must bill hourly).

Many practice management programs include the ability to use or create a client portal. A client portal allows lawyers to securely share files, including documents and invoices, and other matter-related information with clients, generally through the firm's website. In some cases, firms use third-party sites such as ShareFile, sometimes branded for the firm, to store the data.

When a message is sent through the client portal, the recipient gets a notification. There are many advantages to implementing a client portal. First, messages sent through the portal are secure, so client confidentiality is preserved. The security inherent in the client portal is often more robust than lawyers typically use when sending email. Clients must log in with their username and password to access the portal, so concerns about shared or employer-owned email accounts are eliminated.

In addition to the security advantages, communicating through a client portal can provide clients with quick and easy answers to their most common questions with little to no interruption of the lawyer's regular daily work. Clients can easily see the status of their matter, view documents, and even schedule or view appointments.

By using the client portal as the main mode of communication, lawyers can eliminate duplicate modes of communication, including text, email, and telephone messages, which can provide the added advantage of keeping a record of all client communication in one central location that can be accessed at the client's convenience. With a secure client portal, clients have 24/7 access to their file, to the calendar to see upcoming appointments or court dates, or to view, collaborate on, and/or sign documents.

Some lawyers who are particularly tech savvy can develop a series of systems using other applications that can work effectively for a solo practice. But once that solo practice expands—even just with the addition of a part-time paralegal or other staffer—many of those systems will flounder or fail as a result of an inability to share information or adequately train another person on how those systems work. In addition, although using several different applications, programs, or systems can be effective, it is less likely that information will be able to be shared across those programs or linked to one another effectively, creating the necessity to enter the same information in several different programs.

Purchasing (and being trained on how to use) practice management and document software is an investment in your practice. The up-front costs involved should be easily outweighed by the gains in productivity, time, and organization, especially if you're not a true solo and you need to share information with staff and other attorneys, or if you anticipate that you may need to do so in the future.

WRAP UP

Systematizing repetitive tasks or processes within your office can go a long way to creating a more consistent client experience. In addition, creating these systems and procedures will allow you to stop thinking about logistics and what needs to be done next and focus instead on providing excellent client service and doing the best legal work you possibly can.

Lawyers waste a lot of time searching for documents and files because they don't have good file and case management systems in place or they do not realize how helpful search technology can be. Creating protocols for naming and saving files and documents can go a long way, but implementing software programs for case or document management automates these processes to create a much higher level of functionality.

We've heard countless lawyers tell us, "I would tell anyone who is starting their own practice to invest in practice management software from the very beginning. It's the easiest and best way to stay organized. They may not think they need it right away, but it's an investment worth making, and it's much easier to have it ready from the start and enter each client as they come, rather than having to convert later when you've got a lot of clients and other work to focus on." Whether you're starting out or not, consider practice management software.

CHAPTER 8 ACTION STEPS

1. Make a list of the major components of each client matter your office handles, as well as the nonbillable components of your work, including marketing, business development, and client acquisition. Over time, ask the people responsible for each of those elements to write down the major steps involved in each. For example, if client intake is handled by both lawyers (interviewing clients in person or by phone) and staff (taking basic client information, entering it into the computer, etc.), ask each one to list the steps they undertake in their portion of the task. Circulate the lists around the office for input and clarification, and then memorialize the finalized lists by creating procedures and checklists and saving them in a centralized location where all employees can obtain access to them. Refine as necessary.
2. Develop your protocols for file organization, naming, and storage and require that all firm employees use the same system.
3. Investigate case and document management software programs. A simple Google search will provide a list of the most popular case and document management software, and most of these companies provide free webinars or one-on-one demonstrations to allow you to see the program in action and determine which of these programs would work best for your practice and which ones have features that appeal to you. If you decide to implement these programs, get training both at the time of the installation and periodically to refresh your skills and learn about new features.

Part II

DOING 90 MINUTES OF WORK IN 60: WAYS TO USE TECHNOLOGY TO INCREASE PRODUCTIVITY

INTRODUCTION

In Part I of this book, we discussed overarching strategies to manage your activities on a day-to-day basis. In Part II, we will show you how to use the tools and technology you already have in your practice to their maximum advantage so that you can work more efficiently.

Chapter 9

MAXIMIZE YOUR USE OF EXISTING TOOLS

Lawyers are competitive. By the very nature of their profession, lawyers want to win, and their clients hire them to win or, at a minimum, to get the best possible results. So, imagine a scenario where lawyers lose—or fail miserably—again and again and again. Certainly, you would think that if lawyers knew that they were facing a difficult challenge, they would do everything possible to confront it and to overcome it. Yet, when that challenge involves technology, you would generally be wrong.

Think about this. When Dan's sons graduated from high school, as expected, they and their classmates were required to be proficient in various subjects, including math and English. They were also required to demonstrate proficiency in Microsoft Word, Microsoft PowerPoint, and Microsoft Excel. But there was one crucial difference. They took years of classes in the substantive subjects. They took no classes devoted to the software and only a few classes where the programs were mentioned, even in passing. Yet they were *expected to be* capable of using those products. In reality, they had to learn how to use the software by themselves.

In retrospect, their lack of software training was no different from what happens in all types of offices—including law offices—all the time. While knowledge of the law is a prerequisite for lawyers and staff must know their job duties, all of these people are *expected to know* how to use Outlook and Word and multiple other programs. Even when it comes to legal-specific software, many offices expect their staff to learn to use the program through osmosis.

Was your staff trained in law school, or college, or paralegal school, or even high school, how to use these programs? In most cases, the answer is no. Law firms and other businesses assume that their employees are proficient in these products—as though their staff emerged from the womb innately knowing how to use the software. In many cases, computers, let alone the software, did not exist when these people graduated from college or law school. As a result, most computer users have never been taught how to use the technology they so heavily rely upon or, if they were, it was merely in passing. Many are self-taught and have likely picked up bad habits along the way. And even those who did receive some training likely did not receive training in how to use these programs efficiently within a law practice.

In fact, as one tech commentator has written, "Adults have worn their computer illiteracy as a badge of pride for many years now so it shouldn't surprise anyone that their children share their digital inadequacies. Moreover, neither group is even willing to *try* to solve a problem when they encounter it."[1] Lawyers are an ideal example of this theory. These well-educated and intelligent people act as though the mere sight of a computer scares the stuffing out of them, or the thought of learning how to use these tools better is something that is beyond their otherwise impressive intellectual abilities. The problem is that people assume that just because they grew up without these tools, they can't use or learn to use Word, Excel, etc., better. And that's just not true. Similarly, in our experience, many who grew up with the tools never truly learned how to use them efficiently, especially in a professional context. Using these programs to complete classroom assignments or projects is a far cry from using them in a courtroom or for client work.

In addition, for whatever reason, lawyers and law firms continue to place little emphasis on assuring that they and their staff get the most out of the technology they own, including basic programs such as Microsoft Outlook and Microsoft Word that are so critical to the efficient operation of their offices. And when it comes to more advanced technology, in our experience, lawyers seem to prefer to avoid it, rather than to learn how to use it to increase productivity and get better results for their clients. The reason is probably the simple one—most people prefer to avoid change.

Even the amendment to the comment to Model Rule of Professional Conduct 1.1 that requires lawyers to "keep abreast of changes in the law and its practice, *including the benefits and risks associated with relevant technology*,"[2] has

1. Baldur Bjarnason, *Computers Are Too Difficult and People Are Computer Illiterate*, Studio Tendra (Aug. 14, 2013), http://studiotendra.com/2013/08/14/computers-are-both-too-difficult-and-people-are-computer-illiterate/.
2. Model Rules of Pro. Conduct r. 1.1 cmt. [8] (Am. Bar Ass'n 2022) (emphasis added).

had little discernible impact on the profession. As a result of this amendment, most firms haven't suddenly investigated and implemented technology such as case management or litigation management software that would improve their efficiency and, potentially, help them get better results for their clients. And most firms haven't suddenly acknowledged that teaching their lawyers and staff how to use such basic programs as Outlook and Word would allow them to improve efficiency quickly and inexpensively.

The lack of change should not be surprising. The Model Rules of Professional Conduct were released in 1983—before computers were commonly used. The Rules do not mention "technology" because in 1983 technology of the type we have today was something for *Star Trek*, not for real life.

While the COVID-19 pandemic helped raise awareness of the need for improved technology and enhanced training, once the pandemic ends, many firms will almost certainly revert to the way they used to work, in other words, with paper and as little technology as possible. How much of a permanent tech bump will occur is a matter for debate.

Whenever Dan has addressed this issue with lawyers and law firm staffs or during presentations, he always gets a chuckle when he uses the following analogy: Lawyers would not want to receive medical care from a physician who won't use those "newfangled MRIs" because the technology wasn't invented by the time the doctor graduated from medical school. Yet lawyers think nothing of avoiding almost every form of technology, not because it wasn't around when they were in law school—law schools still don't teach a lot about technology—but for other reasons that are just as nonsensical.

The aversion to change is a primary reason lawyers and their staff are less competent at using the technological tools they need to help them serve their clients better. And just like not prioritizing wastes time, so does using technology inefficiently. If a lawyer spends five minutes struggling to format a paragraph in Word or doesn't realize that using Outlook's Reading Pane can save lots of time, those precious minutes add up to weeks or months of wasted time over the course of a year.

This reality was brought into focus in a series of articles by D. Casey Flaherty[3] in which he reported the result of his audits of Kia Motors's outside counsel's competency with technology. The results were probably shocking to many lawyers—every associate at each of the nine firms tested failed the test, which required them to complete mock assignments using Word, Microsoft Excel,

3. D. Casey Flaherty, *Kia Motors Tests Outside Counsel Tech Skills*, Law Tech. News (Jan. 24 & 25, 2013), https://www.law.com/legaltechnews/almID/1202585496232/.

and Adobe Acrobat. Flaherty concluded that "all of the associates approached the assignments in ways that would have required five to 15 times longer than necessary. At $200 to $400 per associate hour, such inefficiency suggests . . . that, indeed, waste is a righteous concern."[4]

Although there are exceptions, by and large, lawyers tend to ignore technology. Even after the pandemic forced lawyers to work virtually—at least for a time—and to rely on technology to run their practices, Allison is still working with lawyers today who run their practices off of spreadsheets that are nothing more than a digital version of paper processes they have been using for decades. Dan has spoken with managing partners who boldly boast that until their clients require them to become more tech savvy, they are happy, and thriving, doing things the old way. But if Kia Motors is a client, they may not have that chance. And if Kia Motors is any indication of client attitudes overall, it's time for lawyers to stand up and take notice.

In short, lack of proficiency with technology not only leads to inefficiencies, but it can also lead to ethical complaints and loss of clients. You can find numerous recent examples in the news of law firms—even large, well-supported law firms—that failed to properly redact pleadings or inadvertently disclosed previously confidential information because they weren't properly trained on how to use their technology. Modern clients expect their lawyers to be proficient in using technology.

Moreover, as Dan wrote years ago, "Attorneys often recommend that their clients make business decisions that may cost significant amounts of money, yet those same attorneys are often reluctant to make the decision to invest even small amounts in the technology necessary to improve their practices. On the other hand, attorneys tell numerous stories about how they informed clients that if they had come in for a consultation, they would have avoided a far more expensive lawsuit. By ignoring technology, or trying to do it for 'free,' lawyers do the same thing with technology."[5] In other words, rather than hire competent staff or consultants to help select, install, and train their staffs in technology, attorneys often do without or try to do it themselves, despite their lack of competence in the area.

Not much has changed. After all, Casey Flaherty couldn't find one law firm, or apparently even one attorney, who had the rudimentary skills needed to use the software so essential to their jobs. Consider the reality: Lawyers spend years learning how to be lawyers. They surrender months of their lives preparing to

4. *Id.*
5. Daniel J. Siegel, *Legal Technology: Investing in Technology Will Pay Off in Law Firms' Futures*, The Legal Intelligencer (May 22, 2008).

take the bar exam and devote at least 12 hours a year to taking continuing legal education courses. But those same lawyers won't spend one hour in all of that time learning how to use Microsoft Outlook, the email program utilized by more firms than any other. Why?

Why does this matter? Look at law firm staffing. Many firms do not employ even one secretary or assistant per lawyer. Similarly, the days of merely dictating a letter or a brief are long past. Instead, lawyers often type their own letters, and many prepare their own briefs, contracts, and other documents. Yet law school doesn't even introduce them to the basic programs needed to function as a lawyer from a technical perspective, and neither do their law firms. As a result, the clients, who expect their attorneys to have minimum levels of proficiency, become frustrated at how much time attorneys are wasting and how much that time-suck costs their companies. After all, the old adage "time is money" still applies to law firms.

While there are still firms in which at least some of the attorneys do not prepare their own documents and reports, preferring to allow staff to undertake those tasks so that the attorneys may concentrate on doing legal work, staff rarely receive the training necessary to prepare those documents in an efficient manner either. Where these tasks are billed to clients on an hourly basis (whether at an attorney rate or a paralegal rate), clients have every right to complain about the lack of technological competency. But firms that are not billing on an hourly basis should be equally concerned about their lack of technological competence because the more efficient they are, the bigger the impact on their own bottom line.

Flaherty's conclusions are still instructive today. He conceded that he employed partners whom he relies upon "for sage advice on esoteric topics [and] would continue to turn to these lawyers even if [he] discovered that they were disembodied heads locked in a closet, and incapable of turning on a computer." He contrasts that reality with the fact "that many commonly billed legal tasks are both essential and labor intensive. The proper use of technology cuts down on the labor required." Plus, because labor equals costs, he considers how well law firms "deploy labor-saving technology."[6]

Even now, years after Flaherty's revelations took many in the legal world by surprise, there is much to be done. In 2022, we still see lawyers and staff using rudimentary technology, wasting time with inefficient methods and undertaking tasks that could be streamlined easily.

6. Flaherty, *supra* note 3.

This is not an earth-shattering revelation. Just think about projects at your home. Are you replacing your heater? When you obtain costs from various contractors, if all things are equal, won't you choose the least expensive proposal? That is what Kia did.

A FIVE-STEP PLAN FOR IMPROVING TECHNOLOGICAL COMPETENCE

So, how can law firms bridge this technological chasm?

Here is our five-step plan:

1. Don't cut corners;
2. Reduce, and preferably eliminate, your reliance on paper while taking the steps needed to utilize digital technology (after all, virtually everything done in law offices and businesses is tech-based, not paper-centric);
3. Train yourself and your entire staff on the programs your firm regularly uses, such as Microsoft Outlook, Word, and Adobe Acrobat;
4. Use legal-specific programs and train, and preferably retrain, yourself and your entire staff how to use these products; and
5. Engage your staff in every step of the process.

Step 1: Don't Cut Corners

Maximizing the use of technology helps make you more profitable, but it may require an investment up front. As we explained earlier, technology can save you money. If you bill at $150 per hour but can save six minutes a day using a computerized case management system, which is a highly conservative estimate, a $1,500 investment pays for itself in less than five months.

There are many ways you should use technology as though it were an additional employee—one who doesn't have to be given a salary, benefits, and days off. First, consider hiring a technology support person rather than letting everyone "do it themselves." If a full-time support professional costs the firm $75,000 per year, that's only $36 an hour, a far lower cost than the time your lawyers will waste trying to do things themselves, and less than the cost of outsourcing. If your firm doesn't have that large a budget or that great a need (have you ever quantified the value of a qualified support professional?), consider contracting with a support company to perform the role on a fixed hourly, monthly, annual, or other basis and let your staff do what it does best: practice law.

Second, hire a consultant to help you recognize where technology can improve your workflow. It may be that your network needs to be upgraded or that you simply need additional software. Or perhaps your staff isn't well trained. There are network consultants who can spot the inefficiencies in your systems; similarly, there are law office workflow experts who can show you how to get more out of the programs you have or introduce you to products that can improve your efficiency, your results, and your bottom line.

Finally, create a budget, just as you do for marketing and other areas (we hope). This will help you plan for upgrades and avoid surprises.

Step 2: Reduce—or Preferably Eliminate—Your Reliance on Paper

If there is one thing that the pandemic taught us, it is that you waste time every time you handle paper. When you work remotely, paper files are useless, and if you actually had the files, then no one else could use them. Everything needed to be digitized when everyone worked remotely.

Even if you return to your office, it takes time to get up from your desk, locate a file, go back to your desk, and then (hopefully) find the item you're looking for. And of course, if an old client calls and the file is in storage, it can take days or weeks to find what you need, not to mention the costs charged by file storage services and how poorly organized and inefficient you look to the client. (Consider how much of a dinosaur you look like if you can't access information when websites can tell you what you bought ten years ago with just a few mouse clicks.) If you store everything electronically and cut the paper umbilical cord, you can find everything quickly from wherever you happen to be.

It is estimated that every lost piece of paper costs a law firm $120, that 15 percent of all paper handled in businesses is lost, and that 30 percent of all employees' time is spent trying to find lost documents. That's why there are two needs. One is to digitize every document in your firm to assure that every member of your staff can access what they need when they need it. Second, firms need to go "less paper" (not paper-free; it is unlikely that we'll ever be completely paper-free). As we have already seen, with proper scanning, file naming, and file storage systems, you reduce clutter, improve efficiency, and cut costs, including long-term file storage costs that often choke firms.

Step 3: Train Yourself and Your Entire Staff on the Programs Your Firm Regularly Uses

Ask yourself the following questions:

- Do you really know *how* to use the software programs, including Microsoft Windows, Word, WordPerfect, Outlook, and Adobe, that are so essential to everything you do?
- Does your staff really know *how* to use those same software programs? Have you and your staff ever received training—real training, where a trainer demonstrates how to use the programs—on these items?

If you cannot honestly answer yes to each of these questions, it's time to get your staff—and you—training.

There is simply no substitute for training. No one emerges from the womb knowing how to use Outlook or graduates from college with a degree in Microsoft Word. Yes, it takes some time and commitment to train everyone in the firm, but the results will be tangible. A good trainer will generate lots of "I didn't know I could do that" moments, revelations that will lead to improved efficiency. Just as you would train a new lawyer to be sure they know about the area of law in which they are practicing, you should do the same with the technology they will use.

In addition to training, there are resources available to help you and your staff learn how to use these programs more efficiently. For example, the Law Practice Division distributes a series of e-books as guides for some of the most popular programs used by lawyers, including *Microsoft Word for Legal Professionals, Microsoft Outlook for Legal Professionals, Microsoft Excel for Legal Professionals,* and more. Dan's latest book, *The Ultimate Guide to Adobe Acrobat DC,* Second Edition, with coauthor Pamela Myers (also published by the Law Practice Division), is another useful resource. We recommend that these publications be used as a supplement, rather than in place of training.

Step 4: Use Legal-Specific Programs

Find out what software exists to help your firm be more efficient. It may be case or matter management software, document management or document assembly software, or a litigation tool that helps you annotate transcripts quickly and more effectively than doing it with sticky notes and highlighters. These products improve workflow and provide better results for your clients, while allowing you to take on more matters without hiring more staff. Remember, technology is or should be your "invisible" staff.

Jim Calloway, the Oklahoma Bar Association Practice Management Advisor, offered some important and timeless criteria for selecting law firm software:[7]

- **Know Thyself**—Make a list of the features you want before looking at specific products. Rank the features in order of their importance to you, and then begin the search.
- **Test Drive the Application**—The best way to pick software is to try it and see if it works for you. Dan calls this "playing" with the software. While it's important to test all software, it's particularly important to use case management, litigation support, and time and billing software, because it's more difficult to move to a different product once you've committed to one.
- **Search for Some Reviews**—Don't trust the lawyer next door. Many times, that same lawyer hasn't even used the software, their staff has. Get references from the vendor, read independent reviews, and look for information online. Technolawyer.com can be a terrific resource, as can your bar association's practice management advisor, if there is one.

Step 5: Engage Your Staff in Every Step of the Process

The most ambitious plans will fail if the people implementing them refuse to cooperate. Staff, at all levels, need to know what you are doing and why. Inform them, ask for input, and let them know you are investing in them. Then follow these steps, which Allison outlined in her "Simple Steps" column in *Law Practice Magazine*,[8] to implement your plans:

- Set goals.
- Consider your existing systems and devices to ensure that any new technology will be compatible with what the firm is currently using.
- Find out what works and what doesn't and use that information as a baseline.
- Form a committee comprised of members of each user group to help select the new product or service, including those who use or will use the technology.

---

7. Jim Calloway, *Picking the "Best" Law Office Software*, OKLA. BAR ASS'N MGMT. ASSISTANCE PROGRAM (2003, 2006).
8. Allison C. Shields, *Introducing New Technology to Your Law Firm*, LAW PRACTICE MAG., Jan.–Feb. 2018, at 14–17, https://dashboard.mazsystems.com/webreader/53663?page=16.

- Do your homework and try out demos, read reviews, and contact other users to help assure you make the right decisions.
- Obtain buy-in and address opposition head on.
- Create an implementation plan, starting with a pilot group.
- Train every user.
- Implement the software or service.
- Get feedback and make revisions based upon the feedback.
- Continue to train your staff.

We can't come to every office and teach every attorney and every staff member how to use technology, but in the following chapters we provide tips about how to use the most common law office software more efficiently. The genesis of these tips is a highly popular program Dan has given for decades called "How to Do 90 Minutes of Legal Work in 60 Minutes," which was one of the inspirations for this book. The theory of the program is simple: if you learn and use one technology tip/shortcut that saves you 15 seconds, four times a day, you will save more than 250 minutes (over four hours per year) from one tip alone. When you learn lots of other shortcuts and add the time savings from those actions, you are suddenly saving hours and hours, if not days and weeks, of time—simply doing what you already do much more efficiently. Dan's program is very popular because it shows people how to use the software *they already have*—just better. It's like discovering a new route to work that saves you 15 minutes each way. That adds up to 2½ hours per week, or more than 125 hours (six days) per year, less time being stuck in your car. That's the beauty and simplicity of learning how to do more in less time.

CHAPTER 9 ACTION STEPS

1. Determine where your firm has knowledge and skills gaps with respect to technology and ascertain whether those gaps can competently, efficiently, and effectively be filled in-house or whether outsourcing is needed.
2. Obtain the necessary training on all essential programs for all attorneys, employees, and staff.
3. Eliminate as much as possible your firm's reliance on paper.
4. Make technological competence a responsibility of all firm employees and institute rewards for excellence and sanctions for failure as you would with any other job requirement.

Chapter 10

TAKING CONTROL OF EMAIL, TEXT MESSAGES, AND OTHER ELECTRONIC COMMUNICATIONS

Improving your efficiency happens in many ways. For example, earlier we explained how to set goals and prioritize your work, planning ahead to get the most from each day. We then focused on why it's important to eliminate distractions and clutter. Next, we helped you recognize that maybe, just maybe, you shouldn't be shouldering the entire load and that you'll benefit by delegating. Then we offered strategies for getting everything accomplished. After exploring those issues, we began to focus on systems, that is, the Rules of Procedure for your office. We then talked about global ways to use technology, including electronic filing systems, and how practice management and document management software programs can organize, store, cross-reference, search for, and retrieve electronic documents.

In this and the following chapters, we have arrived at all of the "techie"-related tips that you can use to make your computer work *for you*. In this chapter, for example, we will demonstrate how to streamline your email use in Outlook, and later on we will provide tips to streamline your use of Contacts and Tasks.

Because email, text messages, and other electronic communications are among the biggest time-wasters lawyers deal with on a daily basis, we'll start by talking about managing those items in general. Later, we'll give you some tips on using the most popular email client for lawyers: Microsoft Outlook. Of course, we recognize that it takes time to wade through all of these tips. We've included screenshots of most of them to make the tips easier to understand and implement.

Let's get started.

EMAIL AND TEXT MESSAGE MANAGEMENT

Email, and now text messages, may be the biggest form of electronic clutter we face on a daily basis, and keeping up with it can be a major hassle. Email is commonly cited as one of the biggest time-wasters in modern offices. It can be overwhelming, and its sheer scope makes it one of the worst enemies of productivity. While not a complete list of all email tips, the following tips can help you get more control over your Inbox and ensure that important messages don't get lost. Many of these tips also apply to text messages and other electronic communications.

Your main goal when managing your email Inbox is to touch email messages as few times as possible (preferably only once) and to keep the Inbox as clear as possible so that you are dealing with only the most recent, relevant messages.

1. **Delete liberally—and quickly.** If a message is junk or a coupon or advertisement you won't immediately act on, delete it (advertisements, specials, and coupons will come around again). Don't let junk mail sit around and clutter up your Inbox. If you haven't gotten into the habit of deleting emails right away, you may have a lot of email backlog to take care of. To do that more easily, Ben Schorr, Microsoft expert and author of several books, advises:
    a. Temporarily sort your Inbox by "From" rather than by date. You will likely be able to batch-delete a number of messages or move several at once to a client file or other archive or storage method.

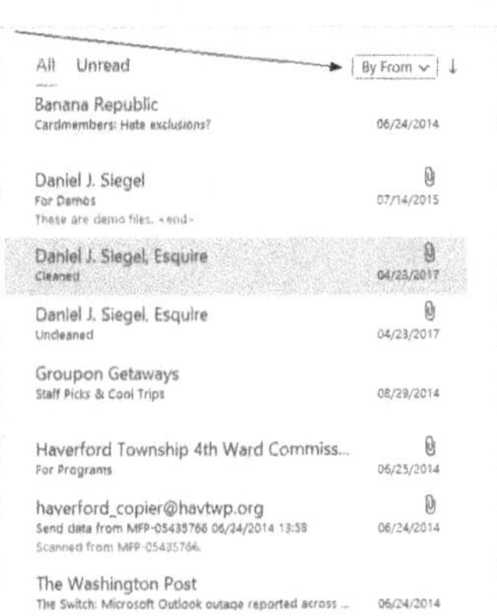

b. Next, sort by "Subject." This will group related messages together, and again, you may be able to delete several at once, such as emails scheduling appointments that already took place, duplicate messages, or emails that are part of a string.

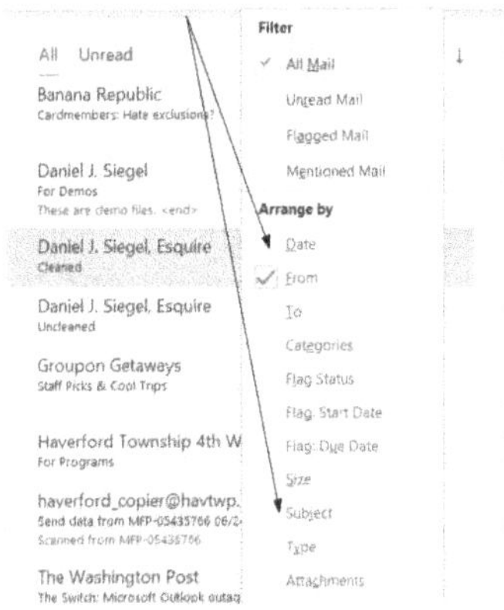

c. Finally, sort your Inbox in reverse date order—the older the message, the less likely it is that it will be important and the easier it will be to delete.

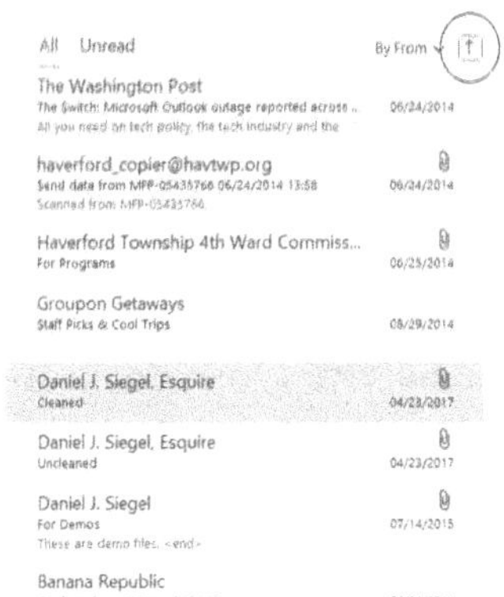

2. **Remove yourself (unsubscribe) from three email lists per day.** That's right. If you don't really participate in an email list, get off it. No one will hate you for it, and if you discover that you really need to be on it, then resubscribe.
3. **Separate tasks from emails.** Don't use your email Inbox as your to-do list. As more and more email messages arrive, it becomes harder and harder to keep track of those to-dos. If an email represents a task that you need to complete, move it to Tasks (to do this in Outlook, just drag and drop the message onto Tasks; the body of the email will remain

intact as part of the task). Alternatively, you can create to-do lists and/or action folders for those emails or use third-party tools that help you manage emails as tasks, such as Toodledo (http://www.toodledo.com/), ClickUp (https://clickup.com/), or Remember the Milk (https://www.rememberthemilk.com/). Just get them out of your Inbox.

4. **Move appointments to your calendar.** If you are keeping an email simply as an appointment reminder, get the information into your calendar right away and toss the email. (Again, if you use Outlook, just drag and drop the message to your calendar and all of the information in the email will stay with the appointment.)
5. **Delegate.** If the email requires action by someone else, forward it to that person right away with a note. Then eliminate the original email from your Inbox by deleting or moving to an alternate folder for follow-up or convert it into a task for follow-up. You can also share email Inboxes with another person in your organization so you can just drag an email from your Inbox to theirs; just remember to keep the item marked "unread" when you drag it so they can easily spot it.
6. **Keep only business email in your business email account.** Don't clutter your regular email Inbox with newsletters, subscriptions, etc. Create a separate email account for those so they're not in the way of your main personal or business messages. Make a separate shopping email account so promotional emails, shipping confirmations, etc., go to that account. There are many free email services you can use for this purpose, including Google's Gmail. Or create rules and folders to automatically move these messages out of your Inbox.
7. **Respond immediately.** Don't make the mistake of "reviewing" your emails and planning to go back and respond to them later. It just creates extra work and may result in important client messages getting lost or forgotten. If you're going to review your emails, respond when you first read the message if at all possible. If you cannot respond immediately, either turn the email into a to-do or put it in an action folder with all of the other messages that need your attention so that you don't have to search for it later.
8. **Don't review email first thing in the morning.** Doing so is the best way to ensure that your day will get out of control. For most lawyers, urgent messages don't arrive via email overnight or first thing in the morning. If that's the case for you, schedule a specific time to blast through email after you've already tackled your most important task of the day. If your clients *do* tend to send urgent emails before you arrive at the office, limit

yourself to a quick skim of your Inbox to ensure no such urgent messages have arrived, and then move on to another task.

9. **On the other hand, if your practice demands it, review email first thing in the morning—within limits.** We're not big fans of "one size fits all" approaches, and we recognize that for some, email overflow is a nightmare, while others consider it a badge of honor. And some practices may require you to review email first thing in the morning, or you won't be able to concentrate on anything else. Email overflow is like a pot boiling over; you can never catch all of the water, and, in the process, some things are spilled and never the same. While we don't prefer this option, which is counter to the one directly before it, if you *must* review email first thing in the morning, set defined limits (for example, limit your review to 30 minutes and then move on to more productive work) and perform your review in conjunction with these other tips.
10. **Convert email to tasks.** While using your Inbox as a to-do list seems like a good idea, it isn't. It means that you have a never-ending list whose end you cannot see. By merely dragging an email onto the Task icon in Outlook, you can instantly create To-Dos with deadlines. This helps eliminate the metastasis of your Inbox and creates a manageable way to follow up at the time you desire. Even better, if you use case management software, your To-Dos can be linked to the programs and, if necessary, reassigned to others.
11. **Don't use your Inbox as your filing cabinet.** Any email message that must be saved belongs in the appropriate file, not in your Inbox. If the email is correspondence relating to a client matter, it should be filed in the client's electronic file. If it is a bill, it should be filed with your financial documents, etc.
12. **Don't let email be a constant interruption.** Schedule specific times to review email rather than checking it constantly throughout the day, unless you're waiting for something particularly urgent or your practice is truly emergency based. If you're waiting for a particular email, don't get caught up in answering all of your email or reading less urgent email over and over during the day; simply scan periodically for the one message you are waiting for and leave the rest for your designated email time.
13. **Keep your emails short and request a specific action or response.** If you're brief, those who respond to you are likely to be brief as well. Give good instructions and tell them what you expect and how and when they should respond. If you put more than one request in a single email

message, number them. This will make your email review much more efficient and eliminate additional questions, clarifications, and long email threads.

14. **Know when email is not the appropriate medium for your communication.** Email is fast and easy, but it isn't always appropriate. Sometimes picking up the phone to speak with a client or walking down the hall to see a colleague is a much more efficient way to accomplish a task or to get the answer you need than ending up in an endless back-and-forth exchange of email messages. A good example of this is scheduling a meeting, particularly if there are several attendees. Use a scheduling tool such as Doodle.com or Calendly.com or use the Meeting Poll (Find Time) feature in Outlook to find a time that works for everyone.
15. **Flag or color code important email.** Some email is more important than others. As a result, it can be helpful to flag emails that require immediate attention or that might otherwise get lost in your cluttered Inbox. You can also create rules to automatically flag email from certain people so that you can see them as soon as they arrive. Outlook also allows you to apply conditional formatting to messages; under the "View" tab, click "View Settings" and then "Conditional Formatting" to apply special formatting to some messages. For example, Allison likes to color code messages from important clients so that she can see them right away when viewing her Inbox. She sets conditional formatting for messages from specific people so those messages arrive in bold and in a different color than other messages.

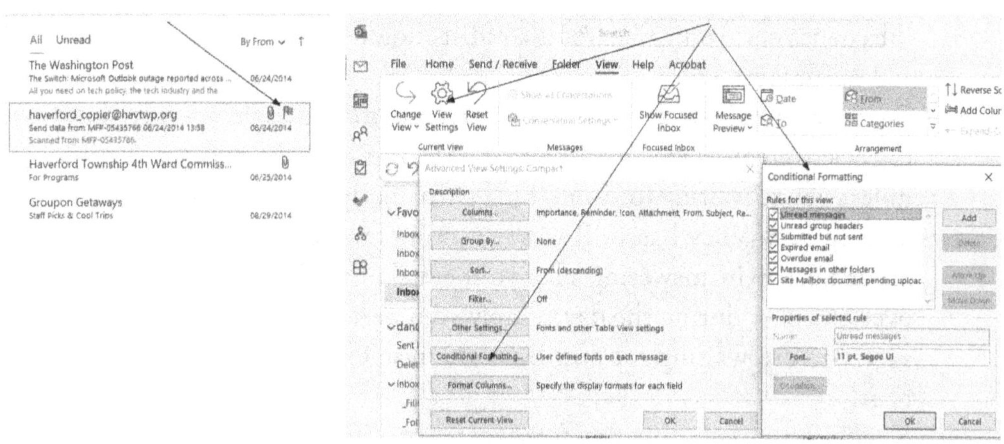

16. **Decide how or if you are going to use text messaging and other forms of electronic communication.** Remember, a client file is the property of a client. If you do not have the ability to preserve a form of communication, such as text messages, avoid using it. If the disciplinary authorities come calling, or the client asks for a copy of the file, excuses why you couldn't produce the items will fall on deaf ears.
17. If you determine that email or other electronic formats are an appropriate method of communication for your purposes, remember these rules:
    - Treat electronic communication the same way you treat any other client communication. All messages should be properly written and spell-checked and look professional. Use complete sentences with appropriate punctuation.
    - All communications, including electronic communication, are part of a client's file and should be saved with the file. Do so: it's not only good practice, but it could also be the documentation you need to avoid or combat a disciplinary claim.
    - Move electronic messages with dates directly to your calendar.
    - Create folders and set up rules, favorites, and filters for your electronic messages so that they are automatically routed to the correct folder. For those who belong to several email lists, forums, etc., or who need to respond to specific people's emails, this rule is absolutely critical to managing your Inbox. You should create rules that automatically route email from certain sources or about certain subjects to specific Inbox folders or to others in your office. That way, listserv email is removed from all the client email, and you can look at it another time. Similarly, email from banks can be forwarded to your office manager or other person, as necessary. Finally, you can set up Outlook to flag or conditionally format email from certain people, so they stand out from the rest.
    - Use case management software. Most case management programs will allow you to save incoming emails directly to a client's file and ask if you want to save outgoing emails to a client's file as well.
    - Don't create paper versions of your email. Just file the electronic version.
    - If you don't want to use folders and need to save emails, consider using Adobe Standard or Professional, which will create a Portfolio containing specified emails (from particular emails or Outlook folders) and attachments. Then you can remove these items from Outlook. Regardless, the best thing to do is to be able to delete emails from your Inbox.
    - Act on email that can be addressed immediately.

- If the communication is something that requires action by someone else, forward or assign it to that person right away. If the email is one you need to save for a file, move it into that file folder and get it out of the Inbox. If it's a task that needs to be done by you, move it to Tasks (the body of the email will remain intact as part of the task). Create to-do lists and/or action folders or file trays.
- Get a planner, preferably electronic (you can always print it out if you must), or a paper-based one, and enter appointments and any necessary notes right away and delete the email.

Use Microsoft Viva

If you are like most users, Microsoft Viva suddenly appeared in your email without warning, having been enabled by your employer. Your first thought might have been "What is this?" Or, "Why does Microsoft know all of this?" Or, like Allison, "Oh no, another useless message to clog up my Inbox!" Microsoft describes Viva as "an employee experience platform that brings together communications, knowledge, learning, resources, and insights in the flow of work. . . . Powered by Microsoft 365 and experienced through Microsoft Teams, Viva fosters a culture that empowers people and teams to be their best from anywhere."[1] What we have discovered is that Viva is a hugely helpful tool.

On a typical day, each of us receives a Microsoft Daily Briefing, with a summary of our schedule and any To Dos, listing any Tasks due today. Viva also often suggests that particular documents may be related to a meeting or appointment on your calendar for that day. For example, Allison often receives Daily Briefings that not only remind her of an upcoming appointment, but also suggest the agenda that might apply. The Daily Briefing includes "Recommended" actions such as "Start the day calm and focused," followed by "Breathe in. Breathe out. Try this short meditation from Headspace."[2]

To maximize the potential of the Daily Briefing, make sure that you are also maximizing the underlying features of Outlook, such as flagging or adding tasks to your calendar. This way Viva can pull the information into one concise package for you.

We also receive a Viva "monthly digest" with surprisingly helpful insights. First, the email includes the "Insight of the month," which informs us about "[t]he people you spent the most time communicating with outside working

1. Microsoft Viva, https://adoption.microsoft.com/en-us/viva/ (last visited Aug. 1, 2022).
2. Emails on file with author.

hours." One monthly insight explained, "Establishing common quiet hours with no meetings or email can lead to better teamwork."

The email also suggests that we "[t]ake a deeper look," for example, explaining that Dan had "25 Quiet days spent without significant activity outside your working hours." There was also "7% Collaboration time spent in meetings, emails, chats, and calls weekly." There is also a list of "top collaborators," that is, "the contacts with whom you've spent the most time in the last month."[3]

Viva will often suggest that you schedule focus time, which, as we have already seen in Part I, can be an invaluable productivity tool. When you choose to schedule it, Viva blocks that time off on your calendar like an appointment.

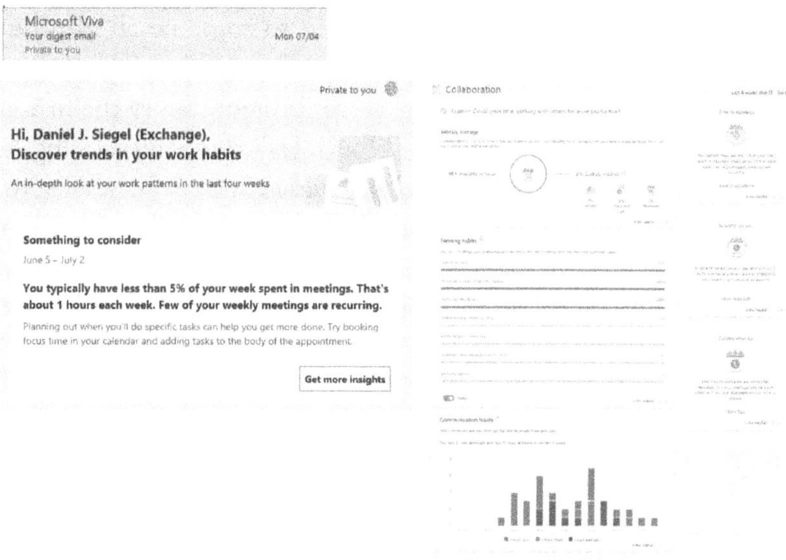

For those who want to know more about how it works, Viva is a hybrid product that merges the utility of Teams with the benefits and features of Outlook. Viva bills itself as an employee experience platform that has five components:[4]

- Viva Connections
- Viva Insights
- Viva Learning
- Viva Topics
- Viva Goals

3. Emails on file with author.
4. *Help Your Employees Thrive with Microsoft Viva*, https://www.microsoft.com/en-us/microsoft-viva (last visited Aug. 1, 2022). Note: some features require an additional subscription fee per user.

Viva Connections allows businesses or law firms that use SharePoint to provide employees with a customized dashboard containing news and information and a place to connect with others within the organization.. The goal of connections is to strengthen firm culture and build a sense of teamwork. Many of these features are for larger firms or organizations, allowing them to create employee resource groups and town halls, focusing on engaging employees wherever they are located.

Viva Insights is the component that is useful to everyone, from small firms to the largest. Insights personalizes the Teams and Outlook experience, providing reminders of the upcoming day's events and deadlines. Insights also helps everyone manage time, including making sure they take breaks, etc.

Viva Learning is a feature that is designed to combine all of a business's learning resources in a single space. Available tools include LinkedIn Learning, Coursera, Microsoft Learn, edX, and whatever content library the firm has.

Viva Topics has been described as AI for today's companies. Using AI, Viva Topics identifies, processes, and organizes content to make it easier to locate or to find related information. Topics can also integrate with other third-party services.

Viva Goals allows teams to collaborate on goals that align with the organization's strategic priorities and track progress on those goals.

MICROSOFT OUTLOOK TIPS AND TRICKS

Outlook is the most popular email program for lawyers, yet many lawyers don't use most of the available features to help them manage the flow of email. These tips will help you to process your email more efficiently and perform email-related activities with as few clicks as possible.

Tips for Streamlining Your Inbox

Use the Reading Pane

The Reading Pane is the key to saving time reading and processing email. Reading email by clicking on one message after another is very time consuming. Using the Reading Pane makes it so much easier and quicker. But the key is putting the Reading Pane on the right. Here is how to set it up:

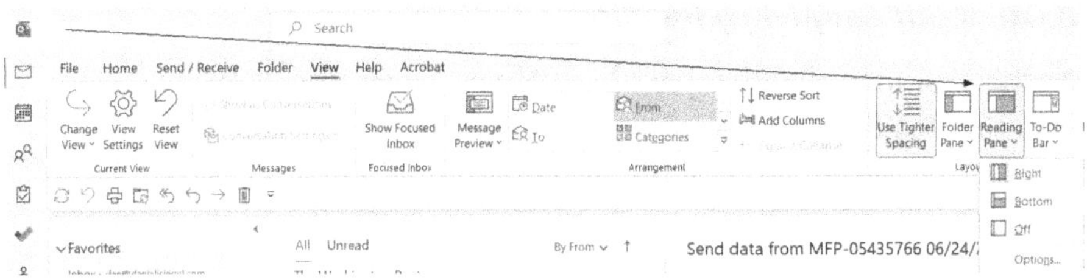

On the View tab, in the Layout group, click Reading Pane and then click Right or Bottom.

Mark Messages as Read after Previewing in the Reading Pane

Because you can view messages without opening each one, you can also set Outlook to mark messages read either when you view, after you view, or after you view them for a specific amount of time. But you don't have to do it manually. Instead:

- Click the File tab.
- Click Options.
- Click Advanced.
- Under Outlook panes, click Reading Pane.
- Select the checkbox at "Mark items as read when viewed in the Reading Pane" and then enter a number in the "Wait n seconds before marking item as read" box.

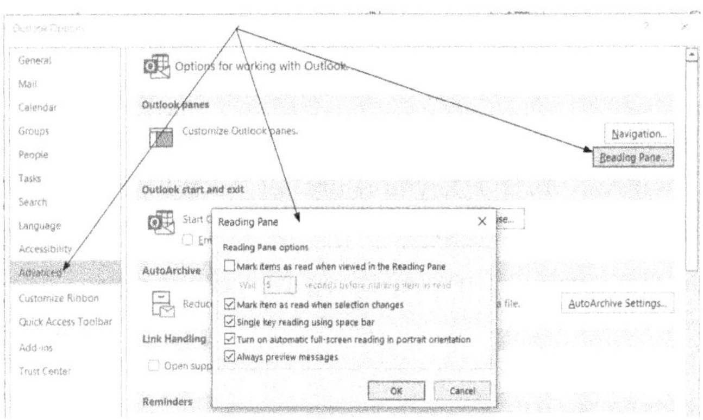

Turn On or Off Single Key Reading

Single key reading using the space bar lets you move quickly through your messages in the Reading Pane. Each time you press the space bar, the Reading Pane content scrolls down one page. At the end of the item, the next unread item in your message list appears.

Switch to Your Inbox or Outbox

Switching between your Inbox and Outbox quickly can save time. Fortunately, there's a shortcut to help you move between the mailboxes quickly.

- To go to your Inbox, press CTRL+SHIFT+I.
- To go to your Outbox, press CTRL+SHIFT+O.

There are also a series of shortcuts to move between the various Outlook windows, which are included in the appendix. The following are the most popular:

- To go to Email, press CTRL+1.
- To go to your Calendar, press CTRL+2.
- To go to your Contacts, press CTRL+3.
- To go to your Tasks (To-Dos), press CTRL+4.

Delete Email Messages Permanently

By default, deleting emails is a two-step process: you delete the email, and it goes into a trash folder, which needs to be purged later. To delete emails permanently in one step:

- Select the email message that you want to delete.
- Hold down the SHIFT key and press DELETE to permanently delete the selected email message.
- Confirm the deletion in the dialog box that appears when you close Outlook.

Find Email Messages Quickly

Ideally, all of your email messages will be either moved to the appropriate file elsewhere on your computer or deleted and won't be languishing in your Inbox. But we know that rarely is the case and that often you will need to search for messages in your Inbox (or sent items). You can quickly search for a specific email message in Outlook. In the Search box, type your subject, that is, the word or phrase you are looking for. For example, to find an email message from Allison Johs, type "from: Allison Shields Johs" (or just Allison Shields to see all messages in which her name appears). This search request quickly lists email messages from that person but not messages that contain her name.

This tip also works for other criteria, such as folders. For example, searching for "folder: clients" quickly lists only those folders that contain "clients" as part of the subject.

You can also make important email messages stand out by using color categories, as mentioned earlier. Click the View tab and then click View Settings, then Conditional Formatting. Here, you can change the color of Unread emails in your Inbox (the default is blue) or change the font and color of all emails in your Inbox. You can also click Add to create your own rules for different kinds of emails.

For example, if you want emails from specific clients to appear in a different color in your Inbox so you can find them easily, create the rule, choose the font and color for the message, and then click Conditions to set the conditions for the rule (by choosing the client's name or email address in the "from" field), similar to the way you would set up Rules and Alerts in Outlook.

Follow Up on Email

Sometimes you need to take action or follow up on an email, but you can't do so right away. You can flag a message by using the INSERT key. Select the message that you want to flag, and then press INSERT. This will flag the item and let you insert a start date and due date. If your To-Do Bar is active, the item will also appear in your task list.

While using flags to follow up can be helpful, if you flag too many messages, the flag becomes useless. And since the default flag is "today," flags become difficult to differentiate on your task list and you run the risk of creating yet another never-ending to-do list. You can change the default flag or create custom flags that can help your messages stand out. Right-clicking on the flag gives you options to customize the flag and due date, add reminders, and more.

Create Reminders to Follow Up on Email You've Sent

In addition to flagging emails you receive for follow-up, you can also set up reminders to follow up on email you have sent. When drafting an email, click the Follow Up flag in the Tags group in the Message tab. By default, Outlook will place a flag in your To-Do Bar tasks for this email message with the current date and time. Click the down arrow next to the Follow Up flag in the Tags group and click Set Reminder to change the start and due dates and to add a reminder.

Use and Create Outlook Quick Steps

So often, we need to schedule an appointment as the result of receiving an email. Outlook Quick Steps can make that task—and so many others—easy. When you use Outlook Quick Steps to create an appointment from the email, the appointment can include the email text in the appointment notes, making it easier to remember why you scheduled the meeting in the first place. Let's see how it's done.

You must configure some Quick Steps the first time you use them. Even for new users, creating most new Quick Steps is easy and intuitive. All you have to do is click on one of the down arrows on the bottom right corner of the Quick Steps section of the Ribbon bar and let Outlook walk you through the process step by step. Plus, when you go to the Quick Steps group in the Home tab, you will see that Outlook has already created some Quick Steps that you can use. If you want to modify an existing Quick Step from the Outlook default or from those you have created, do the following:

- In the Outlook Home tab, in the Quick Steps group, click the More arrow at the side of the Quick Steps box, then click Manage Quick Steps.
- In the Quick Step box, click the Quick Step you want to change, then click Edit.
- Under Actions, change or add the actions you want this Quick Step to perform.
- You can also assign a keyboard shortcut to the Quick Step using the Shortcut key box.
- To change the icon for a Quick Step, click an icon next to the Name box, click an icon to select it, and then click OK.

To create a new Quick Step, do the following:

- In the Outlook Home tab, in the Quick Steps group, click the More arrow at the side of the Quick Steps box and click Create New.
- Under Actions, select the action you want the Quick Step to do. In our example, we want to create an appointment with the text of the email. Scroll down under Appointments and choose "Create appointment with message text."
- In the Name box, type the name for your new Quick Step (perhaps "Appointment with text").

- Outlook will assign an icon for your Quick Step based on the action you choose. If you would like to change the icon, click the icon button next to the Name box, and then click OK.
- Click Add Action for any additional actions.
- You can also assign a keyboard shortcut to the Quick Step using the Shortcut key box or add tooltip text that will show when your mouse hovers over the Quick Step.
- Click Finish when you have completed constructing your Quick Step.

When you create new Quick Steps, they appear at the top of the gallery on the Outlook Home tab in the Quick Steps group. You can rearrange your Quick Steps using the Manage Quick Steps dialog. One caveat, however. If you want to use a Quick Step to move messages from one folder to another, be aware that Outlook requires you to specify the folder before you can use the Quick Step.

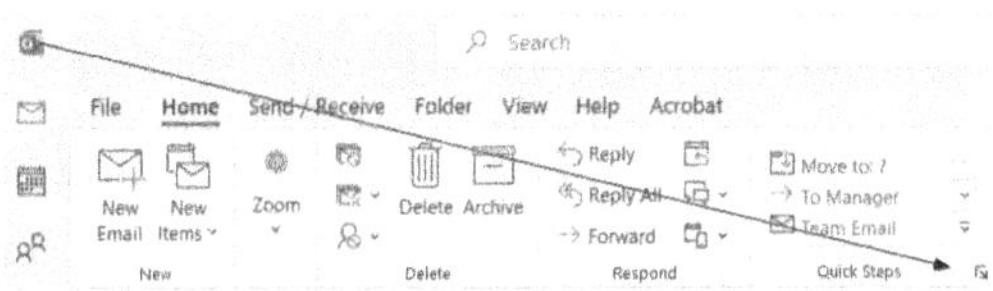

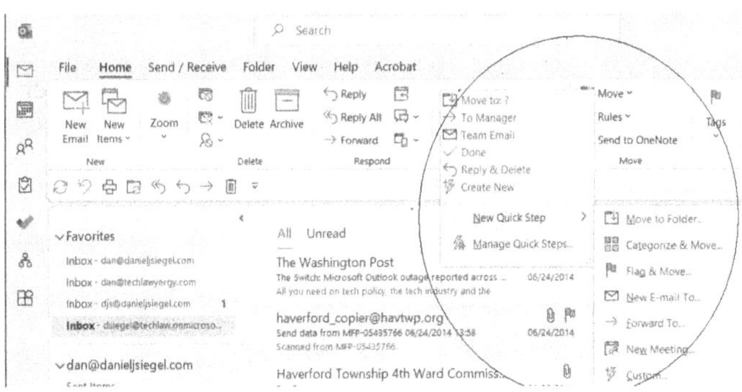

Use and Create Outlook Quick Parts

Do you find yourself repeating the same information over and over in email messages to different people? Don't keep reinventing the wheel—use Outlook's Quick Parts (not to be confused with Quick Steps!).

Lawyers who need to insert large blocks of text into an email message—for example, directions to their office, a list of documents clients should bring to their first appointment, or answers to frequently asked questions—can do so easily using Quick Parts in Outlook.

First, type the text once into a new email message, then select the text and click the Quick Parts icon on the Insert tab and save it to the Quick Part Gallery so it is available for use again in the future. When you want to insert that block of text again, click on Quick Parts and choose the appropriate Quick Part to insert.

Create a Rule

Outlook uses Rules to automate common tasks. They're easy to create and can be used to streamline email-related tasks you perform regularly. Here's how to create a rule from a template or from scratch:

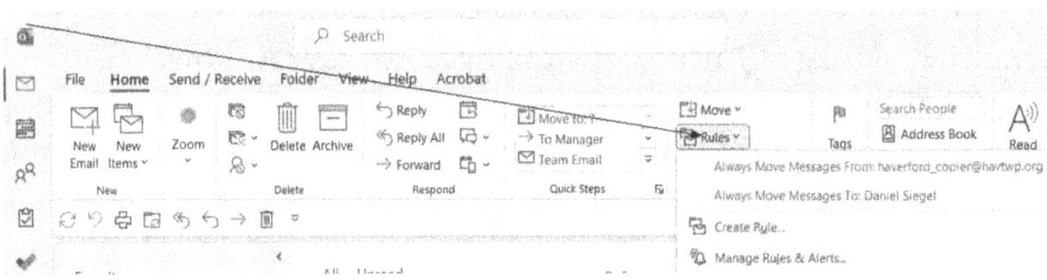

- In the Navigation Pane (the column on the left side of the Outlook window that includes buttons for the Mail, Calendar, and Tasks views and folders), click Mail.
- On the Tools menu, click Rules and Alerts.
- If you have more than one email account, in the "Apply changes to this folder" list, click the Inbox you want.
- Click New Rule.
- Do one of the following:
  - use a template with prespecified actions and conditions and select the template you want; or
  - create the rule by specifying your own conditions, actions, and exceptions.

To have this rule apply to all your email accounts and Inboxes, select the "Create this rule on all accounts" checkbox on the last page of the Rules Wizard.[5]

There are other ways to create rules as well. Here are some examples:

5. To learn more about creating Rules in Outlook, we refer you to another Law Practice Division book: Chris Fortier, The Lawyer's Guide to Office Automation: Tools and Strategies to Improve Your Firm and Your Life (2023).

Create a Rule Based on a Message in a Folder (Great for Listservs)

- Open the folder that contains the message.
- Right-click the message you want to base the rule on.
- Click Create Rule.
- In the Create Rule dialog box, select the conditions and actions you want to apply.
- To add more conditions, actions, or exceptions to the rule, click Advanced Options and then follow the rest of the instructions in the Rules Wizard.

Create a Rule Based on a Name or Subject (Including Flagging the Sender)

- Open the message you want to base a rule on.
- On the toolbar, click Create Rule.
- In the Create Rule dialog box, select the conditions and actions you want to apply.
- To add more conditions, actions, or exceptions to the rule, click Advanced Options and then follow the rest of the instructions in the Rules Wizard.

Use Outlook Search Folders to Find Email, Attachments, and More

Many Outlook users do not know about, let alone use, Outlook's Search Folders feature. This feature allows users to keep email in a particular folder while also "placing" it in a virtual search folder.

A Microsoft Search Folder is a virtual, frequently changing folder that lets users view all email items matching specific search criteria in one place. For example, the Unread Mail Search Folder allows users to see all unread email in one folder, even though the messages might be saved in different folders across your mailbox. Unfortunately, Search Folders can't include search results from multiple Outlook data files (.pst).

For example, suppose you are on a bar association listserv and want to be able to view all of the emails from the listserv at one time, without moving them to a dedicated folder using Rules. For many users, moving email to another folder, without still seeing it in the Inbox, means that they do not look at the emails or at least don't think about looking at them. Using Search Folders permits the email to remain in sight in the Inbox but also provides the opportunity to see the messages segregated; deleting the email from either location deletes it from both.

How to Create a New Search Folder

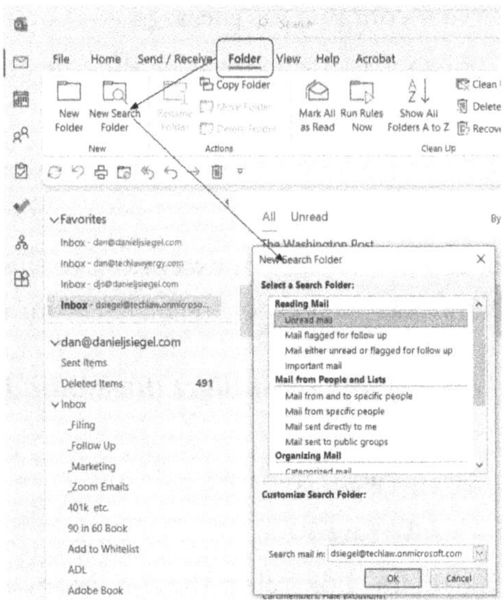

There are two types of search folders: Predefined Search Folders and Customized Search Folders.

Create and Use Predefined Search Folders

Select the Folder menu. In the New group, select New Search Folder or click Ctrl+Shift+P.

From the "Select a Search Folder" list, click the Search Folder you want to add. To view some of the predefined Search Folders, you may have to scroll to the end of the list. If the predefined folder has customization options, those will display under Customize Search Folder. If you have more than one account in Outlook, you can specify which account to search. Use the "Search mail in" box to pick the email account you want to search. Then select OK.

Create a Customized Search Folder

Select the Folder menu. In the New group, select New Search Folder or click Ctrl+Shift+P.

From the "Select a Search Folder" list, scroll to the bottom of the dialog and click Create a custom Search Folder. Select Create a custom Search Folder. Under Customize Search Folder, click Choose. Then type a name for your custom Search Folder. Next, click Criteria and select the options you desire. The Messages tab contains criteria about the message's content or properties. These include sender, keywords, and recipients. The More Choices tab contains criteria to select other features of the message, including importance, flags, attachments, or categorization.

Finally, the Advanced tab permits you to make even more detailed selections, a process you can repeat for each criterion you want to include in this search folder. Next, click OK. From there, you can click Browse to select each folder you want searched. Clicking OK will close each open dialog box.

Choose a Signature for Different Recipients in Microsoft Outlook

Why do lawyers, and lots of other people, use the same signature on every email? Is the fact that we're having lunch really confidential? Is the meeting notice really something that requires a disclaimer that you aren't providing tax advice? Of course not, yet it seems that everyone uses the same email signature for every email. And if, God forbid, you end up being sued—can you really claim that the disclaimer on your email should prevent a liability claim when it is the same for every recipient? We wouldn't want to be that test case. Instead, create different signatures for different purposes.

To create a new signature, open a new message and click Signature under the Insert tab. The signature dialog will open, allowing you to create and name your new signature.

If you want to use a different email signature for different recipients (for example, one for clients and one for other attorneys) or different purposes (for example, one signature for email messages related to legal matters and another for more general messages, such as bar association committees), once the different signatures have been created, you can change signatures with two mouse clicks.

Right-click your signature and then click the other signature that you want to use.

You can also add the signature dropdown to the Quick Access Toolbar, and every signature you have in Outlook will appear under the down arrow next to the signature icon. To add the signature dropdown to the Quick Access Toolbar, right-click on Signature under the Insert menu and choose Add to Quick Access Toolbar. We will discuss the Quick Action Toolbar in more detail in the next chapter.

Use the "Send From" Command

The "Send From" or "Share" command can help you save time switching programs when you are working on something that you need to send to someone, even if you don't use Outlook. In most Windows-based programs, under

File, you will find the "Send From," "Share," or a similar command. This feature enables you to send the item you are working on to another person with your default email program. Just select the command and it should open an email window/dialog and insert the file as an attachment. Then you can write your message, address your email, and send it without having to switch to your email program. *Remember to save the attachment before hitting the command so that you send the correct/latest version.*

Turn Off Email Notifications

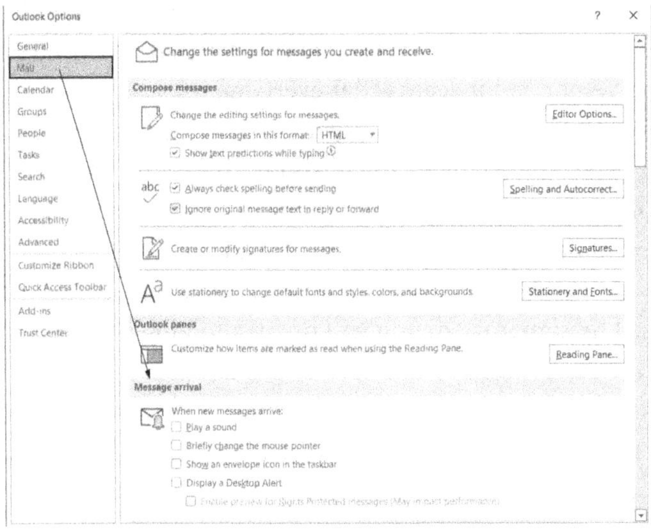

If you receive a lot of email (what lawyer doesn't?), then the email notification icon is a pain in the you-know-what. So turn it off:

- Click File, click Options, click Mail, and then go to Message Arrival.
- Clear the "Display a New Mail Desktop Alert" checkbox.

Never Print an Email

Sometimes an email message is a piece of correspondence that should be saved because it relates to a client's matter. As we mentioned earlier, your Inbox is not the right place to store these email messages. Email is electronic mail, which means it was meant to be created and stored on a computer. There is no reason to print it and save it in a hard copy. Instead, save it electronically. There are many strategies you can use, including:

- Use your case management software.
- If the email isn't client related and you just need the email temporarily, create folders in your email software. Create them logically, that is, by client or topic, and move the email there to avoid cluttering up your Inbox.
- Alternatively, save the email into a PDF package or portfolio in Adobe Acrobat.

Use Adobe Acrobat to Save Email

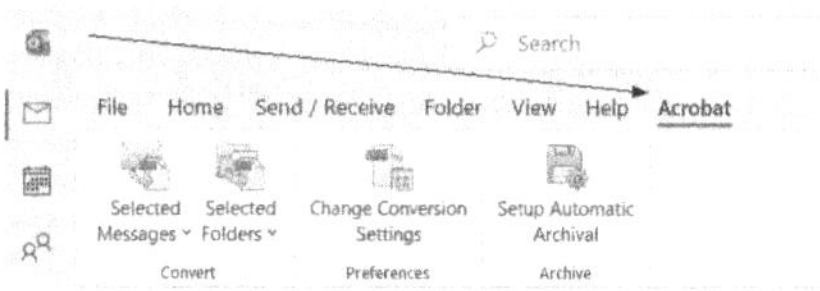

While Adobe Acrobat is generally considered a program to create or work with PDFs, it is also a terrific way to save email, assuming you don't have case management or document management software. Here's how.

Specify Whether Email Messages Become Merged PDFs or PDF Portfolios

A merged PDF simply combines PDFs into one large file, whereas a Portfolio keeps them separate. It's like the choice of either putting everything in one folder or having separate folders for each item.

In Outlook, choose Acrobat > Change Conversion Settings. Do one of the following to select whether your PDF will be a single document or a Portfolio:

- To convert and merge email messages into a PDF as sequential pages in one document, deselect Output Adobe PDF Portfolio When Creating a New PDF File.
- To assemble converted email messages as components of a PDF Portfolio, select Output Adobe PDF Portfolio When Creating a New PDF File.

Convert an Open Email Message to PDF

Acrobat > Convert to Adobe PDF.

You can also convert a different file to PDF from within an open Outlook email message if the "Attach as Adobe PDF" toolbar is shown. Clicking this button opens a series of dialog boxes for selecting and saving the new PDF and also starts Acrobat, if it is not already running. The resulting PDF is attached to the open email message.

Convert Email Messages to a New PDF

Select the individual email messages.

- Choose Adobe PDF > Convert Selected Messages > Create New PDF.
- In the "Save Adobe PDF As" dialog box, select a location, type a file name, and click Save.

Add Email Messages or Folders to an Existing PDF

Select the individual email messages or folders.

- Choose Adobe > Convert Selected Messages > Append to Existing PDF, or Adobe PDF > Convert Selected Folders > Append to Existing PDF. (Note: If you have already created one or more PDF Portfolios, you can choose from recently created PDF Portfolios in addition to the "Append to Existing PDF" option.)
- Locate and select the PDF or PDF Portfolio to which you want to add the converted emails and click Open. **Important:** Do not type a new name for the PDF. If you do, a warning message appears telling you that the PDF was not found. Click OK and select a PDF without changing its name.
- If a message appears alerting you that the existing PDF was created using an earlier version of PDFMaker (see next section), do one of the following:
  - To create a PDF Portfolio from the original PDF archive, click Yes and select a name and location for the new archive. (The default name adds _Portfolio to the original PDF file name.) When the conversion is complete and the Creating Adobe PDF dialog box closes, the new archive opens in Acrobat.
  - Click No to cancel the process.

Note: For PDF Portfolios of email converted or migrated in Acrobat 8 or later, only new messages—that is, messages that are not already part of the PDF Portfolio—are appended.

Convert Email Folders to a New PDF

Adobe Acrobat PDFMaker can convert multiple folders to PDF in one procedure. It is not necessary to select the folders at the beginning of the process because you can select them in a dialog box that appears automatically.

- Choose Adobe > Convert Selected Folders > Create New PDF.
  - In the "Convert Folder(s) to PDF" dialog box, select the folders. Then select or deselect the "Convert This Folder and All Sub Folders" option.
- In the "Save Adobe PDF File As" dialog, select a location and name for the PDF Portfolio.

When the conversion is complete, the new PDF opens in Acrobat.

CHAPTER 10 ACTION STEPS

1. Spend 30 minutes setting up your email to work more efficiently in the future using folders, Rules and Alerts, and Quick Steps and customizing your Quick Access Toolbar.
2. Start developing the habit of deleting unnecessary emails immediately and moving email messages out of your Inbox to more appropriate places (such as your Calendar or Task list or the client's computer file). Alternatively, create Search Folders to be able to review multiple emails at one time based on criteria you specify.
3. Set aside 30 minutes a week to clean out your email using the email management tips in this chapter.

Chapter 11
IMPROVING YOUR TECHNOLOGY IQ

"I didn't go to law school to learn how to use Microsoft Word." "I'm a lawyer, not a geek." "Really, you think I should know how to use computers?" We have heard lawyers say these statements too many times. And while they are correct that they didn't go to law school to be geeks, it is also true that doctors didn't go to medical school to learn about technology. And it is also true that when Dan graduated from law school, the personal computer didn't exist. In fact, when the latest version of the Model Rules of Professional Conduct was approved in 1983 (yes, roughly 40 years ago!), technology was so new that the word "technology" doesn't appear in the Rules.

Things change. How many of you want to go back to the days of paper copies of *Shepard's Citations* or not having smartphones, including GPS?

How many doctors graduated before there were MRIs? And how much of medicine has changed in the last decade, much of it because of technology, let alone over the past few decades? And for lawyers, in the old days, as some call them, every lawyer had a secretary and/or a paralegal. That isn't the case anymore, and that's our point. To be a competent lawyer, your technology IQ must be higher than it was a decade or perhaps four decades ago. You wouldn't go near a doctor who didn't use MRIs because they weren't around when the doctor graduated medical school, would you?

While technology doesn't help lawyers save lives, it does help them provide better services more efficiently. Yet many lawyers still don't understand why they need to learn technology. As Casey Flaherty has said, lawyers leverage their legal expertise through process and technology. Both have changed dramatically since all of us graduated from law school, with no end in sight.

And remember, even if you consider yourself a tech Luddite, you know more than you realize, just not enough. You know what "electronic discovery" and "ESI" are, you have a sense of what a gigabyte and megabyte are, and most lawyers these days understand what metadata is. Lawyers also have to know about redaction, PDFs, and even AI—artificial intelligence. These words and acronyms are part of the legal lexicon.

Similarly, technology training for lawyers and staff should be commonplace so that every person working in a legal organization has a baseline of competency. One technology company wrote in 2018 about the five benefits of technology training," and those tenets have not changed. In fact, their conclusion is really the introduction: "Training is a necessary aspect of your technology solutions and planning. As we become more and more reliant on technology, it's important that your employees know how to utilize the solutions that your business is investing in."[1]

They then offer five reasons to support their belief in training, which we repeat verbatim:[2]

1. **It saves money.**—Employees that are properly trained spend less time troubleshooting and more time on productive and revenue-driving tasks.
2. **It saves time.**—When employees are knowledgeable about the applications they use, they can work quickly and finish projects faster.
3. **It fosters a competitive edge.**—Companies that can use all their solutions effectively are likely to outperform those that struggle to understand the basics. And, since you're saving time and money, you can re-allocate those measures to innovative projects.
4. **It boosts confidence.**—Confident employees are better employees. When people know how to efficiently do their job, they are much more likely to be happy in their position, resulting in less turnover for your business.
5. **It allows for team building.**—Training requires employees from different departments to learn and work together. More experienced users can jump in and help those around them, and employees get a glimpse of how other departments work.

1. *5 Benefits of Technology Training*, ProTech Servs. Grp. (July 11, 2018), https://www.psgi.net/5-benefits-of-technology-training/.
2. *Id.*

This summary is common sense, and it's essential to understand the need for and to have staff learn about technology if you are truly serious about doing more in less time. And if you have already invested in the technology, why not reinvest in training and using it more wisely before changing to new tech, new systems, and new learning curve investments?

In the remainder of this chapter, we will provide a few of our favorite tips that you can use immediately to work better with electronic files, rename directories and files easily, and search for documents, whether or not you're using practice management or document management software.

Mostly, we'll demonstrate countless ways to use the products that most law offices use—Microsoft Windows, Microsoft 365 (including Microsoft Word), and Adobe Acrobat—that are, or should be, the foundations of your office's technology.

We don't expect you to adopt every tip here. What we hope is that as you read these tips, you'll recognize that these and the other software programs you are using have many features and shortcuts you never knew about and that you can do so much more with them by merely learning a few of these tips.

Computer software is generally designed by geeks or nerds, not by the end users, and this can be frustrating. With these tips, we hope that you take back control of your computers and do things the way you want to, not how some geek who works for Microsoft thinks you should do them.

Let's get started.

MICROSOFT WINDOWS TIPS

Use the Quick Access Toolbar

The Quick Access Toolbar is often overlooked, but it is one of the most helpful and easy-to-use tools in various Windows and Office applications. Users customize the Quick Access Toolbar to include commands, buttons, and options that provide instant access to their favorite tools.

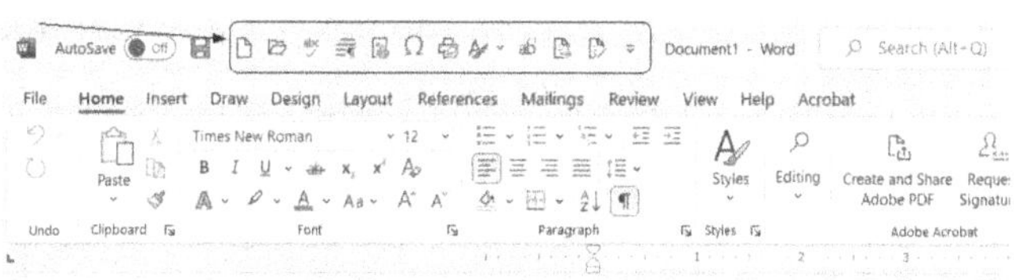

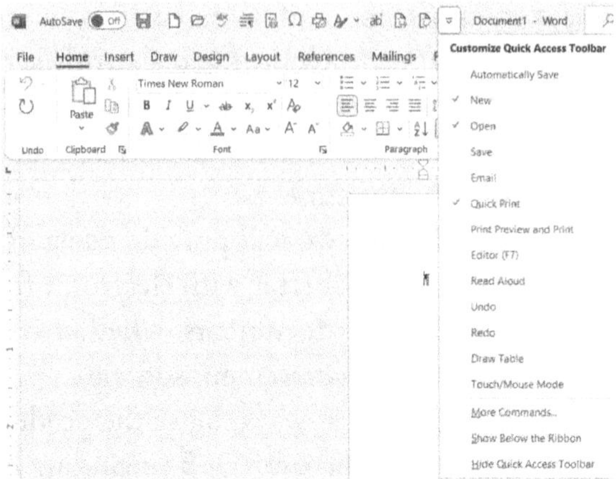

By default, the Quick Access Toolbar is at the top of the File Explorer and Office and other windows throughout Windows. You can, and should, configure it to display the commands and other options you frequently use. Once a button is added to the Toolbar, all you do is click or tap it to use the corresponding action directly from the toolbar.

By default, the Quick Access Toolbar contains only two buttons and an arrow that opens a dropdown menu. Click or tap the arrow to open the menu, which will display the full list of default commands. You can add any of those by just clicking on a command on the list to check or uncheck it.

The magic is adding and using commands to the Quick Access Toolbar, with these tips from Microsoft.[3]

Add a Command to the Quick Access Toolbar

- On the ribbon, click the appropriate tab or group to display the command that you want to add to the Quick Access Toolbar.
- Right-click the command, and then click Add to Quick Access Toolbar on the shortcut menu.

Add a Command That Isn't on the Ribbon to the Quick Access Toolbar

- Click Customize the Quick Access Toolbar > More Commands.
- In the "Choose commands from" list, click Commands Not in the Ribbon.
- Find the command in the list, and then click Add.

3. You can find many more tips at https://support.microsoft.com/en-us/office/customize-the-quick-access-toolbar-43fff1c9-ebc4-4963-bdbd-c2b6b0739e52 (last visited Aug. 3, 2022).

Remove a Command from the Quick Access Toolbar

- Right-click the command you want to remove from the Quick Access Toolbar, and then click Remove from Quick Access Toolbar on the shortcut menu.

Move the Quick Access Toolbar

The Quick Access Toolbar can be located in the upper-left corner on the title bar by default. To move it, just:

- Click Customize Quick Access Toolbar.
- In the list, click Show Below the Ribbon or Show Above the Ribbon.

Export a Customized Quick Access Toolbar

Once you have commands how and where you like them, export them to another computer and use them there, saving the time to recustomize.

- Click the File tab.
- Under Help, click Options.
- Click Quick Access Toolbar.
- Click Import/Export, and then click Export all customizations.

Import a Customized Quick Access Toolbar

To import your customized Quick Action files, just:

- Click the File tab.
- Under Help, click Options.
- Click Quick Access Toolbar.
- Click Import/Export, and then click Import customization file.

Open the Task Manager Faster

Admit it, CTRL+ALT+DELETE is your default keystroke when you want to go to Task Manager and shut down an ornery program that won't close. But the problem is that this command *used* to take you there. Now it takes you to a blue screen that makes you click again to go to the Task Manager. There's an easier way. To go directly to the Task Manager, press CTRL+SHIFT+ESCAPE instead.

Searching for Electronic Files Without a Case or Document Management System

Saving files—on your computer—doesn't do you any good unless you can find what you need when you need it. That's why naming files and storing them in a logical manner is so vital. Once you've established good naming conventions for files, folders, and documents, retrieving them on your computer should be much easier. Thankfully, there are many tools that can be used to help you to locate electronic documents and files.

Where to Start Searching for Files

There are lots of ways to find files on your computer. Most of the time you'll start by using the search tools that appear at the top of every folder you open. But there are a few tools you should know about.

The Search Box

Generally, the quickest way to find a file is to use the search box at the top of the folder window. Just type in the name to begin the search. There is also a virtually identical search box at the bottom of the Start menu that you can use to find files. Using the search box, you can search by file name, kind of file (e.g., document), type of file (e.g., doc file), tag, or author.

File List Headings

When you want to find files that have similar criteria (e.g., they're Word documents or were created the same day, etc.), you can use the headings above the file list to filter, stack, or group your files. Use the dropdown box next to the heading to select this way of viewing files, which can be a huge help sometimes. Allison uses the Date Modified dropdown frequently to see files in specific folders in reverse date order to find the most recent files easily.

Use the Search Folder

Using the Search Folder is the best way to find files that are stored in multiple folders/directories. The nice part about using this method is that there is an Advanced Search option, and you can save your searches and use them again. You can search by name and many other criteria. Find the advanced search features under the Search tab once you have run your initial search.

Rename Directories and Files

When searching for files, the results appear in alphabetical order by default, so you may have to scroll quite a bit to find files that begin with letters that are later in the alphabet. But you can move files or folders by renaming them.

The best method to ensure that a particular file always appears at the top of the file list is to rename it with an underscore or other symbol at the beginning of the file name, which will move it to the top of the alphabetical pile.

Windows users can also rename their files and directories by using one of the following four methods:

Method 1

- Highlight the file or folder you want to rename.
- Right-click the file or folder and click Rename on the menu that appears.

Method 2

- Highlight the file or folder you wish to rename.
- Press the F2 key on the keyboard.

Method 3

- Highlight the file or folder you wish to rename.
- Click File at the top of the window and select Rename from the list of available options.

Method 4

- Highlight the file or folder you wish to rename by single-clicking the file.
- Once it is highlighted, wait a few seconds and click the file again. A box should appear surrounding the file or folder name and you should be able to rename the file.

Renaming Multiple Files or Folders at Once

- Open Explorer.
- Select all the files you want to rename.
- Press F2 and type the new name for the files. For example, typing "test" will rename the files to test, test(1), test(2), test(3), etc. If you have set your computer to display file extensions, also type the name of the file extension you're renaming.

MICROSOFT 365 (PREVIOUSLY CALLED MICROSOFT OFFICE) TIPS

These tips apply to all of the MS Office applications, in particular, Word, PowerPoint, and Excel. While some of the commands work in Access and Publisher, we're confining our tips here to the big three.

Keep Important Documents/Files Handy All the Time

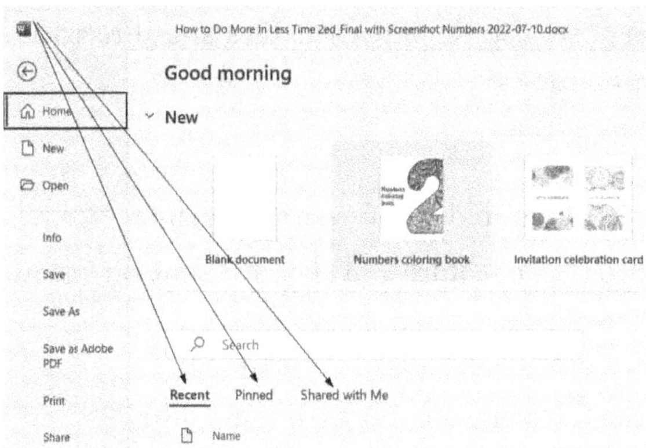

The Recent Documents list is one way to keep important files or documents at your fingertips whenever you need them. To find the Recent Documents list, click either the File or Office button. Click the pushpin icon next to the file name to pin that specific file to the Recent Documents list. When you click the pushpin icon, it changes in appearance to show that the pin has been activated for that document. Doing this makes the document/file always accessible at a click.

You can change the number of documents/files in the recent documents list. To do so:

- Click the File or the Office button, then click [Program] Options (for example, Word Options).
- Click Advanced.
- Scroll down to the Display section, and you will see the section that gives you the option of changing the number of recent documents displayed.

Inspect and Remove Metadata Using the Document Inspector Tool

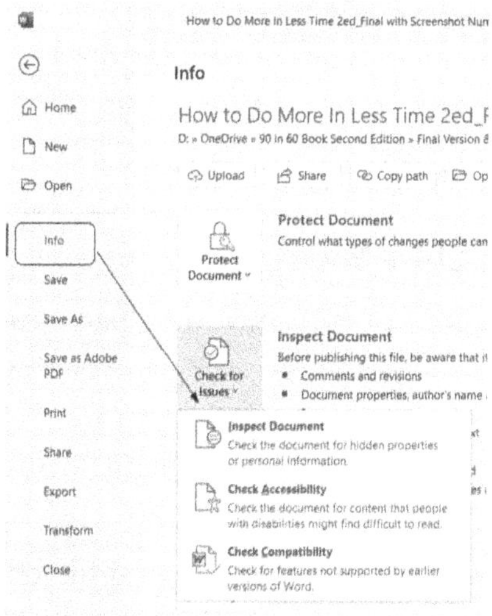

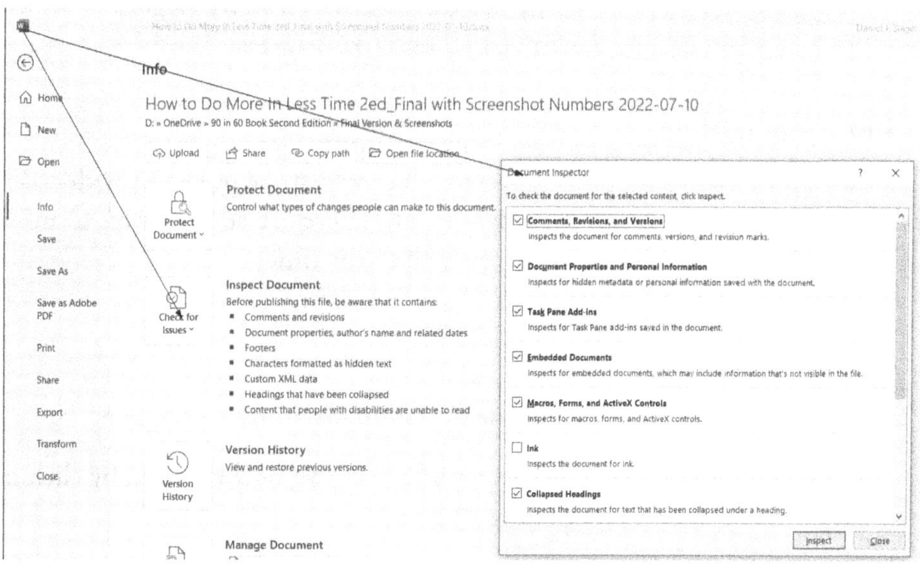

- To access the Document Inspector, save your document.
- Then click either the File or Office button, and then click Inspect Document.
- Depending on the program you are using, this tool searches for different types of content, including comments, unresolved tracked changes, and headers and footers.

- Review the results and decide what you want to remove from your document.
- Keep in mind that some types of content the Document Inspector finds (such as custom XML data) may be required for the document to function properly.

Preview Formatting before You Apply It

A "theme" is a set of design elements, including backgrounds, colors, and fonts, that give your document or presentation a professionally designed feel. They are located on the Design tab.

- You can preview many types of document formatting before you apply them.
- Point to a Style to see font, color, and graphic effect formatting changes all at once throughout the document. For more advanced users, this preview function works for Themes or the SmartArt Styles gallery to preview a variety of formats for your SmartArt diagram.

Minimize the Ribbon

Sometimes the ribbon can take up too much screen space or can provide a distraction when you're working on a document. There are several ways to minimize the ribbon if you don't want to see it all of the time:

- Double-click any tab name.
- Press CTRL+F1.
- Right-click any tab name for the option to minimize the ribbon.

You can also choose to display a simplified version of the ribbon by clicking on the up arrow to the far right of the ribbon.

Adding Line Breaks without the Bullets

When you are creating a bulleted or numbered list, you may want some items to appear in the list without a bullet or without increasing the number. To create a new line without a bullet or new number, press SHIFT+ENTER. The next time you press the ENTER key, however, the new line will continue the bulleted or numbered list.

MICROSOFT WORD TIPS

As we have mentioned before, the default settings built into your software aren't necessarily the settings that will work the best for you. The same is true for Microsoft Word.

Customize the Default Word Document Template

Whether you realize it or not, when you start Word, it opens the new document using a template called the Normal template. This template is really Word's "memory." It's where Word saves all of your default settings, including your default styles, AutoText, macros, toolbars, and other customizations that determine the basic look of your documents. Word's default document template may not be set up the way you want your documents to look, but you can customize the Normal template or create additional templates of your own.

- First, make a copy of the default template in Word, which is saved in C:\Users\user name\AppData\Roaming\Microsoft\Templates for Office 365 users. It may be in a different place depending upon which version of Word you are using.
- Create the document that you want to use as a new template: choose your fonts, heading styles, etc.
- Save the document on your desktop (so you can locate it easily) as a macro-enabled template by choosing Word Macro-Enabled Template as the file type.
- Close all open windows/documents in Word.
- Replace the default template in the location where you found the original default template, and your new template will now be the default. (Don't forget to delete the document from your desktop.)

Change Default Document Formatting

To change the font and paragraph formatting defaults for the open document or all new documents based on the active template, do the following:

- Press CTRL+SHIFT+ALT+S to open the Styles pane (or click the dialog box launch icon in the Styles section on the Home tab).
- Click the Manage Styles icon at the bottom of the pane to open the Manage Styles dialog box.

- On the Set Defaults tab of the dialog box, change font and paragraph formatting as needed. Then, at the bottom of the dialog box, click the option to apply settings either only to this document or to new documents based on the active template.

Predefine the Format for Pasting in Word

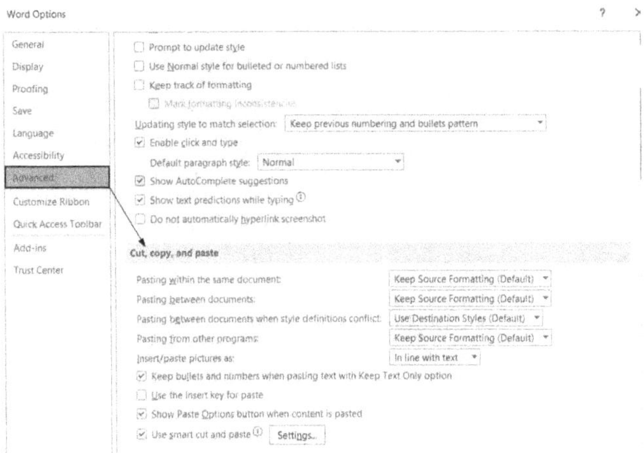

In a Microsoft Word document, each time you paste some text or an image, you can select the format (source formatting, destination formatting, or text only) by clicking the clipboard icon. You can also set the default paste formatting mode:

- Go to File > Options > Advanced or click Set Default Paste on the Home tab under Paste.
- Scroll to "Cut, copy, and paste" and choose your preferences.

The pasted text and images will now be formatted automatically according to your settings.

Change the Smart Quote AutoCorrect Setting

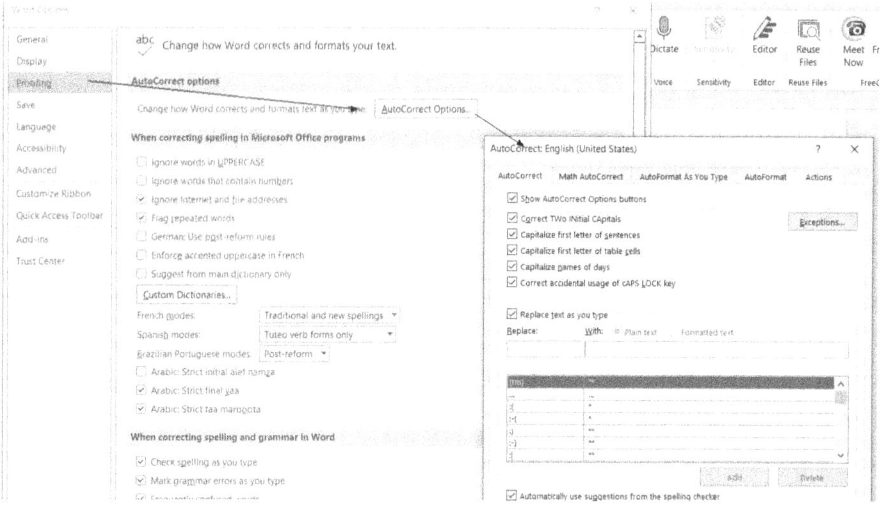

Word sometimes uses "straight" quotation marks (also called "dumb" quotes) instead of true typographic quotation marks ("smart" or "curly" quotes). For consistency, it's best to use one style, generally smart quotes. Here is how you change this setting:

- Click the File or the Office button.
- Click Word Options.
- Click Proofing, and then click AutoCorrect Options.
- Click the AutoFormat tab.
- Clear the "Straight quotes with smart quotes" checkbox.
- Click the "AutoFormat As You Type" tab.
- Clear the "Straight quotes with smart quotes" checkbox.
- Click OK twice.

Now that you have customized Word to work better for you, here are some tips that will help you to work more quickly and efficiently within the program.

Find Tooltips for Keyboard Shortcuts

When working on a document, you can save time any time you don't take your hands off of your keyboard to use your mouse. If you press and hold the ALT key, tooltips appear above the commands in the ribbon at the top of the page. You can then press the appropriate letter for a simple keyboard shortcut without needing to use the mouse.

Using Quick Parts

The Quick Part Gallery is a gallery where you can create, store, and find reusable pieces of content, including AutoText, document properties such as title and author, and fields. It's great for saving phrases, pleading parts, signatures, and just about any other information you type again and again. You access Quick Parts from the Text menu on the Insert ribbon.

AutoText

You'll probably use AutoText the most because it's reusable content that you can store and access again and again. Click AutoText to access the AutoText gallery. You can save AutoText by selecting the text you want to save/reuse, clicking AutoText, and then clicking Save Selection to AutoText Gallery. By filling in the new building block information, you store the content you save to use again.

After you save a selection to the Quick Part Gallery, you can reuse it by clicking on Quick Parts and selecting the item from the gallery. Or, when you start typing a saved phrase, Word will prompt you to hit ENTER if you want to insert the saved text.

Document Property

Click Document Property to choose from a list of properties (really metadata) that you can insert in your document, such as Author, Company, Subject, etc. This information stays with your document.

Field

Use the field codes option to insert fields that can provide automatically updated information, such as the time, title, page numbers, and so on.

Building Blocks Organizer

Have a large brief to complete? Or are you working on some other large project? Then you should consider using Building Blocks Organizer to shorten the time it will take. This feature contains numerous Building Block galleries, such as Headers, Footers, Cover Pages, etc., to help organize your document.

Click Building Blocks Organizer to preview all of the building blocks available to you in Word. You can also edit properties, delete, and insert building blocks from this menu.

Rearrange Paragraphs in Word

- Click the paragraph that you want to move.
- Hold down SHIFT+ALT and move the paragraph up or down by using the arrow keys.

Each press of an arrow key causes your selected paragraph to jump over one adjacent paragraph.

Use the Navigation Pane

You can also move sections of your document around using the Navigation pane. Use the Navigation pane (under the View tab) to search for—and jump to—specific terms within the document or to easily move parts of the document around. If the document contains headings and subheads, you can easily cut and paste large sections of the text and move them around within the document by dragging and dropping the headings within the Navigation pane, which will move the entire section at once.

Save Tables in Word for Use in the Future

There may be times when you want to use the same table more than one time, either in the same document or in a future one. Regardless, you can save it so you don't have to create it from scratch the next time. First, you'll need to save the table:

- Select the table that you want to save.
- On the Insert tab of the ribbon, click Table, point to Quick Tables, and then click Save Selection to Quick Tables Gallery.
- In the Create New Building Block dialog box, give the table a name, classify it with some basic parameters, and then click OK.

To reuse a saved table:

- Position your cursor where you want to insert a saved table into your document.

- On the ribbon, click Insert, click Table, and then point to Quick Tables.
- From the list, click the saved table you want to use. This table will now be inserted into the document.

Remove All Hyperlinks in a Document at Once

If you want a document with no hyperlinks at all, rather than removing them one at a time, select the entire document using CTRL+A. Then press CTRL+SHIFT+F9, and all of the hyperlinks will be gone.

Edit Long Documents Quickly

It can be tedious to scroll through a document to find the spot where you last worked. Fortunately, you can move to the location quickly. Here's how: Use the shortcut SHIFT+F5 to go back to wherever you were working last.

Split Documents

If you ever wanted to see two different parts of a document at the same time, this tip is for you. Just follow these instructions to work on a large document in parts by splitting the screen:

- On the View tab, click Split.
- Next, click the screen where you want the split to appear.
- You can then navigate parts of the document separately in each window.

Find Out How Many Lines or Words You Have Typed

Right-click the status bar, and then select a parameter to view line details or the number of words typed.

MICROSOFT EXCEL TIPS

Microsoft Excel may be the program that lawyers have the least familiarity with, and for many, it is the least intuitive of the Microsoft 365 programs to work with.

Copying a Worksheet

Here's how to copy a worksheet to another place in your Excel workbook:

- Click the tab of the worksheet that you want to copy.
- Leave your mouse pointer on the tab.

- Press and hold down the CTRL key.
- Press and hold down your left mouse button and drag the worksheet that you want to copy to the left or right. Watch for the little black arrowhead that follows your mouse pointer as you drag left or right.

When you release the mouse button, Excel inserts a copy of the worksheet where the arrowhead is pointing.

Customize Records Sort

You can customize how you sort your records within an Excel worksheet by using a filter. To activate a filter:

- Click Filter on the Data tab.
- Click the filter arrow on the column that you want to sort.
- Point to Sort by Color, and then click Custom Sort.
- Create a customized sort order:
  - In the Sort dialog box, under Column, click the dropdown arrow next to "Sort by" and choose the field that you want to be sorted. Values should appear in the Sort On field.
  - In the Order field, click Custom List. This will open a window that offers an entirely custom sort list.
  - In the left pane, list the values (each separated by a comma) in the order that you want them to be sorted, and then click Add.
  - In the right pane, select the list you've created, and then click OK.
  - In the Sort dialog box, click OK.

Your records will now be sorted according to your customized list.

Fit a Printout onto a Set Number of Worksheet Pages

- Click the Page Layout tab on the ribbon.
- In the Scale to Fit section, in the Width box, type the number of pages you want the printout to span horizontally.
- In the Height box in the same section, type the number of pages you want the printout to span vertically.

Move the Cursor in Any Direction When Entering Data

By default, the cell pointer moves down when you press ENTER after entering data in a cell. You can change the direction in which the cell pointer moves.

- Click the File or the Office button.
- Click Excel Options, and then click Advanced.
- Select the "After pressing Enter, move selection" checkbox if it isn't already selected, and then on the Direction menu, click the direction in which you want the pointer to move.

Also, when working in a document, you can make the pointer move in the opposite direction from the one you've chosen by holding down the SHIFT key while you press ENTER.

Enter the Same Value into Multiple Cells Simultaneously

- Select the cells into which you want to enter the value.
- Type the value in the active cell.
- Press CTRL+ENTER.

Type Data into a Series of Cells Simultaneously

- While holding down the CTRL key, click all the cells in which you want to enter the same text (or value).
- Type the entry, and then press CTRL+ENTER.
- The text will be added to all the selected cells.

Paste into Nonsequential Cells in Excel

Sometimes, you want to copy a formula or piece of data into a series of nonsequential cells. You can do this quickly without having to paste into each cell individually.

- Copy the data from the source cell.
- Hold down the CTRL key as you click to select each destination cell.
- After all the cells are highlighted, paste the data by pressing CTRL+V.

You have to paste only once.

Enter a Series of Data

- Type the first value in the series into a cell.
- Type the second value into a cell below or to the right of the first cell.
- Select the cells.

- Drag the Fill Handle (a black square that appears at the bottom right corner of the last selected cell) over the cells into which you want to extend the series.

Enter a Fraction in a Cell

To enter a fraction, simply prefix it with a zero and a space. To display the fraction one-third, type 0 1/3. This will display 1/3 but will have an underlying value of 0.33333333.

Copying Data from a Table in a Web Page

To import a data table on a website:

- Copy the URL (address) of the page.
- In Excel, on the Data tab, in the Get External Data section, click From Web.
- In the New Web Query dialog box, paste the URL into the Address box.
- Select the table that contains the data that you want to work with, and then click Import.
- In the Import Data dialog box, indicate where you want the data to appear, and then click OK.

Zooming to Fit a Selection

- Select the range of cells that you want to focus on.
- Click the View tab, and then click Zoom to Selection.

Identify Duplicates

If you have ever seen a spreadsheet and realized, or just worried, that there were duplicate entries, which could throw off your data or lead to other problems, there are ways to identify the duplicates. Here's how:

- Click the Home tab on the Ribbon.
- In the Styles section, click Conditional Formatting.
- Select Highlight Cells Rules.
- Click Duplicate Values.
- Pairs of duplicates will then be highlighted, and you can choose which of each pair to delete.

Add Rows and Columns to Worksheets

To add a row or column:

- Select any row or column.
- Press the CTRL key at the same time as the PLUS SIGN (+) key on the numeric keypad.

To delete a row or column:

- Select the row or column.
- Press the CTRL key at the same time as the MINUS SIGN (-) key on the numeric keypad.

Change the Color of Every Other Row

Spreadsheets can be difficult to read. To make reading easier, change the color of every other row.

- Select the range of cells you wish to format.
- Click Format > Conditional Formatting.
- In the dropdown box, select Formula Is.
- In the box type: =MOD(ROW(),2)=0
- Click the Format button and then click the Patterns tab.
- Select a color for the shaded rows and click OK twice.

View All the Text in Your Columns

- Select the columns where your text appears by clicking the column headings.
- To resize the columns to fit, double-click in the column heading, exactly on top of the border that divides any of the two columns you selected.
- All of your selected columns are resized based on the longest text string in each column.
- Of course, sometimes this can make your columns too wide. As a result, you may want to highlight the column (or cell), right-click, select Format Cells, and click "Wrap text" under the Alignment tab.

Change the Color of a Sheet Tab

- Right-click the sheet tab.
- Click Tab Color.
- Click the color from the palette that appears.

MICROSOFT POWERPOINT TIPS

Select a Slide Layout

- On either the Home tab or the Insert tab, click the New Slide icon.
- Select a layout option from the Add Slide gallery.
- On your new slide, click a placeholder to add text or slide content.

Move Pictures Around Quickly

To move pictures around quickly in PowerPoint, just drag one picture over another. The top picture will become transparent, letting you position it accurately over the bottom picture.

Use the Design Assistant

If you use Microsoft 365, you have the added feature of the Design Assistant, which can help you create more attractive presentations. Simply add your text and images to your slide and click on the Design Assistant.

Delete Slide Notes before Sending Copies of a Presentation

By using Document Inspector, you can delete all the slide notes in a presentation instantly, making it easy to send your slides to others.

- Click the File or the Office button, point to Prepare, and then click Inspect Document.
- Click Inspect.
- Click Remove All next to Presentation Notes.

You can also choose to remove invisible on-slide content, personal information, comments, and custom XML data.

Save this version of your presentation separately so that you do not write over the original version and lose your notes!

Use Presenter View

Presenter view allows you more control over your presentation, including the ability to show slides out of sequence. It also includes a blackout button that lets you blacken the screen for the audience while maintaining your view of the presentation and your notes on your own monitor. Presenter View allows you to run your presentation from one monitor and let the audience view it on another monitor or a projector.

Enter the PowerPoint Slide Show Mode Beginning at Any Point

To start your slide show with the current or selected slide, press SHIFT+F5.

Move to Specific Slides during a Presentation

When a presenter quickly zooms through slides in order to make up time or to find information, it distracts from the presentation and annoys the audience. To make this method more effective, before giving your presentation, print out the outline of your slides with page numbers on them or simply make a list of the slides with their corresponding numbers. Use this as a guide during your presentation. To jump to a specific slide, type the slide number and voila, you are there.

ADOBE ACROBAT STANDARD AND/OR PROFESSIONAL TIPS

While many lawyers are familiar with the *free* Adobe Reader, the Standard and Professional versions of Adobe Acrobat are the game changers, that is, using these programs can dramatically improve your efficiency and productivity. In fact, we believe that every lawyer and every support person needs Adobe Acrobat (either Standard or Professional). Plus, the program is essential to going paperless.

Add Bookmarks to a PDF File

To create a bookmark, open the page where you want the bookmark to link to and right-click to add a bookmark.

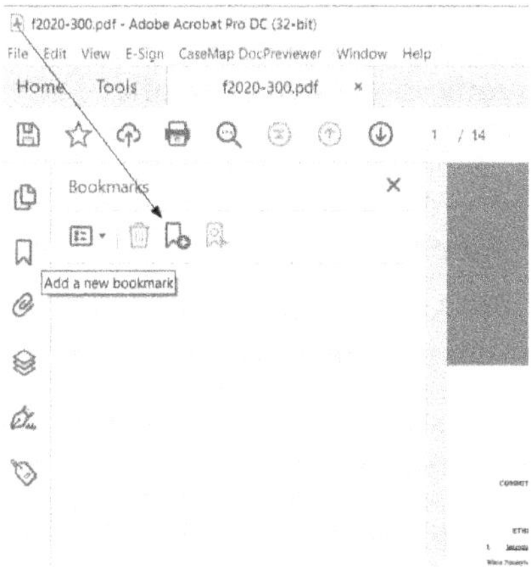

Or you can use the Select tool to create the bookmark:

- To bookmark a single image, click in the image or drag a rectangle around the image.
- To bookmark a portion of an image, drag a rectangle around the portion.
- To bookmark selected text, drag to select it. The selected text becomes the label of the new bookmark.
- You can edit the label.
- Click the Bookmarks button and select the bookmark under which you want to place the new bookmark.
- If you don't select a bookmark, the new bookmark is automatically added at the end of the list.
- Choose New Bookmark from the options menu.
- Type or edit the name of the new bookmark.

Add Menus to the Task Panel

It is important to know that, by default, not all menus are included on the task panel. You can add them easily by clicking on View > Tools and selecting the additional menus you desire to see.

View Thumbnails

As in previous versions, you can view thumbnails of pages, bookmarks, and signatures on the left side of the screen.

Clicking on the ribbon, paper clip, or pen icons on the left side of the screen shows Bookmarks, Attachments, and Signatures in the left panel.

To close the panel, you click the small Collapse button. There is a corresponding collapse button on the menus on the right.

Arrange Pages in a Document

The Page Thumbnail view is especially useful for arranging pages in a document. You can drag and drop pages to rearrange them within the PDF and can easily copy between two open PDF documents by dragging the pages from one document and dropping them onto the Page Thumbnail panel in the second.

Customize the Quick Tools Toolbar

Adobe Acrobat Professional still permits users to customize the Quick Tools toolbar, as in previous versions, by selecting the Customize Quick Tools button on the toolbar. Using this feature, or by right-clicking on the toolbar, you can select the additional features you wish to have displayed on the toolbar.

Save PDFs

As with virtually every Windows-based program, you will open, close, and save files in Adobe using the File menu.

This is also the menu from which you determine how you save PDFs, that is, the specific format you will use. This is particularly helpful because the menu allows you to perform a variety of functions, including save as PDF/A, the standard used by some courts for e-filing. You can also reduce the size of the PDF file through this menu.

This menu provides other important options as well. For attorneys, one of the most helpful is the Reader Extended PDF menu that permits you to create forms and other documents and send them to clients. The clients, who need to have only the free Adobe Reader, can then fill out the form, save it, and return it by email.

In addition, this menu allows you to convert PDFs to Word, image, and other formats and to use many of the actions that automate the manner in which Adobe can process your documents.

Navigation and Customization

The Edit menu offers you the option of customizing the software so that it works the way you want it to, not how the programmers think you want it to. To access these features, go to Edit > Preferences and the Preferences tab opens. This is the location where you make your selections.

The most popular features—Commenting, Documents, Full Screen, General, and Page Display—are at the top, but the other options can be equally as important.

Commenting

From this menu, you select the font used in comments and specify how the comments will act and appear.

Documents

This window provides settings for how Adobe will save documents and whether it will remove hidden information (including metadata) by default. It also shows how Adobe handles redacted files, that is, whether it renames them by default. You can, of course, always remove metadata and other hidden data manually using the Protect tab on the Task Bar.

Full Screen

This window provides you the opportunity to customize how documents open, appear, and navigate by default. In most cases, you can modify these for any particular document without having to modify your preferences.

General

From this window, you can modify some of the program's most common settings.

Page Display

Every user tends to prefer a different method of page display, that is, whether you see one or two pages and whether the program displays the full page, fits the page to the width of the screen, or some other setting. You can modify your defaults here.

You should also review and modify the other categories of preferences to be sure that the program works for you. Among the most important of these categories are **Identity** and **Internet**.

Identity—From this screen, you specify the default data that will appear in the metadata of the file, that is, the name, title, and organization of the PDF's "author." Many users prefer to leave this blank so that no identifying information appears in the document's metadata. Others include the information to avoid any questions about who created the document.

Internet—This screen controls how or if documents appear in your web browser. By unchecking "Display PDF in browser," for example, any PDFs you open on the internet will appear in Adobe (not the browser window), making it easier to save and edit.

Adobe also offers numerous keyboard shortcuts, enabling you to perform many tasks quickly. You can locate the tools from the Help menu or by going to https://helpx.adobe.com/acrobat/using/keyboard-shortcuts.html.

Create PDF Documents

You can create PDFs in several ways with Adobe Acrobat.

First, you can select Create on the opening screen in Acrobat, or you can use the File menu to select the way you will open a new file.

Next, you can create an Adobe PDF from other programs, for example, Word or Excel, as you would print to any other printer. Simply select Adobe Acrobat from the list of printers and the document will print to a file that you can then save.

You can also create a PDF from existing documents directly from Windows Explorer without opening the document by right-clicking on the file and selecting Convert to Adobe PDF.

Microsoft Office programs link directly with Adobe Acrobat Professional, allowing you to convert a document created in Word, Excel, Outlook, or PowerPoint to a PDF without leaving the program.

Convert PDF Documents to Other Formats

You can also convert a PDF document to Word. It may not be an exact reproduction of the document, but the quality continues to improve with each version. Just select File > Save As > Microsoft Word and you are done. Then open the document in Word.

There are other options. For example, you can export a PDF as rich text, a generic word-processing format that can be used by most word processors; XML, the format used in newer word processors; or a spreadsheet. You can also save your document as an HTML or web-based format or as a picture (usually a JPG or JPEG). Finally, you can save a document as a generic txt, or TXT, file. With text files, you have two options—plain or accessible. With plain text, each paragraph retains its formatting (hard returns at the end of the paragraph); with accessible text, each line from the PDF becomes a line (with a hard return) in the generic document. Thus, you probably prefer plain text.

Create PDFs from Multiple Files

The days of having to merge multiple files into one large PDF are over. Using PDF Portfolios, you can assemble PDF files (including PDF forms) as well as non-PDF files into a single Portfolio. Merging PDFs into a Portfolio is the equivalent of making a stack of documents in separate folders, rather than creating a PDF document that is the equivalent of having a pile of documents that were merely placed into a stack.

In a PDF Portfolio, files are not modified when packaged, permitting signatures and security options to stay intact. Documents within a Portfolio are viewed in the same window, so that you can scan through documents quickly without scrolling through all the pages of the document to get to the next one and without the need to create bookmarks. It is also easy to delete or extract documents from a Portfolio. Finally, you can search and print the current or selected document, or all documents, from within the Portfolio.

Creating a PDF Portfolio takes only a few steps, and the choices you make in the Combine Files wizard determine whether the files are merged into a single PDF or combined into a PDF Portfolio.

- Choose Create > Combine Files into Single PDF.
- Next, in the Combine Files wizard, do any or all of the following:
  - To add individual files, click Add Files, navigate as needed, select the files, and click Add Files.
  - Repeat these steps, if necessary, to add files in other locations.
  - To select all of the files in a specific location, click Add Folders, navigate to the needed folder, select it, and click OK.

You can also change the order of the files in the Portfolio using the Move Up, Move Down, and Remove buttons to adjust the file sequence, if necessary. In the top right-hand corner of the Combine Files screen, you can select whether to create a single PDF or a PDF Portfolio. At the bottom right of the screen, you can choose the file size to create. (There are many options and methods to create a Portfolio. For more detailed instructions about these options, use Adobe's excellent Help found in the program.) Once your files are in the correct order and you have the appropriate format and file size, click

Create. A status dialog box will appear, showing the progress of the file conversions. Some source applications may start and close automatically.

When the conversion is complete, the document opens and permits you to change the layout of the Portfolio. You can add additional files through Layout > Add Content > Add Files; you can review the thumbnails and rearrange the documents if necessary. When you are satisfied with the final product, click Save and select a name and location for the PDF Portfolio.

Read and Work with PDF Files

Now that you have documents saved as PDFs, you can begin to use the features that make this such a powerful product. Some of the most significant tools for lawyers are the ability to make scanned PDFs searchable, to index multiple PDFs, and to annotate documents.

Search

One of the biggest benefits of receiving legal documents such as medical records as PDFs rather than as hard copies is the ability to search the records for a particular word or phrase in an instant, rather than shuffling through a stack of papers. If you have scanned in medical records or opposing counsel's brief and try to search it, you won't be able to search immediately, because scanning a document to PDF is like taking a picture of the document. You wouldn't be able to edit the text of a picture, so you can't edit the text of the scanned document. You need to make the text editable, and you do so by using the OCR function.

OCR stands for "optical character recognition" and denotes a type of computer software that translates images of text into editable and searchable text. In Adobe, you can OCR a freshly scanned document or a previously scanned document (in some cases, such as when documents are converted from Word to PDF format, the OCR process is completed simultaneously). OCRing will take typewritten text (not handwriting) and recognize it so that you can search within the PDF.

OCRing documents in Adobe is done through the Tools menu and is found under Recognize Text. You can select the option to recognize text in the file you have open, or you can make multiple files searchable.

When you select In This File, a Recognize Text dialog box appears, prompting you to select an option under Pages to determine whether you want to OCR the whole document or just a particular section. You may also, if you desire, click on Edit and open the Recognize Text Settings dialog box to select the options you want to use.

These settings are extremely important and should be edited. The default PDF output style is Searchable Image, which means that Adobe may actually change the appearance of certain characters so that they match the internal fonts stored in Adobe.

We do not recommend using the Search Image or the Clear Scan setting. Clear Scan will revise fonts to appear the same as the closest font within Adobe. In contrast, the Searchable Image (Exact) setting preserves the original fonts so that the output is identical in appearance to the original, which is critical for most attorneys. Fortunately, once you change this setting, Adobe remembers it every other time you use it.

Once a document has text that can be searched, there are multiple ways to search for words and phrases.

A valuable corollary to OCRing documents is the ability to index and search them. From within a PDF, you have two choices: Find or Search, both of which are found either on the toolbar or in the Edit menu on the top left of the Adobe Acrobat window.

- The **Find** command will search for the word or phrase one instance at a time.
- The **Advanced Search** command brings up a separate window, which searches for every instance of the word or phrase in the current PDF and creates a list, allowing the user to go directly to each instance. Advanced Search offers other options as well, including Whole Words Only and the ability to search comments.

The real strength of Adobe is its ability to index groups of documents, including multiple files or directories, and permit a global search of all the documents, with the immediate display of each instance of the word or phrase in every document indexed.

An Index can be created by clicking on Tools > Document Processing > Full Text Index with Catalog.

The program then prompts you to select the files to be indexed and the location of the index file, as well as other indexing parameters. To search an Index (Indices are PDX files, not PDF files), just open it (by double-clicking on the file name or opening it from the File > Open menu, remembering to change the file parameters from *.PDF to All Files so that the PDX file will be displayed). Then type in the word or words you are searching for and wait for the results.

Annotate PDF Documents

Once you have indexed and searched a document or documents, you may want to annotate the instances of words or phrases. Adobe allows you to use the same tools you would use to annotate paper documents with sticky notes and highlighters in the PDF.

The Annotation options are found under Comment > Annotations; once you find them, simply click on the tool you want and click where you want to insert the note into the PDF or select the text to annotate.

Each of the icons represents a different way to annotate the document. For example, clicking on the Sticky Note tool permits you to click anywhere on the page and insert a sticky note with a text box.

You can also see that the sticky note will show up in the comments list, which makes it easy to navigate to the annotations in a document. Or you can build your index to search annotations.

Below the Annotations section is the **Drawing Markups** section, which is useful for drawing attention to certain sections of a document. Using the different tools in this section, you can circle information, put an arrow in the document, or create a callout box as part of the document.

Back in the Annotations section, the Stamp tool in Adobe Acrobat Professional includes many preloaded stamps such as "Approved," "Confidential," and even "Sign Here." This tool also permits you to create custom stamps from various formats, including PDF, JPEG, and bitmap files. To add an image to a PDF, just paste the image into the document. Pasted images have the same characteristics as other stamp comments; each includes a pop-up note and editable properties.

To create a custom stamp, select Stamps in the Annotations section of the Comment menu. Then click Show Stamps Palette. Then click Import and select the file you want to use and then click Select. If the file has more than one page, scroll to the page you want, and then click OK. Choose a category from the menu or type a new category name, name the custom stamp, and then click OK. The real advantage of stamps is that they can be used to create headers and footers, backgrounds, and watermarks and be saved for use in other documents. A stamp can be as large or small as you want it to be.

Other Customizing Tools

You can also remove or update existing headers, footers, watermarks, and backgrounds; shrink content to accommodate headers and footers; and preview changes in real time. These tools are found in the Tools menu under the Pages section under Edit Page Design.

To add page numbers, select Header & Footer and then select Add Header and Footer. Once page numbers are applied, you can update them by selecting Update or remove them by selecting Remove. Once you select Add Header & Footer, the Add Header and Footer box appears. This screen permits you to select the font and size of any text in the header or footer. You can also control the page margins. If you select Appearance Options below the font, you can instruct Adobe to shrink each document so that the page number does not overlap the document information.

To add the page number, you click in the location you want the page number to appear, for example, Left Header Text or Center Footer Text, and click Insert Page Number. To the right, you can control the format of the page number and date.

Just as in Word and Excel, any text you put in the header and footer shows up on each page. Thus, if you are preparing an Appellate Reproduced Record, you can type "R. " and then click Page Number to get the correct numbering format of R. 1, R. 2, etc. You can also save these settings for later use.

If you want to send clients a draft document, which clearly shows it is a draft, you can use the Watermark tool. You access the **Watermark** tool just below the Header and Footer tool. When you click Watermark > Add Watermark, a similar window appears.

You can select the option to have the watermark load from text you type or from a file you select. The text or image will then appear on every page of your document. You can apply watermarks to multiple documents and can save settings you use frequently.

Adobe offers different tools depending upon the type of document you are working with. For example, perhaps the document you are working with is not a stack of records but a form downloaded from a website. Adobe Acrobat Professional permits you to type on the form as if you were using a typewriter. If it is a form you will use again and again, you can create form fields in the document so that you can type into it without using the typewriter tool. Also, if the form uses fonts you have on your system, you may be able to type directly into the document.

The following tools are found in the Content section of the Tools menu.

Add Text & Images permits you to simply start typing anywhere in a document that has searchable text. In previous versions, this was called the Touch Up Text tool. If the form is still a "picture," use Add or Edit Text Box. Once you click on the tool, a window titled Typewriter will pop up and you can click anywhere on the PDF and begin typing. The window contains features to change the font, size, and spacing of the text you type.

Once you have your document the way you want it, you can **Save** and **Print.** Both of these functions are in the File menu and can also be added to the Quick Tools toolbar.

When printing, you have several options. You can elect to print the document as it shows on your screen, print it without markups or annotations, or print only the markups and annotations. Although these second two options may sound odd, they are fantastic for legal professionals.

Using the **Print Form Fields only** option, you can scan a form to PDF, type on the form using the typewriter tool, and then print the "typewritten" text back onto the original paper form.

Work with Forms in Acrobat

As discussed earlier, you can use the typewriter tool to fill out forms, but Adobe Acrobat Professional also gives you the ability to automatically or manually create forms, distribute forms, and manage the data received from forms. Acrobat also comes with LiveCycle Designer form creation software as a standard feature and has improved the form field recognition features. The Forms tools are found under the Tools menu in the Forms section. The More Form Options field allows you to import and export data received from forms.

In order to obtain data from clients or other individuals to import or merge, you can use forms you create or can highlight existing fields, which allows Adobe to select the areas the software recognizes as form fields. Once you have created a form, you can send it to anyone, even if the person has only Adobe Reader. One of the great frustrations users had with prior versions was that they could not save any documents filled in with Adobe Reader; they had to print the document to retain the changes. There are several options for allowing users with Adobe Reader to modify PDFs.

If you have a form you want users with Adobe Reader to be able to save, you save the form as a Reader Extended PDF in the File menu. By enabling additional features, you permit users with Adobe Reader to save. You can also permit users with Adobe Reader to use the Typewriter feature and to comment on the PDF by selecting different options in the Reader Extended PDF menu.

Bates Numbering

If you are producing documents for discovery, it is also useful to Bates number the documents. Bates numbering allows you to place a unique identifying number on every page of every document so that there is no confusion later. With Adobe, you can Bates number one or many documents and save and reuse the Bates numbering formats.

Adobe makes it easy to apply these identifying labels to a batch of related documents. Bates numbers appear as a header or footer on each page of each PDF in the batch and are created in virtually the same manner as page numbers. Adding Bates numbers, which you create in a wide range of styles, is simple; Bates numbering is found in the Tools menu in the Edit section.

As with page numbering, once you click Bates numbering, you are prompted to determine whether you want to Add or Remove Bates Numbering. If you select Add Bates Numbering, you are then prompted to identify the files to add Bates numbers to in the order they should appear. Once you have selected the files, you are prompted to add the Bates numbering in the style and in the location on the page you would like it to appear. You can also save the settings you use for future projects.

Get It and Send It Electronically

Since Dan opened his own firm in 2005, he has never provided discovery or other materials in paper form. Instead, he sends the items either as email attachments or on a CD. This enables him to Bates number every item using Adobe Acrobat Professional (assuring no one claims something was missing) and to reduce or nearly eliminate the costs of printing, copying, postage, envelopes, and the time involved.

Another advantage is that when you receive a document related to a client's case, you can scan it, save it, and then send it to the client, further reducing the number of copies made and paper used. It's more economical all around.

Metadata Removal

Another function in the Protect section involves metadata removal. Most common software programs, including Microsoft Word, Excel, and PowerPoint, contain metadata, or "information about data." This can include names of individuals who worked on a document, editing time of the document, and more. Adobe also contains metadata, although not the same data that was contained in the original document or other object that was converted to a PDF format. There may still be reasons, however, that you would want to remove the metadata from a PDF.

With Adobe Acrobat, you can easily view an object's metadata by using the Remove Hidden Information tool in the Protect section. The metadata is displayed in predefined groups of related information. You can display or hide the information by clicking the plus and minus signs (Windows) next to the group. (Adobe calls each group a schema name.) If a schema does not have a recognized name, it will be listed as Unknown. The XML name space is contained in parentheses after the schema name.

Adobe Acrobat has taken metadata removal a step further with the **Sanitize Document** function. With one click, you can remove metadata, embedded content and attached files, scripts, hidden layers, indexes, stored form data, review and comment data, hidden data from previous saves, and other information. Selecting Remove Hidden Information gives you a chance to review the information you are removing, whereas Sanitize Documents removes all the hidden data with one click.

Additional Features

The **Action Wizard** in Adobe has improved upon the Batch Processing feature of previous versions. This wizard permits you to automate a series of frequently performed tasks. By applying one or more routine sets of commands to files, users save time and keystrokes by using an automated sequence, that is, a predefined series of commands with specific settings performed in a specific order that can be applied in a single step. You can apply a sequence to a single document, to several documents, or to an entire collection of documents.

You can create your own action by selecting Create New Action, which will allow you to choose actions from the tools available in the Tools menu. You can also select from Adobe's preloaded actions. For example, Prepare for Distribution will prompt you to apply a header and footer, a watermark, and bookmarks to an open file and will then remove hidden information (metadata) from the file.

Here are some other actions you might want to consider using.

Password Protected Envelopes

With this feature, you can add security to any document by storing it in an encrypted envelope, which is called a security envelope, and sending it as an email attachment. This method is especially useful for sending secure file attachments without modifying the attached files. When the other user opens the security envelope, they can extract the attachments and save them to disk. The saved files are no longer encrypted when saved. To use this feature, go to the Tools menu under the Protect section and select More Protection and then Create Security Envelope.

Then just add the files you want to attach, select an envelope template, select a delivery method, and select a security policy from the list of available policies (or create a new policy, if needed). From there, just follow the on-screen instructions to complete the security envelope. If prompted, provide your identity information. Finally, type an email address in the message that appears and click Send, or save the security envelope to send later.

Document Passwords

For added security, you may desire to place a password on a document or to restrict another user's ability to edit, copy from, print, or perform other functions with the document. To do so, go to File > Properties > Security.

To change the type of security, click on Security Method and select the type of security you desire, generally Password Security. This will bring up the Password Security > Settings dialog, which allows you to specify the encryption (security level), password (Adobe even tells you how strong the password is), and other permissions. Just follow the prompts.

Of note, at this location, and when you use the Save As > Reduced Size PDF menu, you can specify with which prior versions of Adobe your PDF will be compatible.

This is an important setting because, unlike you, many other computer users only have the Adobe Reader or are using an earlier version of Adobe Acrobat. Thus, it is recommended that you make documents compatible with the latest version possible. Otherwise, you may discover that your PDFs cannot be opened by other users. Please also remember that when you change version compatibility, certain features may be disabled, so be careful when doing so.

As you can see, it isn't hard to improve your technology IQ, and the benefits are clear, but it does require you to be a bit adventurous and discover how to accomplish more in less time. If you improve your technology knowledge, you will be

- more productive—after all, saving 15 minutes a day with these tips translates to having more than 60 additional hours per year to do other things;
- more profitable—if you can get more done, you can bill more and increase your revenues;
- less stressed—knowing how to use your technology will reduce your stress and provide you the chance to get back some time and achieve a better work-life balance.

Chapter 12
TIMESAVING TIPS TO MAKE YOUR COMPUTER DO WHAT *YOU* WANT

In this chapter, we continue with more tips and shortcuts designed to save time, including tips on using the internet effectively, tips for using technology in litigation, configuring your computer to work better for you, and other shortcuts. If you adopt only a handful, you will save days, and perhaps even weeks, of time simply doing your work more efficiently. And the best part is, no computer skills are required.

SEARCH WISELY: USING GOOGLE MORE EFFICIENTLY

Everyone uses Google. Well, almost everyone. When looking for something on the web, most searchers rarely do more than type a brief query (a word or short phrase) into the search box on the main Google page. But you can obtain better, more tailored results by tweaking your queries just a little. Here are some of our favorite search shortcuts and features (sample queries appear in boldface).

Specific Phrases

When you place quotation marks around a group of words, like **"book shelf"**, Google will display only results that include that phrase. Of course, by default, the results you get will be based on the order of the words you entered. So if you search for **"shelf book"** instead, your results will differ. Similarly, when you place the plus sign in front of one word (without a space), Google will display results that include only the word you typed. For example, a search for **+siegel** will display only those web pages that include Dan's last name.

Specific Pages in a Site

The query "[word/phrase] site:" before a URL (a web address) allows you to search for something within a specific website. Google will display any page at that site that contains the searched word or phrase. For example, the query **siegel site:www.americanbar.org** will return every page or link on the American Bar Association's website that references Dan's last name.

Specific File Types

Google can display results for a specific word or phrase in a document that exists in a particular format, including Microsoft Excel (xls or xlsx), Microsoft PowerPoint (ppt or pptx), Microsoft Word (doc or docx), portable document format (pdf), PostScript (ps), rich text format (rtf), ShockWave Flash (swf), and text (ans, txt). For example, **siegel "pdf"** displays only documents in PDF format that contain Dan's last name.

Excluded Terms

If you include a minus sign (without a space) before a word, Google knows that your results should exclude web pages that contain that particular word. Google also knows the difference between the minus sign and hyphenated words. For example, **former presidents –carter** will display websites discussing former presidents not named Carter.

Wild-Card Searches

The asterisk, or wild card, instructs Google to treat the symbol as a placeholder for unknown words and display only the most relevant results. Unlike other programs, in Google the asterisk works only on whole words, not on parts of words. For example, **attorney * jones** will search for web pages that contain the words "attorney" and "jones" with a word or name between them, like "attorney Cyrus Jones."

OR

If you want results to include one of a few words, use the word "OR" (in all capital letters). Google will display results with one or more of the desired words. You can also use the | symbol instead of "OR." For example, **sotomayor OR scalia** or **sotomayor | scalia** will display pages containing one of those names or both.

Definitions

If you type "define:" at the beginning of a query, Google will return sites that include a definition of the word or words you entered. Note that the definition will be of the entire phrase you entered, not just the first word. For example, **define:summary judgment** will return a list of several websites that offer a definition of that phrase.

Words in URLs

The term "allinurl:" at the beginning of a query yields a display of sites whose web address includes the specific words entered. Try querying **allinurl:justice department** to see what I mean.

Synonyms

If you place the tilde symbol immediately before a word in a query, Google will display websites that include synonyms for that word. For example, when you search for **~vehicle parts**, you will see results that include auto parts stores, etc.

Saved Versions of Websites

Typing "cache:" along with a URL (with no space between the two) will display the page as it appeared the last time you visited it—the cached version. To see your cached version of Google's home page, type **cache:www.google.com**.

Website Links

Placing "link:" before a URL will display pages that have hyperlinks (clickable links) to the specified page. Try this: **link:www.americanbar.org**.

Similar Sites

When you place "related:" before a URL, Google will display web pages that have content similar to that found at that address. See what a search for **related:www.americanbar.org** turns up.

Website Information

Using "info:" in a search will yield links to information and to searches about a particular site. For example, **info:www.americanbar.org** brings up a description of the ABA and a link to its home page, and it offers several ABA-related search options.

Google Calculator

Google includes a sophisticated built-in calculator that works by entering the desired calculation into the Google search box or the Google toolbar (an add-on to most web browsers). The calculator can perform basic arithmetic (addition, subtraction, multiplication, and division), advanced math (trigonometry, logarithms), and computation of units of measure and conversions (currency, weights, distances). You can find excellent examples at www.googleguide.com/calculator.html.

Weather

When you type "weather" and the name or zip code of a specific place, Google will display the location's weather. I type **weather 19083** or **weather Havertown, PA** to learn what weather conditions to expect in my area.

USE BUILT-IN KEYBOARD SHORTCUTS

Keyboard shortcuts are combinations of two or more keys that, when pressed, can be used to perform a task that would typically require a mouse or other pointing device. Keyboard shortcuts can make it easier to interact with your computer, saving you time and effort as you work with Windows and other programs. Most programs also provide accelerator keys that can make it easier to work with menus and other commands. Check the menus of programs for accelerator keys. If a letter is underlined in a menu, it usually means that pressing the ALT key in combination with the underlined key will have the same effect as clicking that menu item. Pressing the ALT key in some programs, such as Paint and WordPad, shows commands that are labeled with additional keys that you can press to use them.

Special Characters

A special character is a character, like the section (§) or paragraph (¶) symbol, that is not located on your keyboard. You can insert special characters by using Character Map or by pressing a combination of keys on your keyboard.

Using Character Map

Character Map lets you view the characters that are available in a selected font. Using Character Map, you can copy individual characters or a group of characters to the Clipboard and paste them into any program that can display them.

- Open Character Map by clicking the Start button. In the search box, type Character Map, and then, in the list of results, click Character Map.
- Click the Font list, and then click the font you want to use.
- Click the special character you want to insert into the document.
- Click Select, and then click Copy.
- Open your document and click the location in the document where you want the special character to appear.
- Click the Edit menu, and then click Paste (or CTRL+P).

Using the Keyboard to Create Special Characters

You can also create special characters by typing a series of keys in conjunction with the ALT key.

- Ensure that the NUM LOCK key has been pressed to activate the numeric key section of the keyboard.
- Press and hold the ALT key.
- While the ALT key is pressed, type the sequence of numbers (on the numeric keypad) that corresponds to the character you want to type. An excellent resource for viewing all the available options is at https://www.alt-codes.net/.
- Release the ALT key and the character will appear.

There are some gaps in the numerical sequence of ALT character codes because either those elements do not exist or they are duplicates of elements listed elsewhere.

Some word processing programs will not recognize all of these ALT functions.

EXPLORE YOUR COMPUTER: USING WINDOWS EXPLORER MORE EFFECTIVELY

Windows Explorer is the tool used to view files on a Windows computer. Just click on the Computer icon (it could be called This PC or some other name on your computer) and it will open the file tree. From there, you can locate a file or folder or navigate to another folder or location. Once you have the file tree open, you have many options for viewing the list of files:

- Icon views
  - Extra large icons
  - Large icons
  - Medium icons
  - Small icons
- The icon views place the emphasis on icons, although file titles are also shown.
- List view

  The list option shows the title of the file accompanied by a very small icon. Dan finds this view the most helpful because it allows you to view more files in a window than any other way, so you see more and scroll less.
- Details

  The details view shows you not only the icon and title but also the date the file was last modified, as well as the type and size of the file. Allison finds this view to be the most effective for her; it has the information she needs but is still small enough to fit many items on one screen.
- Tiles

  The tiles view is similar to the icon views in that it displays icons, sorted alphabetically into vertical columns, but in addition to icons and titles, this view lists the file type and size as well.
- Content

  The content view displays medium icons in a vertical column with title, author, date modified, and size of the file.

Once you've chosen your preferred view, right-click to sort files (e.g., by name or date) to view them more quickly and efficiently.

Chapter 13 ORGANIZING YOUR REMOTE WORKSPACE TO GET WORK DONE MORE EFFICIENTLY AND ETHICALLY

WELCOME TO A NEW WORLD OF REMOTE WORK

Despite the desires of traditional employers, and certainly many law firms, the COVID-19 pandemic transformed the way we work. Now, not only is much of the workforce able to accommodate remote work, but the ability to work remotely has also become a criterion employees use to decide which jobs to take and which to leave or reject. In many ways, the pandemic also highlighted the previously overlooked skills of employees who worked part-time and remotely before the pandemic.

Over the years, we have met many lawyers who worked remotely and had to adjust their work schedules, not because they arose with the roosters, but because of their need to juggle their work lives with other commitments such as childcare, that is, the thing commonly known as their personal lives. Many conceded that they had to perform familial gymnastics to hide their "problems" from the powers-that-be who would determine their futures in their firms.

What we also saw was that the overwhelming majority of the firms they worked for did not appreciate these lawyers, whose loyalty remained despite the obstacles they faced. Then came COVID-19, and everyone had some "problems." A 9-to-5 schedule is far more challenging when you need to deal with

Zoom classes for toddlers and many other adjustments. Consequently, firms had to adapt and allow staff to modify their schedules and their working hours to accommodate those "problems."

The quarantines of COVID-19 have destroyed the validity of the justifications traditionally offered by law firms for why everyone in a firm must work full-time in a brick-and-mortar office, particularly during "traditional" business hours. Report after report emphasizes that assignments were completed and that lawyers did not show a decrease in productivity. The success of remote work, and the increased willingness of courts to conduct hearings and other proceedings remotely, changes the dynamic of law firm life and highlights the value of attorneys who can adapt, are comfortable with the technology needed to work remotely, and can produce high-quality work product, regardless of where and when it is created.

Suddenly homebound during the pandemic, previously office-based workers had to take on the role of quasi-teacher, babysitter, daycare worker, and more. They may also have had to care for aging relatives or family infected with the coronavirus. No one could hide it. It meant that work schedules had to become more flexible. After all, if a kindergartener's Zoom classes were at 1 p.m. and one parent was scheduled to give a presentation to their CEO at that time, the other parent's work schedule had to "wait" until kindergarten class was over.

As childcare and other issues became daily interruptions, firms were forced to recognize that their staff had private lives. As firms now adopt a more remote workforce, the tables have turned. To thrive, firm leaders will need to recognize that their existing remote staff was highly productive because they learned to be efficient schedule jugglers years ago. They learned in order to survive.

What was often lost on firms before the pandemic, however, was that lawyers who work remotely or reduced hours have traditionally been more adept at juggling schedules and maximizing their efficiency. They also knew how to use technology and didn't have to learn what GoToMyPC was or how to use basic software. They had to learn or they would not have been able to work competently in a remote environment. They had also created dedicated workspaces from which to work, a necessity in the postpandemic world.

Lawyers accustomed to working remotely either did not have to adapt to new technology at all during the pandemic or adapted more easily than many of their counterparts. To them, remote access, videoconferencing, and other indicia of the quarantine were just another day at work. According to Global Workplace Analytics, a consulting firm that helps employers understand and prepare for the future of work, an estimated 56 percent of the U.S. workforce holds a job that is compatible or partially compatible with remote work. The company predicts "that the longer people are required to work at home, the greater the adoption we will see when the [pandemic] dust settles."[1]

In sum, the pandemic has taught law firms many lessons, including:

- Lawyers and staff have personal lives, which they have silently and successfully juggled seemingly forever.
- Childcare is virtually nonexistent, and the need to juggle children and work will continue for the foreseeable future.
- Lawyers and staff will continue to have to balance these and other demands with the need to do their jobs.
- Law firms will need to allow lawyers and staff greater flexibility as to when they will accomplish their work.
- Firms that remain rigid in the demand that staff work traditional hours will discover that many lawyers and staff will leave because the traditional on-site law firm model is no longer viable for them.
- Lawyers who have avoided discussing their personal lives with firm management will now be able to confront their firms and demand the flexibility often considered a death knell to the likelihood of becoming a partner.
- Law firms will no longer be able to demand that staff always be in the office, because the pandemic has proved that firms can accomplish much, if not all, of their work remotely.
- The excuse that workers who work remotely are less productive has been disproven.
- The excuse that technology is not adequate to permit remote work on a continual basis has been disproven.

COVID-19 has changed everything. As the legal world adapts to a more remote workforce, firm leaders will have to respond to and accommodate the needs and demands of their remote staff, rather than impose work schedules that ignore their staffs' private lives. This is also an opportunity to revise their old partnership standards and welcome into their partnership the women and other attorneys who have been denied entry despite their productivity. Otherwise, those valuable employees will seek positions at firms that recognize that you can be a loyal and productive employee even if you're not on site or working from the same place they are.

1. *Work-at-Home after Covid-19—Our Forecast*, Glob. Workplace Analytics, https://globalworkplaceanalytics.com/work-at-home-after-covid-19-our-forecast (last visited Aug. 8, 2022).

TIPS FOR CREATING AN EFFICIENT REMOTE WORKSPACE

Setting up a remote workspace isn't as easy as trying to duplicate a traditional workspace within a brick-and-mortar law firm because of the additional challenges posed by distractions that would not normally be present in a traditional law firm environment. Here are some tips on how to create an organized, efficient, and sanity-affirming remote workspace.

Maintain Regular Hours

When you work in an office, you have a schedule, and you need one if you work from home as well. While that schedule may need to be a bit different to adjust for home-based distractions, it is still important to have a regular schedule. In other words, set a basic schedule and stick to it, at least most of the time, with clearly delineated guidelines so that your office (and your clients) knows your availability.

With a clearly set basic schedule, you can maintain your work-life balance, while also building in flexibility to handle the types of interruptions that never came to the office.

Set Ground Rules for Family and Others

When you work remotely, others may equate your presence to automatic availability. You need to specify when they can interrupt and when they can't. For example, you may have meetings, hearings, and other events that require your complete attention and no interruptions. You need to set boundaries and clearly establish signals to let others know when you are off limits and cannot be interrupted.

Take Breaks, as Well as Lunch and Meal Breaks, Just Like in the Office

At work, your firm has to allow you to take breaks, and you need to do the same in your remote office. You need to know the policy on break times and take them. The same applies to meals. Don't allow your office to take advantage and operate under the belief that you need to work every minute every day. Dan has always mandated that his staff take a lunch break every day to clear their heads and take a deep breath.

Ask for What You Need

Just because you are working remotely doesn't mean that you suddenly have to provide your own supplies. Ask for what you need whenever you need it.

It is a firm's responsibility to provide the appropriate supplies to allow you to complete your work. Best practices dictate that the law firm should provide the computer or laptop and other equipment you use to perform work for the firm so that if or when you leave your firm, it is clear who owns what. Having separate equipment also helps make certain that you can keep personal information and communications separate from work-related information and communications.

Create a Dedicated Office Space

Ideally, you should have a separate room that, at least during business hours, is dedicated solely for you to work in, but that isn't always possible. (Dan, for example, does his remote work at the kitchen table.) If it isn't possible for you to dedicate an entire room to your work, you may designate a portion of one room or even a desk or workspace that is devoted just to your legal work.

Wherever your remote workspace is, set up the area where you work so that it clearly demonstrates you are on the clock during the hours you are working. Make sure your family and others recognize that, while working, you and your space are private property and that all client files are confidential and off limits.

Get a Comfortable Chair

You likely spend more time sitting in your office chair than you do occupying any other piece of furniture, perhaps even more than your bed. Having a comfortable chair to work in is essential. Using an uncomfortable chair can lead to back and neck problems and has been likened by some to a form of torture.

Dan has a bad back, and for years he had neck and back problems that required physical therapy. The therapist recommended that he purchase a chair from a store that sells products designed for people with bad backs. Although the chair wasn't inexpensive, it was well worth the expense since his problems went away.

You can't work well if you aren't comfortable and are focused as much on your back pain as your work. Spend the money for a comfortable chair, and don't be afraid to ask your office to pay for it or subsidize it.

Establish "Work Zones"

Decide what happens in every area of your office. You should have a main work area, such as your desk, where you store your PC or laptop, printer, scanner, and other devices; a filing area for work-related materials; and an area for your office supplies. Make sure that the things you need are close to you.

Install Proper Lighting

Lack of good lighting can strain your eyes and lead to vision problems. With proper lighting you can accomplish more at any time of day with less difficulty. In addition, as we've already mentioned, proper lighting is important for presenting a professional appearance for virtual meetings and presentations.

Digitize Everything You Possibly Can

Anything that is digitized (scanned) and backed up can be restored if the worst happens. As a result, scan everything you can; in other words, scan anything and everything related to your office.

In addition, if you are not storing everything in your office's electronic filing or document management system, you need to create a logical folder system for the files. Doing so assures that you can find whatever you need quickly.

Keep Your Space Neat

Daily or at most weekly, throw out (or shred if confidential) material that you don't need or want. Look around. And monthly, go through furniture, equipment, supplies, and other stuff. Then put everything where it belongs.

Prioritize Face Time

We've both worked for law firms with partners who believed that lawyers were only working if they could see them—if we were in the office at the same time the partners were, even if we arrived hours earlier than they did. Remote work can magnify this problem if your bosses subscribe to this theory. To combat this potential problem, you need to show your face at every opportunity. Check in regularly with people in your office, whether by phone, Zoom, or the occasional in-person meeting.

Take Sick Days

When you are sick, take a day off and get better rather than work at less-than-optimum levels or bring your "condition" to work. Remember that days off can do wonders for your long-term wellness and your productivity; it's best to rest and get better so that you can get back to work at full capacity.

Have a Day-Ending Routine

Start your day with a routine and end it with a routine that makes it clear that you have completed your work for the day. While that may not seem possible, it is always helpful to have some routine that signals that you have moved from work mode to home mode. Whatever you decide to do, do it consistently to mark the end of working hours. That might be as simple as logging off of your work computer, closing your office door behind you, packing up your kitchen-table office and putting it away, or changing out of your Zoom-meeting shirt into your T-shirt.

Work Remotely Safely and Ethically

The pandemic caused unprecedented disruption for attorneys and law firms and has renewed the focus on what constituted competent legal representation during a time when attorneys did not have access to their physical offices. In particular, having employees working remotely forced law offices to transform themselves overnight and to finally be cognizant of how they and their staff work remotely, how they access data, and how they prevent computer viruses and other cybersecurity risks. It also forced lawyers working remotely to consider the security and confidentiality of their procedures and systems, including everything from protecting computer systems and physical files to ensuring that the confidentiality of client telephone and other conversations and communications remains protected.

At a minimum, when working remotely, attorneys and their staff have an obligation under the Rules of Professional Conduct to take reasonable precautions to assure that

- all communications, including telephone calls, text messages, email, and video conferencing, are conducted in a manner that minimizes the risk of inadvertent disclosure of confidential information;
- information transmitted through the internet is done in a manner that ensures the confidentiality of client communications and other sensitive data;
- their remote workspaces are designed to prevent the disclosure of confidential information in both paper and electronic form;
- proper procedures are used to secure and back up confidential data stored on electronic devices and in the cloud;
- any remotely working staff are educated about and have the resources to make their work compliant with the Rules of Professional Conduct; and
- appropriate forms of data security are used.

Consider Getting Computer Glasses

Dan swears by his computer glasses. And yes, he wears glasses to work in front of his computer that are different from his "regular" glasses. Why? His optician recommended them, as did his optometrist.

Computer glasses are prescription lenses that are designed to be used while doing work on a computer. They are designed to allow users to focus on a computer screen, which is a different distance than reading material. Equally important, computer lenses are progressive lenses that still allow the wearer to see at a distance should someone walk into the room. They also can block blue light. For example, Dan wears Shamir lenses, which are lightweight and filter 98 percent of blue light at the customary distance for computer users.

Even if you don't wear glasses, you may want to consider nonprescription computer glasses that help block blue light and prevent eye strain.

A CHECKLIST OF ITEMS YOU SHOULD HAVE IN YOUR REMOTE WORKSPACE

Finally, here is a checklist of items you may need to have a properly outfitted remote office:

- Desk
- Chair
- Proper lighting (both to illuminate your work and for online meetings)
- A computer with the software you need to be efficient
- A high-speed internet connection
- Printer
- Scanner
- UPSes (universal power supplies) and surge protectors
- A dedicated work phone
- Backup system
- Storage location
- Paper shredder
- Pens

Working from home should be comfortable and productive. All it needs is some planning and you're on your way.

Chapter 14
USING TECHNOLOGY TO MEET ETHICAL OBLIGATIONS

Working remotely implicates various Model Rules of Professional Conduct that affect an attorney's responsibilities toward clients, potential clients, other parties, and counsel, primarily focused on the need to assure confidentiality of client and sensitive information. Although no Model Rule of Professional Conduct specifically addresses technology and the ethical obligations of attorneys working remotely, the ABA Center for Professional Responsibility released Formal Opinion 498, Virtual Practice, on March 10, 2021, which addresses many of these issues. Other states have also issued formal guidance for attorneys practicing in those jurisdictions. For example, Pennsylvania, where Dan practices, provided extensive guidance in Pennsylvania Bar Association Committee on Legal Ethics and Professional Responsibility Formal Opinion 2020-300, Ethical Obligations for Lawyers Working Remotely. Dan was the primary author of this guidance, which has been cited or adopted by many jurisdictions and provides guidance that also addresses the ethical use of technology, including remote technology.

All opinions agree that, in general, a lawyer is required to make reasonable efforts to prevent inadvertent or unauthorized access to client information. Lawyers should assess the risk with regard to each client or transaction. Special security precautions may be required to protect against the inadvertent or unauthorized disclosure of client information when required by an agreement with the client or by law, or when the nature of the information requires a higher degree of security.

In addition to the opinion, the following Rules apply generally:

- Rule 1.1 (Competence)
- Rule 1.6 (Confidentiality of Information)
- Rule 5.1 (Responsibilities of Partners, Managers, and Supervisory Lawyers)
- Rule 5.3 (Responsibilities Regarding Nonlawyer Assistance)

When working remotely, attorneys and their staff have an obligation under the Rules of Professional Conduct to take reasonable precautions, which are dependent upon circumstances, and may suggest or require that

- Data created or stored remotely is backed up and secured
- Security measures are used so that information sent by electronic mail is protected from unauthorized disclosure (although we recommend encryption, to date, the Model Rules do not require it, according to ABA Formal Opinion 477R[1])
- Firewalls, antivirus and antimalware software, and other similar products are used on all remote devices to prevent the loss or corruption of data
- Handling of information remotely is limited
- The identity of individuals who access a firm's data from remote locations is verified
- A written work-from-home protocol that specifies how to safeguard confidential business and personal information is implemented
- A Virtual Private Network or similar connection to access a firm's data is used
- Two-factor authentication or similar safeguards are used
- All employees are supplied with or must use secure (and, in our view, preferably encrypted) laptops
- Data is permanently saved only on the office network, not personal devices, and if saved on personal devices, reasonable precautions to protect such information are taken
- Every employee signs a written agreement that they will comply with the firm's data privacy, security, and confidentiality policies

1. ABA Formal Opinion 477, Securing Communication of Protected Client Information, was originally issued on May 11, 2017, and the revised opinion, 477R, was issued on May 22, 2017.

- Electronic records containing confidential data, including backups, are encrypted
- The use of smart devices such as those offered by Amazon Alexa and Google voice assistants in locations where client-related conversations may occur is prohibited
- Employees must conduct client-related conversations in locations where they cannot be overheard by other persons who are not authorized to hear this information
- Other reasonable measures to assure that all confidential data are protected are taken
- All communications, including telephone calls, text messages, email, and video conferencing, are conducted in a manner that minimizes the risk of inadvertent disclosure of confidential information
- Information transmitted through the internet is done in a manner that ensures the confidentiality of client communications and other sensitive data
- Employees' remote workspaces are designed to prevent the disclosure of confidential information in both paper and electronic form
- Proper procedures are used to secure and back up confidential data stored on electronic devices and in the cloud
- Any staff who work remotely are educated about and have the resources to make their work compliant with the Rules of Professional Conduct
- Appropriate forms of data security are used

COMMUNICATIONS

When working at home or from other remote locations, all communications with clients must be and remain confidential. This requirement applies to all forms of communications, including phone calls, email, chats, online conferencing, and text messages.

When speaking on a phone or conducting an online or similar conference, attorneys and legal assistants should dedicate a private area where they can communicate privately with clients and take reasonable precautions to assure that others are not present and cannot listen to the conversation.

Similarly, when communicating using electronic mail, text messages, and other methods for transmitting confidential and sensitive data, attorneys must take reasonable precautions, which may include the use of encryption, to assure that unauthorized persons cannot intercept and read these communications.

Avoid Using Public Internet/Free Wi-Fi

Attorneys and staff should avoid using unsecured free internet/Wi-Fi hotspots when performing client- or firm-related activities that involve access to or the transmission of confidential or sensitive data. This includes public unsecured Wi-Fi at hotels, airports, and coffee shops. Remote workers who need to travel frequently may want to invest in a secure mobile hotspot so they do not have to rely on public Wi-Fi connections.

Use Virtual Private Networks to Enhance Security

A VPN, or Virtual Private Network, allows users to create a secure connection to another network over the internet, shielding the user's activity from unauthorized persons or entities. VPNs can connect any device, including smartphones, PCs, laptops, and tablets, to another computer (called a server), encrypting information and shielding your online activity from all other persons or entities, including cybercriminals. Thus, the use of a VPN can help to protect computers and other devices from hackers.

Use Two-Factor or Multifactor Authentication

Two-factor or multifactor authentication is a security method that requires users to prove their identity in more than one way before signing into a program or a website. For example, a user might be required to enter a login name and a password and would then be sent a four- or six-digit code by text message to enter on the website. Entering this additional authentication helps to ensure only authorized persons are accessing the site. Although these forms of enhanced security may seem cumbersome, their use provides an additional layer of security beyond simple password security.

Use Strong Passwords to Protect Your Data and Devices

One of the most common ways that hackers break into computers, websites, and other devices is by guessing passwords or using software that guesses passwords, which remain a critical method of gaining unauthorized access. Thus, the more complex the password, the less likely that an unauthorized user will be able to access a phone, computer, website, or network by guessing the password or using password-cracking software.

Assure That Video Conferences Are Secure

The FBI issued a warning about teleconference hijacking during the COVID-19 pandemic and recommended that users take the following steps "to mitigate teleconference hijacking threats":[2]

- Do not make meetings public.
- Require a meeting password or use other features that control the admittance of guests.
- Do not share a link to a teleconference on an unrestricted publicly available social media post.
- Provide the meeting link directly to specific people.
- Manage screen sharing options. For example, many of these services allow the host to change screen sharing to "Host Only."
- Ensure users are using the updated version of remote access/meeting applications.
- Ensure your organization's remote work policy addresses security requirements.

BACK UP ANY DATA STORED REMOTELY

Backups are as important at home as they are at the office, perhaps more so because office systems are almost always backed up in an automated fashion. Thus, attorneys and staff working remotely should either work remotely on the office's system (using services such as Windows Remote Desktop Connection, GoToMyPC, Remote PC, or LogMeIn) or have a system in place that assures that there is a backup for all documents and other computer files created by attorneys and staff while working remotely. Often, backup systems can include offsite locations. Alternatively, there are numerous providers that offer secure and easy-to-set-up cloud-based backup services. In addition, if your firm uses a cloud-based document management system, the system may have built-in document and backup recovery.

2. Press Release, FBI Boston, FBI Warns of Teleconferencing and Online Classroom Hijacking during COVID-19 Pandemic (Mar. 30, 2020), https://www.fbi.gov/contact-us/field-offices/boston/news/press-releases/fbi-warns-of-teleconferencing-and-online-classroom-hijacking-during-covid-19-pandemic.

SECURITY IS ESSENTIAL FOR REMOTE LOCATIONS AND DEVICES

Attorneys and staff must make reasonable efforts to assure that work product and confidential client information are kept confidential, regardless of where or how they are created. Microsoft has published its guidelines for a secure home office, which include:[3]

- Use a firewall.
- Keep all software up to date.
- Use antivirus software and keep it current.
- Use antimalware software and keep it current.
- Do not open suspicious attachments or click unusual links in messages, email, tweets, posts, or online ads.
- Avoid visiting websites that offer potentially illicit content.
- Do not use USBs, flash drives, or other external devices unless you own them or they are provided by a trusted source. When appropriate, attorneys should take reasonable precautions such as calling or contacting the sender or supplying party directly to assure the data are not infected or otherwise corrupted.

Never Leave Your Devices or Laptop in the Car

Because we are mobile, we often take devices with us. And the stories of leaving devices in cabs and other locations are common. Thus, remote workers should keep work laptops and devices with them at all times. That means all the time, because thieves often observe parking areas, just waiting for a new victim. A trunk may be more secure than a back seat, but not much.

3. *Top Tips for Working More Securely from Home*, Microsoft, https://support.microsoft.com/en-us/topic/top-tips-for-working-more-securely-from-home-c3e6c940-43a6-43a3-b780-b8784776c2a8 (last visited Aug. 22, 2022).

Chapter 15

USE CHECKLISTS

WHY CHECKLISTS?

Everyone uses checklists—at home, at the gym, and in lots of other places. Yet when you suggest using checklists at the office, people either balk or act like you're crazy.

We all use checklists and rely upon them for almost everything. In fact, when you think about it, we can't really live without them. We make Christmas lists, shopping lists, lists of guests when planning weddings, and lists for almost everything else we do. Sometimes we write them down, other times we keep them in our heads—but usually when we keep them in our heads, we tend to forget something.

What's worse is how upset we become when we forget or lose a checklist. You feel lost when you leave the supermarket shopping list at home, and how frustrating is it when you want to bake a cake and realize that you forgot to pick up one key ingredient—and the guests are coming in two hours?

That said, the question "Why should law firms use checklists?" is an important one to answer. Many of us—especially the slow or late adopters—"got religion" either by making mistakes, by having the idea bludgeoned into our subconscious, or by reading *The Checklist Manifesto,* Dr. Atul Gawande's truly game-changing book about the critical need for checklists in the medical setting, which explained so well why checklists are essential not only for efficiency but also for saving lives (if you're a doctor) and for eliminating mistakes (no matter what you do).

The summary of the book on the publisher's website really explains why checklists are so vital:

> The modern world has given us stupendous know-how. Yet avoidable failures continue to plague us in health care, government, the law, the financial industry—in almost every realm of organized activity. And the reason is simple: the volume and complexity of knowledge today has exceeded our ability as individuals to properly deliver it to people—consistently, correctly, safely. We train longer, specialize more, use ever-advancing technologies, and still we fail. Atul Gawande makes a compelling argument that we can do better, using the simplest of methods: the checklist.[1]

But stories about checklists always seem to be about other professions. Yes, we can agree that checklists, such as the ones in use for landing planes, have reduced the number of plane crashes. We can also agree that the use of checklists really has saved lives by focusing medical professionals on each step they take, whether they're performing surgery or they're merely conducting "routine" checkups.

So why do lawyers need checklists?

WHY LAWYERS NEED CHECKLISTS

That answer is simple: to avoid malpractice and to allow you to provide the best representation to your clients, so that they remain your clients. In other words, if you miss something like a filing deadline and your brief is rejected, your client's appeal might be dismissed. Or, if you are a real estate attorney and didn't remember to order the title report (yes, people forget things, even something that obvious), then your client will be very unhappy when you have to postpone closing and may not be your client anymore. You get the idea.

And finally, you need checklists because we can't and don't remember everything. To the contrary, we are human. As a result, we need checklists to make sure that we—and this means everyone in the office from the attorneys to the janitor—don't make avoidable mistakes and don't forget to do something.

Checklists ensure that the essential pieces of legal practice get done correctly, every time. Whether it is a list of documents required in a particular type

1. *The Checklist Manifesto*, MITIMCo, https://mitimco.org/portfolio-item/the-checklist-manifesto/ (last visited Aug. 8, 2022).

of case or transaction or accountability for putting in deadlines and statutes, checklists make you more efficient and more effective.

Efficient means you can complete your work in less time. Effective means you do better work. For many lawyers, getting work done more quickly may not be that important—until, of course, a client objects to the amount of time billed, but everyone wants to make sure their work is the best it can be. Rest assured, at some point, someone in your office will make a mistake, and if it's a major error, that's when the lawyer (or the managing partner) will realize that things must change. In the next section, we will discuss a few reasons that checklists make sense even for you.

MALPRACTICE PREVENTION

Let's be honest. Nothing tends to compel lawyers to change how they do things more quickly than the need to avoid malpractice. After all, malpractice claims cost lawyers money and can lead to professional discipline. In 2010, Dan Pinnington wrote an article discussing the biggest malpractice claim risks and how to avoid them.[2] After reviewing the various sources of malpractice, we list next those that could be avoided by using checklists:

- Failure to calendar properly/missed deadlines
- Failure to file documents/no deadline
- Failure to know deadline
- Procrastination
- Failure to obtain client consent
- Conflicts of interest
- Substantive legal errors/failing to know/apply the law
- Ineffective client screening
- Inadequate documentation of work
- Planning errors
- Inadequate discovery/investigation

A simple checklist could eliminate many of these malpractice risks. Consider how Dan's office handles these situations.

2. Daniel E. Pinnington, *Are You at Risk? The Biggest Malpractice Claim Risks and How to Avoid Them*, 36 ABA L. Prac. 4 (2010).

1. Failure to Calendar Properly/Missed Deadlines

Whenever we receive any deadlines, we have a checklist that reminds us to

- First enter the due date (and appropriate reminders) in our case management software
- Scan the notice or item with the confirmed deadline and attach it to the due date reminder in our case management system; andwrite the deadline on the whiteboard in Pam's office (adjacent to our kitchen), so that everyone sees it every time they go to or from the kitchen area

2. Failure to File Documents/No Deadline

We place a "rough" deadline in our system for any matters with a nonspecific deadline, using a checklist that reminds us to

- First enter the estimated due date (and appropriate reminders) in our case management software
- Scan the notice or item with the confirmed deadline and attach it to the due date reminder in our case management system
- Write the estimated deadline on the whiteboard in Pam's office (adjacent to our kitchen), so that everyone sees it every time they go to or from the kitchen area
- Diary the item for a specified time to follow up in determining if a firm deadline has come in

3. Failure to Know Deadline

Whenever we receive any item without a deadline, we have a checklist that reminds us to

- Consult the court or court dockets (or client if we are preparing a brief for another attorney) to determine the deadline
- If we are unable to determine a deadline, enter an estimated due date (and appropriate reminders) in our case management software
- Scan the notice or item with the confirmed deadline and attach it to the due date reminder in our case management system
- Write the estimated deadline on the whiteboard in Pam's office (adjacent to our kitchen), so that everyone sees it every time they go to or from the kitchen area

- Diary the item for a specified time to check again for the actual/firm deadline

4. Failure to Obtain Client Consent

Whenever we require client consent in a matter, we have a checklist that reminds us to

- Schedule either an appointment or phone conference with the client to discuss the matter requiring consent
- After the meeting, confirm the client's agreement/assent in writing

5. Conflicts of Interest

Whenever we have a waivable conflict of interest, we have a checklist that reminds us to

- Schedule either an appointment or phone conference with the client to discuss the conflict
- After the meeting, confirm the client's waiver of the conflict

6. Ineffective Client Screening

Whenever we open a new file, we have a checklist that reminds us to

- Discuss the matter and any reservations about the client with all staff
- Do an internet search for the client
- View any social media pages for the client
- Set up a Google Alert for the client

7. Inadequate Documentation of Work

Our training procedures include a reminder to explain and demonstrate proper time recording of work performed.

8. Inadequate Discovery/Investigation

We have checklists for proper discovery/investigation of different types of matters.

ETHICS AND BEST PRACTICES

When lawyers consider their ethical obligations, they tend to focus on issues like conflicts of interest, confidentiality of client information, and other similar topics. They don't tend to associate checklists with their ethical obligations, but they should.

In 2012, the American Bar Association amended various Model Rules of Professional Conduct, including Rule 1.1 (Competence), which states:

> A lawyer shall provide competent representation to a client. Competent representation requires the legal knowledge, skill, thoroughness and preparation reasonably necessary for the representation.

The comments to Rule 1.1 include the following:

> Thoroughness and Preparation
> [5] Competent handling of a particular matter includes inquiry into and analysis of the factual and legal elements of the problem, and use of methods and procedures meeting the standards of competent practitioners. It also includes adequate preparation. The required attention and preparation are determined in part by what is at stake; major litigation and complex transactions ordinarily require more extensive treatment than matters of lesser complexity and consequence. An agreement between the lawyer and the client regarding the scope of the representation may limit the matters for which the lawyer is responsible. See Rule 1.2(c).
>
> Maintaining Competence
> [8] To maintain the requisite knowledge and skill, a lawyer should keep abreast of changes in the law and its practice, including the benefits and risks associated with relevant technology, engage in continuing study and education and comply with all continuing legal education requirements to which the lawyer is subject.

While the focus of Rule 1.1 is competence generally, the 2012 amendments included comment [8], requiring attorneys to understand the risks and benefits of technology.

Now let's take a step back. Remember:

- Competence, an ethical obligation, includes taking the appropriate steps to avoid making mistakes and prejudicing clients.
- Being certain that you use the appropriate procedures, including checklists, is a part of being competent.

- And when you standardize your procedures, you
  - prevent mistakes,
  - prevent malpractice, and
  - comply with your ethical obligations.

TRAINING STAFF/COSTS

Hiring employees costs money and takes time. A new employee has to learn all of your office's procedures and systems and needs to be able to learn the nuances that differentiate your office from others. And that's on top of learning the substantive aspects of their job and the law. According to an article by the Society of Human Resources Management, the total cost for hiring a new employee can be three to four times the position's salary.[3] These costs include:

- Development costs (e.g., salaries and benefits of personnel, equipment)
- Direct implementation costs (e.g., training materials, technology costs, facilities, travel, equipment, trainer or instructor's salary and benefits)
- Indirect implementation costs (e.g., overhead, general, and administrative)
- Compensation for participants
- Lost productivity or costs of "backfilling" positions during training

Additional costs include the time spent screening resumes and applications, interviewing candidates, and making hiring decisions, as well as the hit to productivity while the new employee gets up to speed and other interruptions to a team or practice group when one member of the team is replaced.

The better you can train your employees and give them tools to succeed in their jobs, the higher your retention rate will be. And the more tools you have in place, the easier it will be when you have to train a new employee, reducing the time it takes them to get acclimated.

Imagine the difficulty facing a new employee, even one who only has to type a letter. The employee has to learn everything from scratch.

- Letterhead:
  - Does the firm use preprinted letterhead, or does letterhead get printed with the letter?
  - If it is preprinted, what are the settings? Is there a template? Is the printer set up correctly?
  - If it is printed, where is the correct letterhead? Is there a template?

3. Katie Navarra, *The Real Costs of Recruitment*, Soc'y of Hum. Res. Mgmt. (Apr. 11, 2022), https://www.shrm.org/resourcesandtools/hr-topics/talent-acquisition/pages/the-real-costs-of-recruitment.aspx.

- Margins:
  - Does the firm use default or custom margins?
  - Is there a firm-wide standard or does everyone do it differently?
- Fonts:
  - Is there a standard or custom font for the body of the letter? What size is it?
- Spacing:
  - Single, double, "memo" format of a space after each paragraph?
- Paragraphs:
  - Does the firm use full justified or left justified margins?
- Signature:
  - How is it formatted?

This all comes before the substance of the letter is even addressed. If you have a checklist that identifies all of these parameters, it will be much easier for the new employee to learn how to complete the letter to your specifications.

Now that we have, hopefully, convinced you that checklists will benefit your office, it is time to create them—and use them.

A NOTE ABOUT TEMPLATES

In addition to checklists, templates are another useful productivity tool that can help ensure that tasks are completed correctly. For example, creating a template in Word (as we discussed in Chapter 11) for letters to clients that incorporates all of the elements outlined in the previous example can help you not only create documents more quickly but also ensure that the formatting is correct every time.

CHAPTER 15 ACTION STEPS

1. Keep a notepad next to your computer and write down everything you do that you do more than once, including case-related tasks, office procedures, etc.
2. After compiling the list for a few days, dedicate some time to figuring out how each of the repetitive items you wrote down could be helped with a checklist.

3. Talk to coworkers and get their feedback on your list and see what items they suggest.
4. Create a list of potential checklists, some of which may be very short, while others will be long.
5. Create a couple of checklists and test them out. Also have coworkers test them out. Then refine the lists.
6. As you create your checklists, think of more, and encourage coworkers to help you. Eventually, you will compile a group of checklists that could be transformed into an office manual.

Chapter 16 WORKING COLLABORATIVELY

Most lawyers and staff work collaboratively to handle client matters. In a traditional office, collaboration could be as easy as stopping by someone's desk and explaining the situation. But when we are working remotely, collaboration is different—for many reasons. At its core, the dynamic of in-person give and take is more intimate and allows the use of verbal and nonverbal communications, from words to body language, to convey thoughts. Remote work is different. It's easy to see why. Think about an in-person meeting and a Zoom meeting. When you are in person, you can see whether the person you are talking to is paying attention, and you can also kibbitz after the meeting. On a remote platform like Zoom, it is not even possible to know if the person is actually looking at you, let alone paying attention. Plus, when a meeting ends in Zoom, the people disappear from your screen, leaving you all alone.

BASIC CONSIDERATIONS FOR COLLABORATION

There are some general rules to help create an effective remote-based team, including the following:

1. Establish communication systems. To collaborate better, remote workers need to communicate efficiently. Systems could include Teams, Slack, or other messaging platforms or a system internal to your firm. The key is that everyone uses the same system and knows how to use it.

2. Set "sprint" and "milestone" goals. In other words, have short- and long-term goals.
3. Set up recurring meetings so that check-ins are regular and don't appear to be merely an excuse for checking up on someone.
4. Emphasize the need for clarity. It is easier to misconstrue tone and facial gestures in a remote work situation, so be attuned to the limitations you face and focus on delivering a consistent, clear message.
5. Create time for friendship and chitchat. While getting work done is essential, don't lose sight of the fact that people often produce better results when they have a more personal rapport with others. So, make time for non-office-related conversations.
6. Be adaptable. When you first began your remote life, you discovered how different your life was. That same realization applies to all of your office. To address this, be ready and willing to adapt, whether because a coworker is dealing with a child-related issue or someone else seems to have a train station behind them.
7. Create opportunities to collaborate.

HOW TO COLLABORATE BETTER WITH A REMOTE TEAM

A 2018 article in the *Harvard Business Review* seemed to presage the pandemic by explaining the issues that arise when a team must collaborate remotely and offering solutions designed to make remote collaboration more effective. But the central theme of the article is one every firm should recognize: "When remote teams communicate well and leverage their strengths, they can actually gain an advantage over co-located teams."[1]

Authors Erica Dhawan and Tomas Chamorro-Premuzic began by asking questions every remote office should consider:

- Why do remote teams demand new collaboration skills?
- What's missing from our texts, emails, conference calls, and other digital communications?

The answer to their questions is body language.

They explain, "Even when we're co-located, the tone of a text or the formality of an email is left wide open to interpretation, to the point that even our

1. Erica Dhawan & Tomas Chamorro-Premuzic, *How to Collaborate Effectively If Your Team Is Remote*, HARV. BUS. REV., Feb. 27, 2018, https://hbr.org/2018/02/how-to-collaborate-effectively-if-your-team-is-remote.

closest friends get confused. These misinterpretations create an anxiety that can become costly, affecting morale, engagement, productivity, and innovation."[2]

The authors are correct. Remote life changes our perceptions and can lead to misunderstandings from even the most minor things. Consider how you feel when you send a text and the immediate reply you are awaiting isn't there. Are they mad? Bored with you? Involved with others? Don't care? Or perhaps it's because the message didn't arrive instantly?

The authors outline three kinds of distance in remote collaboration: (1) physical, that is, in place and time; (2) operational, that is, in team size, bandwidth, and skill levels; and (3) affinity, that is, in values, trust, and interdependency. They then suggest that "[t]he best way for managers to drive team performance is by focusing on reducing affinity distance. Try switching most remote communication to regular video calls, which are a much better vehicle for establishing rapport and creating empathy than either e-mails or voice calls. And design virtual team-building rituals that give people the opportunity to interact regularly and experience their collaboration skills in action."[3]

What the article highlights is that collaboration has many facets, not only the ability to work together, but also the need to build relationships in a less personal medium. Here are some ways to build the process.

1. Establish a Centralized Hub Containing the Tools Your Teams Need

Just as you need a server in your office, your collaborative team needs one central location or hub where everyone can access all of the tools they need to complete their work. The hub, of which there are many options to choose from, should provide all of the tools needed to accomplish any tasks and stay in touch, whether to check on status, ask questions, share materials, or just chat.

With a hub in place, you can also establish guidelines, including:

- The default modes used to communicate (email, video call, etc.), including one default where everyone knows that they can always communicate
- The circumstances in which each mode should be used, and when to use them
- Who should be included on communications
- How often to check in
- How to communicate/respond if there is an urgent matter

2. *Id.*
3. *Id.*

2. Allow for Asynchronous Communications

As we've already discussed in this book, the world has come to expect a response yesterday to every communication, which can cause friction when using communications like email. By not only permitting, but encouraging, asynchronous communication—communication that permits team members to reply when it is most productive or convenient for them—you can free your teams to focus on work when needed with the full understanding that delays are natural and normal.

3. Avoid Perfunctory Video Meetings

Although Zoom and other video meetings have become the norm, don't overuse them. A full day of video meetings can be exhausting, so use them only when needed, for example, when it is important for your team to see one another or to collaborate in real time. If a video meeting is not necessary, consider using another method of communication. If a video meeting is necessary, be sure to invite only those attendees necessary to accomplish the aims of the meeting or whose contributions are necessary to the discussion.

4. Encourage Active Brainstorming

With virtual communications, some people can feel less inclined to talk, while others open up more. But critical thinking is often accomplished through active brainstorming and is most effective with the participation of the entire team. It's critical to discover how to get the most out of everyone, how to actively solicit participation of members who are less forthcoming in a virtual setting, and how to know when it is time to take a break.

5. Change the Team Members for Different Matters

Change and diversity are good, especially for remote teams. Changing or rotating team members lets more people get to know each other and ensures that any personalities with friction do not always have to work together. Mixing up the groups may create different, more positive dynamics.

6. Create Time for Team Bonding

One challenge that has always been inherent in remote collaboration is creating the time to allow everyone to just meet and get to know one another. Bonding remains essential to establishing a strong team; it helps to create trust and increase openness. At a minimum, you should create a nonwork communications avenue to allow for non-work-related chitchat and bonding.

7. Always Honor Successes

When things go well—you win a case, obtain a favorable outcome for a client, receive a positive decision on a motion, land a dream client, etc.—it is important to congratulate those who contributed and publicize their success. This is even more true in a remote environment.

Collaboration can make the power of multiple minds produce exponentially better results. With a bit of honing, the results will be obvious.

Conclusion

Lawyers contend with numerous competing priorities on a daily basis, and as such, productivity will continue to be a challenge for lawyers into the foreseeable future. In this book, we've tried to give you strategies for defining the most important tasks and projects so that you can focus your efforts on the clients and activities that will bring you the highest return and hopefully bring you the most satisfaction in your practice.

In Part I of this book, we provided you with tips on setting goals and planning the tasks required to accomplish those goals. We've talked about strategies to eliminate (or at least limit) distractions and interruptions. We've helped you to clear out obstacles to your success, whether those obstacles are in the form of paper or electronic clutter or bad clients that keep you from doing your best work for those who appreciate (and pay for) it. We've showed you how to get more done by delegating effectively to others, conducting more valuable meetings, using your calendar as a tool to complete important tasks, and creating systems for repetitive tasks or activities to create a more consistent client experience.

In Part II of this book, we walked you through many of the most popular technology platforms and software programs used by lawyers today and showed you some "insider tips" and little-known tricks to help you accomplish your daily work more efficiently, without sacrificing quality or effectiveness.

Although you'll never be 100 percent productive or eliminate distractions completely (lawyers *are* human, after all), we are confident that the strategies, tips, and tricks you've learned in this book can help you get much more work done in much less time, provide better service to your clients, and even improve your profitability.

Appendix

OUTLOOK NAVIGATION SHORTCUTS[1]

To do this	Press
Switch to the **Mail** view.	Ctrl+1
Switch to the **Calendar** view.	Ctrl+2
Switch to the **Contacts** view.	Ctrl+3
Switch to the **Tasks** view.	Ctrl+4
Switch to the **Notes.**	Ctrl+5
Switch to the **Folder** list in the **Folder** pane.	Ctrl+6
Switch to **Shortcuts.**	Ctrl+7
Open **Journal.**	Ctrl+8
Open the **Address Book.**	Ctrl+Shift+B
Go back to previous view.	Alt+B or Alt+Left arrow key
Go forward to next view.	Alt+Right arrow key

1. *Keyboard Shortcuts for Outlook*, Microsoft, https://support.microsoft.com/en-us/office/keyboard-shortcuts-for-outlook-3cdeb221-7ae5-4c1d-8c1d-9e63216c1efd#bkmk_basicnav (last visited Aug. 10, 2022).

To do this	Press
Switch to next open message.	Ctrl+Period (.)
Switch to previous open message.	Ctrl+Comma (,)
Move between the **Folder** pane, the main Outlook window, the **Reading** pane, and the **To-Do** bar.	Ctrl+Shift+Tab key or Shift+Tab key
Move between the Outlook window, the smaller panes in the **Folder** pane, the **Reading** pane, and the sections in the **To-Do** bar.	Tab key or F6
Move between the ribbon and the calendar.	F6
Show the access keys in the ribbon.	Alt or F6
Open split buttons.	Alt+Down arrow key
Move around message header lines in the **Folder** pane or an open message.	Ctrl+Tab
Move between the **Navigation** pane and the calendar.	Ctrl+Tab
Move around within the **Folder** pane.	Arrow keys
Go to a different folder.	Ctrl+Y
Go to the **Search** box.	F3 or Ctrl+E
In the **Reading** pane, go to the previous message.	Alt+Up arrow key or Ctrl+Comma (,), or Alt+Page Up
In the **Reading** pane, page down through the text.	Spacebar
In the **Reading** pane, page up through the text.	Shift+Spacebar
Collapse or expand a group in the email message list.	Left or Right arrow key, respectively

To do this	Press
Go back to previous view in the main Outlook window.	Alt+B or Alt+Left arrow key
Go forward to next view in the main Outlook window.	Alt+Right arrow key
Select the **InfoBar** and, if available, show the menu of commands.	Ctrl+Shift+W
Show the **To-Do** bar (peek).	Alt+V, B, and then C for Calendar, P for People, T for Tasks, or O for Off

WINDOWS OPERATING SYSTEM KEY COMBINATIONS

- F1: Help
- CTRL+ESC: Open Start menu
- ALT+TAB: Switch between open programs
- ALT+F4: Quit program
- SHIFT+DELETE: Delete item permanently
- Windows Logo+L: Lock the computer (without using CTRL+ALT+DELETE)

WINDOWS PROGRAM KEY COMBINATIONS

- CTRL+C: Copy
- CTRL+X: Cut
- CTRL+V: Paste
- CTRL+Z: Undo
- CTRL+B: Bold
- CTRL+U: Underline
- CTRL+I: Italic

GENERAL KEYBOARD-ONLY COMMANDS

- F1: Starts Windows Help
- F10: Activates menu bar options
- SHIFT+F10: Opens a shortcut menu for the selected item (this is the same as right-clicking an object)
- CTRL+ESC: Opens the Start menu (use the ARROW keys to select an item)
- CTRL+ESC or ESC: Selects the Start button (press TAB to select the taskbar or press SHIFT+F10 for a context menu)
- CTRL+SHIFT+ESC: Opens Windows Task Manager
- ALT+DOWN ARROW: Opens a dropdown list box
- ALT+TAB: Switch to another running program (hold down the ALT key and then press the TAB key to view the task-switching window)
- SHIFT: Press and hold down the SHIFT key while you insert a CD-ROM to bypass the automatic-run feature
- ALT+SPACE: Displays the main window's System menu (from the System menu, you can restore, move, resize, minimize, maximize, or close the window)
- ALT+- (ALT+hyphen): Displays the Multiple Document Interface (MDI) child window's System menu (from the MDI child window's System menu, you can restore, move, resize, minimize, maximize, or close the child window)
- CTRL+TAB: Switch to the next child window of an MDI program
- ALT+underlined letter in menu: Opens the menu
- ALT+F4: Closes the current window
- CTRL+F4: Closes the current MDI window
- ALT+F6: Switch between multiple windows in the same program (for example, when the Notepad Find dialog box is displayed, ALT+F6 switches between the Find dialog box and the main Notepad window)

TO COPY A FILE

- Press and hold down the CTRL key while you drag the file to another folder.
- CTRL+C (or CTRL+INSERT)

TO CREATE A SHORTCUT

Press and hold down CTRL+SHIFT while you drag a file to the desktop or a folder.

GENERAL FOLDER/SHORTCUT CONTROL

Keystroke	**Action**
F4	Selects the "Go to a Different Folder" box and moves down the entries in the box (if the toolbar is active in Windows Explorer).
F5	Refreshes the current window.
F6	Moves among panes in Windows Explorer.
CTRL+G	Opens the "Go to Folder" tool (in Windows 95 Windows Explorer only).
CTRL+Z	Undo the last command.
CTRL+A	Select all the items in the current window.
BACKSPACE	Switch to the parent folder.
SHIFT+click+Close button	For folders, close the current folder plus all parent folders.

Index